Lloyd Suh
Once in the Countryside: A Collection of Plays

Lloyd Suh

Once in the Countryside: A Collection of Plays

The Chinese Lady
The Far Country
Bina's Six Apples
Charles Francis Chan Jr.'s Exotic Oriental Murder Mystery
The Heart Sellers

Edited by CHRISTINE MOK

methuen | drama
LONDON • NEW YORK • OXFORD • NEW DELHI • SYDNEY

METHUEN DRAMA
Bloomsbury Publishing Plc
50 Bedford Square, London, WC1B 3DP, UK
1359 Broadway, New York, NY 10018, USA
29 Earlsfort Terrace, Dublin 2, Ireland

BLOOMSBURY, METHUEN DRAMA and the Methuen Drama logo are trademarks of
Bloomsbury Publishing Plc

First published in Great Britain 2026

Copyright © Lloyd Suh, 2026
Critical Essays © Christine Mok and Contributors, 2026

The authors have asserted their right under the Copyright, Designs and Patents Act, 1988, to be identified as authors of this work.

For legal purposes the Acknowledgements on p. 357 constitute an extension of this copyright page.

Cover design by Matt Thame
Photograph by Leo Thame

All rights reserved. No part of this publication may be: i) reproduced or transmitted in any form, electronic or mechanical, including photocopying, recording or by means of any information storage or retrieval system without prior permission in writing from the publishers; or ii) used or reproduced in any way for the training, development or operation of artificial intelligence (AI) technologies, including generative AI technologies. The rights holders expressly reserve this publication from the text and data mining exception as per Article 4(3) of the Digital Single Market Directive (EU) 2019/790.

Bloomsbury Publishing Plc does not have any control over, or responsibility for, any third-party websites referred to or in this book. All internet addresses given in this book were correct at the time of going to press. The author and publisher regret any inconvenience caused if addresses have changed or sites have ceased to exist, but can accept no responsibility for any such changes.

No rights in incidental music or songs contained in the work are hereby granted and performance rights for any performance/presentation whatsoever must be obtained from the respective copyright owners.

All rights whatsoever in these plays are strictly reserved and application for performance etc. should be made before rehearsals to Independent Artist Group of 3 Columbus Circle, 23rd Floor, New York, NY 10019, USA. No performance may be given unless a licence has been obtained. No rights in incidental music or songs contained in the Work are hereby granted and performance rights for any performance/presentation whatsoever must be obtained from the respective copyright owners.

A catalogue record for this book is available from the British Library.

A catalog record for this book is available from the Library of Congress.

ISBN: HB: 978-1-3504-3921-4
PB: 978-1-3504-3920-7
ePDF: 978-1-3504-3922-1
eBook: 978-1-3504-3923-8

Series: Methuen Drama Play Collection

Typeset by RefineCatch Limited, Bungay, Suffolk
Printed and bound in Great Britain

For product safety related questions contact productsafety@bloomsbury.com.

To find out more about our authors and books visit www.bloomsbury.com
and sign up for our newsletters.

Contents

List of Contributors vi

Introduction *Christine Mok* 1

The Chinese Lady 13
Preface *Amy B. Huang* 15
Postscript *Shannon Tyo* 55

The Far Country 59
Preface *Ju Yon Kim* 61
Postscript *Whit K. Lee* 129

Bina's Six Apples 133
Preface *Elizabeth W. Son* 135
Postscript *Jiyoun Chang* 189

Charles Francis Chan Jr.'s Exotic Oriental Murder Mystery 193
Preface *Christine Mok* 195
Postscript *Peter Kim* 293

The Heart Sellers 297
Preface *Lucy Mae San Pablo Burns* 299
Postscript *May Adrales* 347

The Long Answer: A Conversation with Lloyd Suh 349

Acknowledgements 357

Contributors

Lloyd Suh (author) is an award-winning, internationally produced playwright. His plays, which include *The Heart Sellers, The Chinese Lady, The Far Country* (Pulitzer Prize finalist), *Bina's Six Apples, Charles Francis Chan Jr.'s Exotic Oriental Murder Mystery, Franklinland, American Hwangap,* and others, have been produced at Atlantic Theater Company, The Public Theater, Alliance Theatre, Huntington Theater, Milwaukee Rep, Denver Center, Magic Theatre, Berkeley Rep, Children's Theatre Company, Ma-Yi Theatre Company, and the National Asian American Theatre Company, among others. His work has been produced internationally at the Cultural Center of the Philippines and with PCPA at the Guerilla Theatre in Seoul, Korea. Awards include the Steinberg Playwright Award, Guggenheim Fellowship, Herb Alpert Award, Horton Foote Prize, and Helen Merrill Award. He served as Director of Artistic Programs at The Lark from 2011-20. He was elected in 2016 to the Dramatists Guild Council.

Christine Mok (editor and contributor) is Associate Professor of English at the University of Rhode Island. Her work has been published in the *Journal of Asian American Studies, Theatre Survey, Theatre Journal, Modern Drama,* and *PAJ: A Journal of Performance and Art*. She is co-editor with Joshua Chambers-Letson of *Frances Ya-Chu Cowhig's China Trilogy: Three Parables of Global Capital* (Bloomsbury, 2022).

May Adrales (contributor) is an Assistant Professor and Director of the Theatre Program at Fordham University. An accomplished theater director, she is celebrated for bold and innovative productions and has directed over 30 world premieres at theaters across the country, including Manhattan Theatre Club, Lincoln Center, Second Stage, Public Theater, and Goodman Theatre. A Yale School of Drama graduate, she has received the Alan Schneider Director Award, Josephine Abady Award, a Drama League fellowship, and was a Zelda Fichandler Award finalist. She has taught and directed at Yale School of Drama, Brown, A.R.T/Harvard, NYU, and Juilliard.

Lucy Burns (contributor) is an associate professor in the Asian American Studies Department at UCLA. Among their publications are *Puro Arte: Filipinos on the Stages of Empire* and the co-edited collection *California Dreaming: Movement and Place in the Asian American Imaginary*.

Jiyoun Chang (contributor) is a scenic and lighting designer. Broadway: *Stereophonic* (Tony Nominated); *Jaja's African Hair Braiding; The Cottage; KPOP; for colored girls who have considered suicide/when the rainbow is enuf* (Tony Nominated); *Slave Play* (Tony, Drama Desk, Henry Hewes Nominated), Recent: *Walk On Through* (Gavin Creel); *The Far Country* (Drama Desk, Lucile Lortel Nominated). Recipient of the Suzi Bass Award and Obie Award, she has worked at The Public, Roundabout, NYTW, MCC, Signature, ATC, Guggenheim, Alley, Alliance, Berkeley Rep, CalShakes, Guthrie, Old Globe, OSF. Selective scenic credits: *Bina's Six Apples* (CTC, Alliance Theatre); *A Tale of Two Cities* (Alliance Theatre).

Amy B. Huang (contributor) is an Assistant Professor of Theater and Performance Studies at Bates College. Her book project, *Circuits of Secrets on British and American*

Stages, focuses on how theatre's secrecy engages with the power relations and racist imaginaries attached to slavery, settler colonialism, Orientalism, and Chinese exclusion. Her recent research focuses on early Asian American and diasporic theatre artists' conceptions of temporality and history. Her work has appeared in *Theatre Survey*, *Eighteenth-Century Studies*, and *Milestones in Asian American Theatre*.

Ju Yon Kim (contributor) is the Patsy Takemoto Mink Professor of English at Harvard University. She is the author of *The Racial Mundane: Asian American Performance and the Embodied Everyday* (2015). Her current book project is titled "Paper Performance: Suspicion and the Spaces of Asian American Theater."

Peter Kim (contributor) is an actor, director, and producer. He has acted on Broadway, Off-Broadway, and regionally. Film/TV include *BROS*, *The Forty-Year-Old Version*, *The God Committee*, *Saturday Church*, *Margin Call*, *Sex and the City*, *Hackers*, *GEN V*, *Chicago Med*, *Ugly Betty*. Peter is the recipient of TCG's 2020 Rising Leaders of Color grant, a founding member of AAPAC, producer of Radha Blank's exhibition for The Costume Institute's *In America: An Anthology of Fashion*. He is Creative Producer of NAATCO (National Asian American Theatre Company) and holds an MFA from the Yale School of Drama and a BFA from New York University.

Whit K. Lee (contributor) is an actor/singer whose TV credits include *Blue Bloods*, *FBI: Most Wanted*, *Beyond*, *Kaleidoscope*, *Law & Order SVU*, and *Orange Is the New Black*. Off-Broadway, Whit was in *The Far Country* at the Atlantic Theatre Company, and *Assassins* at Classic Stage Company. Some of his regional theatre credits include: *The Doppelganger* at Steppenwolf, *Secret Hour* at Capitol Rep, and *A Christmas Carol* at Actors Theatre of Louisville. His film credits include *Wall Street English* (80-episode sitcom) and *Grounded*. Thank you to my dream team, Manager, Susan Campochiaro Confrey at CBU Management, and his agent, Padraic at JC William Agency for their love and support.

Elizabeth W. Son (contributor) is an associate professor at Northwestern University in the Department of Theatre. Her research interests focus on Asian & Asian American theatre and performance; transnational and diaspora studies; gender-based issues; trauma and memory; and human rights and social movements. She is the author of the award-winning book *Embodied Reckonings: "Comfort Women," Performance, and Transpacific Redress* (2018), among other articles, book chapters, and public scholarship. Son is currently working on her next book titled *Diasporic Care: Holding History of Violence*.

Shannon Tyo (contributor) is an actor, writer, and director based in New York City. Broadway: *Yellow Face*. Off-Broadway: *The Comeuppance* (Signature Theatre), *Regretfully, So the Birds Are* (Playwrights Horizons), *The Far Country* (Atlantic Theater Company), *peerless* (Primary Stages), *The Chinese Lady* (Ma-Yi at The Public), and *Kentucky* (Ensemble Studio Theater). Shannon has received two Obie Awards (Sustained Achievement in Performance, and a Special Citation for the ensemble of *The Comeuppance*), a Lucille Lortel Award for Outstanding Lead Performance in a Play (for *The Chinese Lady*), and a Theater World Award.

Introduction

History Play

Christine Mok

"My really real answer is that if we left for really real we would go to a place I saw once in the countryside."

– Lloyd Suh, *The Heart Sellers*

One of the best-known artifacts in Asian American history depicts a scene that infamously included no Asian Americans. Taken May 10, 1869, at Promontory Summit in Utah, Andrew Russell's "East and West Shaking Hands at Laying of Last Rail"[1] commemorated the "Golden Spike Ceremony" that marked the joining of the Central Pacific and Union Pacific railroads to form the first transcontinental railroad in the United States. Though upwards of twenty thousand Chinese male laborers had built the western part of the tracks, not one appears in the historic image.

After connecting the last tracks with a final spike (which was not in fact gold – the golden one was a bit of theatre and ultimately swapped out[2]), Union Pacific's *No. 119* and Central Pacific's *Jupiter* were driven so close that their cowcatchers nearly touch. Engineers and workmen crowded around. Though there were three photographers on hand for the occasion, Russell's photograph captured the moment for posterity. His photo is a convergence of trains and men in sepia tones. Hats and vests dominate. The metal links of watch chains glint. Because of the long exposure time, some of the figures are smudged, like ghosts. The sky is clear, an empty off-white expanse. Scraggly brush encroaches along the bottom. At the vanishing point, George Booth raises a bottle of champagne while fellow engineer Sam Bradford holds out two more bottles, each reaching towards the other from atop their respective trains, an industrial *Creation of Adam*. In the foreground, Samuel S. Montague, Central Pacific's chief engineer, and General Grenville M. Dodge, Union Pacific's chief engineer, shake hands. Of the 28 men identified on the National Park Service website[3], last updated on July 9, 2021, not a single name is Chinese.

This image, through the presence of absence, offers a metaphor for the erasure of the Chinese from American history.[4] Another exclusion, before the legislative exclusion in 1882, that illustrates the erasure of these figures and their histories. Erasure and absence are key refrains when tracing Asian American history and a reverse archive fever compels historians, writers, and artists to recover pasts, which might, in fact, be irrecoverable. This "urgency of historical recovery stems," as literary scholar Julia H. Lee explains, "not only from the absence of these Asian authored, first-person documentary sources, but also from the generalized perception that Asians do not belong, a long standing feature of Asian racial formation in the United States."[5] Writers Frank Chin and Maxine Hong Kingston turn to fiction, respectively in *Donald Duk* and *China Men*, to contest Russell's photograph. To remind us of what we know. Over 20,000 Chinese workers toiled and died to build the western part of the railroad. They made up 90 percent of Central Pacific's labor force. They were there when, at the first glance or the 100th, they do not seem to be. Even in Russell's "East and West Shaking Hands at Laying of Last Rail."

In a turnabout, historian Gordan Chang[6] and fellow researchers at Stanford University's Chinese Railroad Workers in North America Project identified two Chinese laborers in the crowd, first one, and then a second. One laborer faces the camera. The other is turned away with only the back of a patched coat and hat in frame. They were there to lay the last rails of the track before the pomp and circumstance of the final spike. As fellow historian Madeline Y Hsu notes, "[t]his recently noticed Chinese railroad worker underscores that although laborers like him feature in every Asian American history, they remain cardboard figures about whom very little detail is known. Perhaps so little has been written about Chinese railroad workers because so few traces remain."[7] Yet, Hsu continues: "The most abundant records have proven to be glass, porcelain, metal fragments, and other Chinese artifacts from campsites that are so pervasive throughout the west and southwest, that scores of archeologists have turned up in the course of their everyday work."[8]

To know the Chinese were there, but not to see them. To finally find them but for so little to be known. So little may have been written and even less has been interned in official archives and repositories, but some remains are persistent. The lives of settler immigrants from Asia are embedded in this land. The evidence of their lives are fragments of glass, porcelain, metal, and other – a heritage of miscellany. While archaeologists, in pursuit of other artifacts, might dig these traces up incidentally, there is an abundance. And from this abundance of glass, porcelain, metal, debris, dust, silence, and scraps,[9] Lloyd Suh has crafted an Asian American history on stage.

For the last decade, Suh has written a series of plays that push against the expulsion of Asian bodies from history inviting audiences to not only take notice of the Asian American subjects who came before but, through his extended treatment, assert that attention must be paid. His history plays, collected here for the first time, dig into and ripple out from milestones of geopolitical events, which have shaped the history of Asians in America, to mark the ways that Asians have made history *in* America and on the world stage. The plays explore the consequences of laws like the Chinese Exclusion Act of 1882 and the Immigration and Nationality Act of 1965 (also known as the Hart-Celler Act) on the lives of Asian subjects; how the violences of the Korean War and other US entanglements in hot and cold wars fail to break families and found families. They allow lost figures of history like Afong Moy, the first Chinese woman in America, to reappear and exorcise racist performance and literary practices like yellowface and orientalism. They commemorate Asian American theatre and performance by dramatizing forebears like Frank Chin and Kathy Change to reflect on the political identities and coalitions made possible by the Civil Rights Movement and the Asian American Movement.

In *The Chinese Lady* (2018), *The Far Country* (2022), *Bina's Six Apples* (2022), *Charles Francis Chan Jr.'s Exotic Oriental Murder Mystery* (2015), and *The Heart Sellers* (2023), Suh imagines the lives and experiences of Asian and Asian American subjects. The cycle, and each individual play, insists on the presence of Asian Americans, refusing their absence, to span over 150 years of history, from the 1830s through the 1970s. Across the five plays, which vary in form, magnitude, and genre, Suh works with the remains of history to grapple with the question of what it is to be Asian American, which has animated Suh's work throughout his career.

Suh reimagines Asian America through the history play. He brings obscured figures center stage and foregrounds the complexities of migration and resistance. Though the plays have clear political catalysts like the Chinese Exclusion Act or the Korean War, their attention to character, who, for most narratives of American history, like the two Chinese railroad laborers, are deemed minor, affords a view of history at a granular, felt level where we watch individuals who are deeply affected by the historical events the play takes up but also how they act and thrive under those conditions. The Asian America imagined in the plays counterbalances the weight of their histories with the absurdity and radiance of life. While there is always an eye towards that larger political possibility such a project aspires to, his plays are grounded in their lyricism and materiality – as full of beauty and longing as they are of dust, rain, and smells.

While Asian America provides the materiality for "history," Suh's engagement with history, specifically Asian American history, intervenes in the form of the contemporary history play. This intervention in theatricality exposes a tension between readers and audiences for whom the events of the play are ancestral memories to be excavated and for those learning for the first time (not just *as if* for the first time, which undergirds theatre's iterative ontology). What then does it mean to present these events on stage? "What does it mean to present these events *again* on stage?"[10]

I repeat theatre scholar Freddie Rokem's query, from the preface to *Performing History: Theatrical Representations of the Past in Contemporary Theatre,* with and without the *again* to mark the ways that Asian American history and its very (im)materiality, with its absences, occlusions, and disremembering (the Korean War is often called the Forgotten War), complicates the again-ness of the history play. Rather than a repetition, Suh's history plays offer an instantiation. In her essay "Possession," playwright Suzan-Lori Parks meditates on how African American history shapes her playwriting, and the ways that her plays, in turn, shape African American history:

> And the history of History is in question too. A play is a blueprint of an event: a way of creating and rewriting history through the medium of literature. Since history is a recorded or remembered event, theatre, for me, is the perfect place to "make" history – that is, because so much of African-American history has been unrecorded, dismembered, washed out…I'm remembering and staging historical events which, through their happening on stage, are ripe for inclusion in the canon of history.[11]

Suh uses the againness of theatre to not only "make" history but make "history." If theorist Michel DeCerteau offers a critique when he writes "[T]hus the past is the fiction of the present,"[12] Suh twists that critique back by acknowledging the fictions of the present that render Asian Americans outside of history to offer us the past as an ongoing drama of the present. Following the Western theatrical tradition, the history play's predecessor was the medieval chronicle play, then Suh is chronicling a history for Asian America. His plays are the record. An aphorism of empire and colonization is that "we are here, because you were there." Suh's plays are defiant in their acknowledgement that we are here because our ancestors once were both here and there. They dared to dream—and crossed oceans to make those dreams real. For not only are we, in the words of poet Kinley Simmons, "our ancestors' wildest dreams," our presence today is their sweetest revenge, a testament to their persistence and survival and a reminder of our own capacity for such in times of crisis.

Suh was born in Detroit, Michigan, in 1975, and grew up in the suburbs of Indianapolis, Indiana. Though he arrived at Indiana University, Bloomington, intent on becoming a novelist, he developed an interest in theatre, and playwriting in particular, enrolling in every playwriting course taught by Dennis J. Reardon, who served as the Head of the Playwriting Program at Indiana. Suh graduated with a BA in English and moved to New York City where he earned an MFA in Playwriting at the Actors Studio Drama School at New School University. In addition to his playwriting, Suh has worked at many levels of theatre-making and production, as a founding member and steering committee member of the National Asian American Theater Conference, the artistic director of Second Generation Productions, co-leader of the Ma-Yi Writer's Lab, the largest resident company of Asian American playwrights in the universe, and director of artistic programs at the Lark Play Development Center. He has taught at Hunter College, Columbia University, Atlantic Theater Company's Virtual Global Conservatory, and the Sewanee Writers Conference. He is Professor of Practice at the Lewis Center for the Arts at Princeton University.

Produced nationally and internationally, his published plays include *American Hwangap* (2009), *The Chinese Lady* (2019), *Charles Francis Chan Jr.'s Exotic Oriental Murder Mystery* (2021), *Bina's Six Apples* (2022), *Happy Birthday William Abernathy* (2022), his translation of *Henry V* (2022) for Play On Shakespeare, *The Far Country* (2023), and *Disney & Fujikawa* (2023). He is the recipient of The Harold & Mimi Steinberg Playwright Award, the Herb Alpert Award in the Arts, the Horton Foote Prize, the Helen Merrill Award, Guggenheim Fellowship, and the Lilah Kan Red Socks Award in recognition of an artist's commitment to community service. Suh is a 2023 Pulitzer Prize Finalist in Drama for *The Far Country*.

Suh did not set out to write his century and a half cycle. Instead, each historical exploration led to the next. It all began with the research process he undertook to develop *Charles Francis Chan Jr.'s Exotic Oriental Murder Mystery* for NAATCO. By looking into the history of stereotypes and Asian racialization, Suh read scholarship unavailable to him or not yet written during his undergraduate studies of Asian American history, learning then about Afong Moy. Suh pinpoints his "historical impulse" to his Asian American study undertaken after and outside the university. In an interview with fellow playwrights Sanaz Toossi and Aleshea Harris, Suh notes "there's so much more scholarship around Asian American history than when I was in school, and I kept coming across the stories that just stuck with me, that almost haunted me. I felt like I needed to wrestle with them somehow."[13] Suh explains the discovery and excitement in an interview with director Ralph B. Peña, as he was hailed by his research ("Hey, there's a play there. There's a play there."), and discovers a sense of purpose:

> [Th]e more I dig . . . the more I'm compelled to analyze where it all comes from. Not just as an exercise in excavating the past, because let's face it, a lot of that history is quite bleak and painful. But I'm particularly interested in using the past as a guide to where we come from, so that we can understand where we are now, in relation to that history, and hopefully figure out where to go from there.[14]

For Suh, researching and writing *Charles Francis Chan Jr.'s Exotic Oriental Murder Mystery* was the origin point for his cycle of history plays, where he encounters figures and histories that haunt him and that he wrestles with first on the page and then "in a room with peers and [we] wrestle with this together."[15]

In the week following the opening of *Charles Francis Chan Jr.'s Exotic Oriental Murder Mystery*, which was based on the racial histories of Asian Americans and would inspire the next decade of his work, the racial politics of casting, and how Suh's plays were being produced, took center stage, upstaging even Monkey's antics. Clarion University of Pennsylvania (Pennsylvania Western University, Clarion) cancelled their production of Suh's *Jesus in India*. The student production had cast two white actors and one mixed-race actor in race-conscious roles Suh had written as South Asian, which he only discovered after seeing an image from the production. After first requesting the characters be recast and being denied, Suh withdrew permissions for the production. After the *Pittsburgh Post-Gazette* broke the story about the casting "controversy,"[16] based on statements by Clarion University stakeholders, including the director Marilouise Michel and reprinting an email from Suh to the director, Suh posted a statement[17] circulated on social media and on arts administrator, writer, and advocate Howard Sherman's website. Michel responded with an essay titled "How Racial Politics Hurt My Students," in *The Chronicle of Higher Education*, that argued for a director's right to cast "regardless of race, ethnicity and even gender."[18] Clarion University also put out a statement that their students were being "punished for their race."[19]

These events came just days after playwright Katori Hall published a statement on a Kent State University production of her play, *The Mountaintop*, which double cast the role of Dr. Martin Luther King with both a black and a white actor. In 2015, the backdrop to these college theatre productions were the student protests that broke out across universities, with Yale and University of Missouri capturing the most media attention, over racial discrimination and campus climate. For both Hall and Suh, white actors were cast in non-white roles, the college productions ignored playwrights' permissions, and the institutions fudged their licensing agreements.

Both casting "controversies" reveal the zero-sum mindset of opponents to diversity that is currently playing out politically with devastating effect, using the cover of "reverse racism" to continue the erasure and theft of artists of color, extending the political economies of blackface, brownface, and yellowface. In his statement, Suh wrote that "as a writer of color in a field where representation and visibility are ongoing struggles, I feel a responsibility to provide opportunities for artists of color to be seen, and to protect that work from distortion in the public eye." He continued, "[t]he practice of using white actors to portray non-white characters has deep roots in ugly racist traditions. It sends a message, intended or not, that is exclusionary at best, dehumanizing at worst."[20] Suh connects racist pasts to a contested present. Similarly in her statement, Hall laments the casting of a white actor for King as "yet *another* erasure of the black body" (my emphasis).[21] Both playwrights foreground the ways that the repetition of theatre (by trading in representations and re-presenting them night after night) repeats the violences of exclusion and erasure with the weight of history. Moreover, Asian American theatre history is punctuated by representational crises from the casting "controversies" of Broadway's *Miss Saigon* to La Jolla Playhouse's *The Nightingale* – and almost all productions of Gilbert and Sullivan's *The Mikado*.

I want to draw a line here connecting Clarion University's almost production of *Jesus in India* to the four history plays Suh would go on to write after *Charles Francis*

Chan Jr.'s Exotic Oriental Murder Mystery. What he calls, in an interview with Rich Kelley, "an involuntary impulse to investigate particular moments in history."[22] His insistence on presence in absence and exploring erased histories feels like a rejoinder, such that his cycle of history plays is an extended study on how to tell Asian American history ethically. That these plays brim with characters to be played by actors of Asian descent is another form of reparation and revenge. Rather than bemoan the absence of Asian America or succumb to this history's bleakness and pain, Suh makes Asian American presence non-negotiable, through not just bodies, both that of the actors and characters, but the time and space for Asian and Asian American life to be brought back to life night after night. In doing so, his Asian American history is one of abundance and accumulation. If he was haunted and wrestled with bringing these stories on stage, then we, as spectators and readers, bear witness. This is the "really real" place of Asian America and Suh's cycle of history plays forges its genealogy.

Once in the Countryside is a critical edition of Suh's five history plays, which takes that abundance and accumulation to heart, such that the collection of the plays is an occasion to gather a cast and crew of scholars and artists in conversation with Suh's work. In addition to the scripts, each of the plays is framed for the reader with a critical preface by a scholar of Asian American theatre and performance studies and a postscript by a creative collaborator, a theatre artist who collaborated with Suh on key productions. Scholars Amy B. Huang, Ju Yon Kim, Elizabeth W. Son, Lucy Burns, and I, along with theatre artists Shannon Tyo, Whit K. Lee, Jiyoun Chang, Peter Kim, and May Adrales provide context and insight into the plays and their productions. Following the plays, their prefaces, and postscripts, the collection closes with an interview with Lloyd Suh about his cycle of history plays.

Rather than follow their production history, *Once in the Countryside* is presented in historical order, moving from the life of Afong Moy, the first Chinese woman in America, in *The Chinese Lady,* to the ways that the Chinese in America forged generational belonging in the era of Chinese Exclusion when the United States first restricted immigration based on race in *The Far Country,* which moves from 1909 through 1930. While *The Chinese Lady* takes us on a tour across the US and arrests us in the exhibit space that Afong Moy is stuck in, *The Far Country* shifts between Taishan, San Francisco, and the no man's land of detention at Angel Island Immigration Station in San Francisco Bay. Suh extends his meditation on the experiences of migration in *Bina's Six Apples,* a play for young audiences, which follows Bina, and her family, who are suddenly made refugees by the outbreak of the Korean War. By setting *Bina's Six Apples* in Korea in the fall of 1950, the play looks back to the time and place before immigration to the US for so many Koreans, and at the geopolitics, militarism, and war that propel migrations within homelands and to new ones. The Vietnam War becomes a backdrop when Suh returns to San Francisco in the 1960s for *Charles Francis Chan Jr.'s Exotic Oriental Murder Mystery,* where Suh both exorcises and dramatizes the invention of pan-ethnic coalitional politics of Asian America. The cycle ends with *The Heart Sellers,* which explores the effects of the immigration law that finally repealed the Asian exclusion laws through the lives of two recent immigrants, wives of foreign-trained doctors, each trying to find their way in a new home on the cusp of futures unknown.

The collection opens with the most produced play in the cycle of history plays. Commissioned by Ma-Yi Theatre Company, *The Chinese Lady* co-premiered first in Pittsfield, MA, at Barrington Stage in July 2018, and then in NYC, at Theater Row produced by Ma-Yi in November 2018. During the 2021-22 playgoing season, *The Chinese Lady* was the most produced play in the US.[23] The play begins in 1834 and "conjure[s]"[24] the historical figure, Afong Moy, who was the first Chinese woman in the US, brought (and bought) to be exhibited among porcelain, silks, and rugs by the Carne Brothers and later acquired by PT Barnum as an attraction. Moving from the 1830s through the present moment, Suh's play focuses on Afong, along with Atung, her translator, to present her life, inner life, and afterlife. The two-person play plumbs her hopes and dreams in a series of scenes that double Moy's life on display with the spectacle unfolding before spectators, who might find themselves uncomfortably standing in for audiences past. The play's metatheatrical form informs its canny investigation of the (white) gaze and the possibilities of performance to forge identities and understanding.

For his exploration of the impact of legislative exclusion, Suh's *The Far Country* casts seven actors to play 13 characters who span the years between 1909 and 1930 and traverse continents. From San Francisco, USA, to Taishan, China, and back again (and again), the epic dramatizes the paper son (and daughter) system whereby Chinese immigrants circumvented laws to build lives and create lineages in the United States. These early Chinese in America made themselves Americans after enduring detention and interrogation at Angel Island Immigration Station, which was built expressly to enforce the Chinese Exclusion Act of 1882. Commissioned and produced by Atlantic Theater Company, *The Far Country* had its world premiere at the Linda Gross Theater in NYC in November 2022. It had its Bay Area premiere in April 2024 at Berkeley Repertory Theatre. The play includes transcribed poems by detainees from the walls of the barracks on Angel Island, which is published and copyrighted with permission from *Island: Poetry and History of Chinese Immigrants on Angel Island, 1910-1940,* edited and translated by Him Mark Lai, Genny Lim, and Judy Yung.

While *The Far Country* moves between the US and China to explore both the before and after of migration, *Bina's Six Apples* is a return to the homeland in a prequel to immigration. Set during the Korean War, the fall of 1950, and based on Suh's father's family history, the play, written for a young audience, follows 10-year-old Bina, who has been tasked with carrying 6 apples, when she is separated from her family as they flee their apple orchard for the coast. Along Bina's journey from Geochang to Busan, she meets others who are both and differently impacted by the war. Through each encounter with Mother, Soldier, Boatperson, Merchant, and Boy, Bina evaluates her sense of self and her relationship to others by way of the apples that could sustain a hungry refugee but also represent legacy, inheritance, and her family's livelihood. *Bina's Six Apples* was originally commissioned and produced by The Children's Theatre Company in Minneapolis, Minnesota, in January 2022, with a world premiere that was co-produced by Alliance Theatre in Atlanta, Georgia, in March 2022.

The first history play in this collection that Suh wrote, *Charles Frances Chan Jr.'s Exotic Oriental Murder Mystery,* is a sprawling genre mashup: it is the portrait of an Asian American playwright as a young man in San Francisco during the upheaval of the Vietnam War and the Civil Rights Movement. The play braids two storylines. One is a Charlie Chan murder mystery. The other follows Frank Chan (a thinly veiled Frank Chin) and Kathy Ching in the dawning of an Asian American counterculture. They converge as the characters and the play contend with the enduring legacies of racist stereotypes and practices like yellowface. The play was commissioned and produced by the National Asian American Theatre Company (NAATCO) at Walkerspace in New York City in October 2015.

If *Bina's Six Apples* stages Suh's father's childhood, *The Heart Sellers,* the final play in the collection, speculates an alternative past and future for his mother's new adulthood. Set in a mid-sized US city in 1973, *The Heart Sellers* quietly explores the impact of the Immigration and Nationality Act of 1965, also known as the Hart-Celler Act, on the lives and futures of two 23-year-old women, who have each immigrated to the US as trailing spouses to their doctor husbands. Luna has arrived from the Philippines; Jane, from South Korea. They have left homelands oppressed by dictators (Marcos in the Philippines and Park Chung Hee in South Korea) and arrive in a United States that is on the brink of the Watergate scandal. When the two meet at the supermarket on Thanksgiving, Luna invites her over to her apartment and Jane accepts. The play spools out as one impulsive evening, fueled by wine and roasted sweet potatoes. Commissioned and produced by Milwaukee Repertory Theater, *The Heart Sellers* premiered in February 2023.

The possibility for reparation radiates across *Once in a Countryside* through Suh's imagining of both the reach and limits of Afong Moy's agency in *The Chinese Lady*, and the forging of found families as an unintended consequence of racist legislation in *The Far Country*. In *Bina's Six Apples,* he offers a reparative reading of his own family history by recasting his daughter in his father's life story. Suh rubs the unfulfilled promises of representation against the resilience of racist stereotypes in *Charles Francis Chan Jr.'s Exotic Oriental Murder Mystery*. Finally, *The Heart Sellers* is built whole cloth from a dramaturgy of fulfillment, which Suh previously utilized in single scenes, through the gift of friendship and futures.

Suh's "historical impulse" has propelled this collection of five plays, which insists on Asian and Asian American presence in the face of history's absences. When novelist Min Jin Lee opens her epic *Pachinko* with the line, "History has failed us, but no matter,"[25] she immediately proceeds with a multigenerational story that traces another history through the everyday lives of the Korean diaspora[26] in Japan. This collection of history plays dwells in the insouciant defiance of "but no matter," to offer us what might be "really real" about Asian American history for a future as yet unimagined. I see the same "historical impulse" and insistence on presence and future when Moon Gyet, in *The Far Country,* explains to his mother Low the why of his existence in America – why he remains even as America, and history, has failed him:

Moon Gyet   But I'm trying. I'm trying to . . . make something from it

Low   Make what?

Moon Gyet   A future. Not for me, not for my children either, perhaps, but . . . but maybe. Maybe beyond that. Past what you or I can see. Because they say there is no more gold on Gold Mountain, but yes . . . Yes. There is. There is. And I will find it. This, this is the only path. (111)

Acknowledgements

To the contributors to this collection, May Adrales, Lucy MSP Burns, Jiyoun Chang, Amy Huang, Ju Yon Kim, Peter Kim, Whit K. Lee, Liz Son, and Shannon Tyo, thank you for sharing your experience, expertise, and knowledge. Thank you to Chris Eng for reading my drafts and always offering vital insights, and Jennifer Wang for her cheery acumen. This collection was supported by a subvention grant from the Humanities Center at the University of Rhode Island.

None of this would be possible without Lloyd Suh, and the theatrical worlds that he has crafted. I am thrilled that this volume, which was an audacious aside at the closing night party for *The Far Country,* has come to fruition.

Notes

1   "East and West Shaking Hands at Laying Last Rail." Stanford University Libraries. Accessed March 16, 2025. https://exhibits.stanford.edu/rr/catalog/hx407zx8552
2   "The last spike was an ordinary spike (not a 'golden' spike, which would have been crushed by a sledgehammer's blow)." Robert M. Utley, "The Spike Wasn't Golden," *NYTimes*, 12 December 1999. http://www.nytimes.com/books/99/12/12/reviews/991212.12utleyt.html.
3   "Andrew J. Russell." National Park Service. Accessed August 19, 2024. https://www.nps.gov/gosp/learn/historyculture/a-moment-in-time.htm
4   For David Eng, this moment is one that embodies the erasure of Chinese from American history. See Chapter 1, "I've been (re)working on the railroad: Photography and National History in *China Men* and *Donald Duk*," David Eng, *Racial Castration: Managing Masculinity in Asian America* (Durham, NC: Duke University Press, 2001).
5   Julia H. Lee, "Asian American Settlers, the Neo-Frontier Narrative, and the Problem of History." *Amerasia* (2024): 4.
6   See Gordon H. Chang, *Ghosts of Gold Mountain: The Epic Story of the Chinese Who Built the Transcontinental Railroad* (Boston: Houghton Mifflin Harcourt, 2019) and Gordon H. Chang and Shelley Fisher Fishkin, eds, with Hilton Obenzinger and Roland Hsu, *The Chinese and the Iron Road: Building the Transcontinental Railroad* (Palo Alto: Stanford University Press, 2019).
7   Madeline Y. Hsu, "Asian American History and the Perils of a Usable Past." *Modern American History* 1, no. 1 (2018): 71.
8   Madeline Y. Hsu, "Asian American History and the Perils of a Usable Past." *Modern American History* 1, no. 1 (2018): 71.
9   Saidiya Hartman on the "silence in the archive": "This writing is personal because this history has engendered me, because "the knowledge of the other marks me," because of the pain experienced in my encounter with the scraps of the archive, and because of the kinds of stories I have fashioned to bridge the past and the present and to dramatize the production of nothing – empty rooms, and silence, and lives reduced to waste." Saidiya Hartman, "Venus in Two Acts," *Small Axe* 26 June 2008: 4.
10 Freddie Rokem, *Performing History: Theatrical Representations of the Past in Contemporary Theatre* (Iowa City, IA: University of Iowa Press, 2002), xi.
11 Suzan-Lori Parks, "Possession" in *The America Play and Other Works* (NY: TCG,1995), 4–5.
12 Michel de Certeau, *The Writing of History,* trans. Tom Conley (New York: Columbia University Press, 1988), 10.

13 Rob Weinert-Kendt, "Sanaz Toossi, Aleshea Harris, Lloyd Suh: Finding Form and Who Their Plays Are For," *American Theatre.* July 27, 2023. https://www.americantheatre.org/2023/07/27/sanaz-toossi-aleshea-harris-lloyd-suh-finding-form-and-who-their-plays-are-for/
14 "Chapter One: Ralph B. Peña, Artistic Director, Ma-Yi Theater Company, interviews Lloyd Suh," Accessed August 19, 2024, https://herbalpertawards.org/artist/lloyd-suh-chapter-one
15 "Chapter One: Ralph B. Peña, Artistic Director, Ma-Yi Theater Company, interviews Lloyd Suh," Accessed March 17, 2025, https://herbalpertawards.org/artist/lloyd-suh-chapter-one
16 I place casting "controversy" in scare quotes to put pressure on what might be controversial and what might be consensus. Racist performance practices like whitewashing, yellowface, blackface, brownface, etc. are not controversial in the sense that there is a public or cultural disagreement. It's also not controversial in the sense that such casting practices are rare or anomalous. These practices have long histories.
17 Howard Sherman, "Erasing Race On Stage At Clarion University," Accessed August 21, 2024. http://hesherman.com/2015/11/13/erasing-race-on-stage-at-clarion-university/
18 Marilouise Michel, "How Racial Politics Hurt My Students," *The Chronicle of Higher Education,* November 13, 2015, https://www.chronicle.com/article/how-racial-politics-hurt-my-students/
19 Clarion University, "Issues of Race Shut Down University Play Days Before Opening Night," November 13, 2015, https://www.prnewswire.com/news-releases/issues-of-race-shut-down-university-play-days-before-opening-night-300178610.html
20 Howard Sherman, "Erasing Race On Stage At Clarion University," Accessed August 21, 2024, http://hesherman.com/2015/11/13/erasing-race-on-stage-at-clarion-university/
21 Katori Hall, "Playwright Reacts to the White Casting of MLK in The Mountaintop"," November 9, 2015, https://www.theroot.com/playwright-reacts-to-the-white-casting-of-mlk-in-the-mo-1790861704
22 Rich Kelley, "Lloyd Suh on fathers and sons, Ben Franklin's humor, the American experiment, and FRANKLINLAND," September 20, 2024, https://www.ensemblestudiotheatre.org/est-blog-1/2024/9/20/lloyd-suh-on-fathers-and-sons-ben-franklins-humor-the-american-experiment-and-franklinland
23 Diep Tran, "What 'The Chinese Lady' Can Teach Us About Asian America, Then And Now," *American Theatre,* October 27, 2021, https://www.americantheatre.org/2021/10/27/what-the-chinese-lady-can-teach-us-about-asian-america-then-and-now/
24 Giselle, "Exclusive Q&A: Lloyd Suh from Ma-Yi Theater Company and Public's *The Chinese Lady*," February 16, 2022, https://www.stagerightsecrets.com/lloyd-suh-the-cinese-lady/
25 Min Jin Lee, *Pachinko* (Grand Central Publishing, 2017), 5.
26 One categorization for the Korean diaspora living multi-generationally in Japan is Zainichi Koreans. In her acknowledgements, Lee notes that zainichi is "a term used often to describe Korean Japanese people who were either migrants from the colonial era or their descendants . . . Some Koreans in Japan do not wish to be called *Zainichi* Korean because the term means literally 'foreign resident staying in Japan,' which makes no sense since there are often third, fourth, and fifth surviving generations of Koreans in Japan." Min Jin Lee, *Pachinko* (Grand Central Publishing, 2017), 481.

References

"Andrew J. Russell." National Park Service. Accessed August 19, 2024. https://www.nps.gov/gosp/learn/historyculture/a-moment-in-time.htm

Chang, Gordon H. *Ghosts of Gold Mountain: The Epic Story of the Chinese Who Built the Transcontinental Railroad*. Boston: Houghton Mifflin Harcourt, 2019.

Chang, Gordon H. and Shelley Fisher Fishkin, eds, with Hilton Obenzinger and Roland Hsu. *The Chinese and the Iron Road: Building the Transcontinental Railroad*. Palo Alto: Stanford University Press, 2019.

"Chapter One: Ralph B. Peña, Artistic Director, Ma-Yi Theater Company, interviews Lloyd Suh," Herbert Alpert Awards. Accessed August 19, 2024, https://herbalpertawards.org/artist/lloyd-suh-chapter-one

Clarion University, "Issues of Race Shut Down University Play Days Before Opening Night," November 13, 2015, https://www.prnewswire.com/news-releases/issues-of-race-shut-down-university-play-days-before-opening-night-300178610.html

de Certeau, Michel. *The Writing of History,* trans. Tom Conley. New York: Columbia University Press, 1988.

"East and West Shaking Hands at Laying Last Rail." Stanford University Libraries. Accessed March 16, 2025. https://exhibits.stanford.edu/rr/catalog/hx407zx8552

Eng, David. *Racial Castration: Managing Masculinity in Asian America*. Durham, NC: Duke University Press, 2001.

Giselle, "Exclusive Q&A: Lloyd Suh from Ma-Yi Theater Company and Public's *The Chinese Lady*," February 16, 2022, https://www.stagerightsecrets.com/lloyd-suh-the-cinese-lady/

Hall, Katori. "Playwright Reacts to the White Casting of MLK in The Mountaintop"," November 9, 2015, https://www.theroot.com/playwright-reacts-to-the-white-casting-of-mlk-in-the-mo-1790861704

Hartman, Saidiya. "Venus in Two Acts," *Small Axe* 26, vol. 12, no. 2 (June 2008): 1–14.

Hsu, Madeline Y. "Asian American History and the Perils of a Usable Past." *Modern American History* 1, no. 1 (2018): 71–75.

Kelley, Rich. "Lloyd Suh on fathers and sons, Ben Franklin's humor, the American experiment, and FRANKLINLAND," September 20, 2024, https://www.ensemblestudiotheatre.org/est-blog-1/2024/9/20/lloyd-suh-on-fathers-and-sons-ben-franklins-humor-the-american-experiment-and-franklinland

Lee, Julia H. "Asian American Settlers, the Neo-Frontier Narrative, and the Problem of History." *Amerasia Journal* (2024): 1–16.

Lee, Min Jin. *Pachinko*. Grand Central Publishing, 2017.

Michel, Marilouise. "How Racial Politics Hurt My Students," *The Chronicle of Higher Education,* November 13, 2015, https://www.chronicle.com/article/how-racial-politics-hurt-my-students/

Parks, Suzan-Lori. *The America Play and Other Works*. NY: TCG, 1995.

Rokem, Freddie. *Performing History: Theatrical Representations of the Past in Contemporary Theatre*. Iowa City, IA: University of Iowa Press, 2002.

Sherman, Howard. "Erasing Race On Stage At Clarion University," Accessed August 21, 2024. http://hesherman.com/2015/11/13/erasing-race-on-stage-at-clarion-university/

Tran, Diep. "What 'The Chinese Lady' Can Teach Us About Asian America, Then And Now," *American Theatre,* October 27, 2021, https://www.americantheatre.org/2021/10/27/what-the-chinese-lady-can-teach-us-about-asian-america-then-and-now/

Utley, Robert M. "The Spike Wasn't Golden," *NYTimes*, 12 December 1999, http://www.nytimes.com/books/99/12/12/reviews/991212.12utleyt.html.

Weinert-Kendt, Rob. "Sanaz Toossi, Aleshea Harris, Lloyd Suh: Finding Form and Who Their Plays Are For," *American Theatre*. July 27, 2023. https://www.americantheatre.org/2023/07/27/sanaz-toossi-aleshea-harris-lloyd-suh-finding-form-and-who-their-plays-are-for/

The Chinese Lady

Preface

Spending Time with Afong Moy

Amy B. Huang

In Lloyd Suh's *The Chinese Lady* (2019), Afong Moy, possibly the first Chinese woman to set foot in the United States, slowly comes to the startling and painful realization that her exhibition may not produce the intercultural understanding that she had hoped for. Earlier in the scene, she had excitedly informed audience members (who stand in for the original nineteenth-century American audiences of the exhibitions) that she was in Washington, D.C., and had just met President Andrew Jackson. Yet after re-enacting this meeting for us, Afong Moy begins to realize that the exhibition may actually reflect and reinforce ideas of Orientalism, which Edward Said defines as "a Western style for dominating, restructuring, and having authority over the Orient" (1979: 3). Orientalism is a way of seeing that stresses the binaries and differences between "the familiar (Europe, the West, 'us') and the strange (the Orient, the East, 'them')" (Said 1979: 43). The exhibition works to exotify and dehumanize Asian women until they are animals on view at the zoo, or meat to consume for dinner. Afong Moy hesitantly states of her exhibition, "I am thinking that perhaps ... perhaps it is not good" (40). Her translator Atung then whispers to remind her that we, the audience members, are watching. This moment marks a significant shift in Afong Moy's relationship with the audience. Once spoken to with great excitement and warmth, we now intrude on a private, painful moment. The change might give us pause. What should we be seeing in this moment? Should we even be looking at all? How might this metatheatrical moment pointing to the audiences' spectatorship invite them to consider past and present ways of seeing Asian women? As Atung removes Afong Moy's headdress or loosens her hair, the stage directions note: "*This can take time*" (41). The play quietly gives Afong Moy and Atung time. They take time to think, hope, dream, remember, and grieve. Foregrounding the idea that they must remain unknowable, Suh still works to conjure for Afong Moy and Atung a past, a present, and all the possibilities in between.[1]

To give Afong Moy and Atung time is a radical act. It refuses to accept the elisions in the historical record and historiography as well as the temporal logic behind the exhibitions.[2] Afong Moy arrived in the United States from Guangzhou, China in 1834; this trip was part of a temporary financial agreement that her family had made with the American traders, Francis and Nathaniel Carnes. Upon arrival, Afong Moy became the centerpiece of Captain Benjamin Obear's New York City exhibition, which sought to display and sell imported Chinese goods. The exhibition toured multiple cities including Baltimore, Philadelphia, and Charleston, drawing large crowds of spectators, and inviting the consumption of Chinese goods.[3] Advertisements of these initial exhibitions briefly noted that Afong Moy's interpreter, Atung, worked to translate her statements for white American audiences. In 1848, Afong Moy participated in PT Barnum's exhibitions, appearing alongside performers such as Charles Stratton (advertised as General Tom Thumb). After her last public exhibition in 1851, however, Afong Moy disappears from the historical record. She is unaccounted for in death and census records, leaving it unclear when she died or if she struggled to survive in the United States after performing in numerous exhibitions.[4] In an interview in *Mochi Magazine*, Lloyd Suh explained that in the course of conducting research on Afong Moy, he came to wonder (especially regarding the later parts of Afong Moy's life, after her initial sensational popularity):

> "How did she feel? What did she think about all this?" At the point where history loses her — when she's lost to the record — nobody cared to record it, nobody cared to follow, nobody cared to document [. . .] At that point, after doing all that investigation, sitting with that story and trying to imagine the magnitude of what she went through, I cared. I do. I really cared enough to want to tell people that they shouldn't forget.

So much of what remains of Afong Moy and Atung in archives – the newspaper advertisements and broadsides – freezes them in time, shaping how past and present viewers saw them. The exhibitions and their advertisements place "the burden of liveness" (as conceptualized by the performance theorist, José Esteban Muñoz) on Afong Moy and Atung to perform the live attraction of their exotic otherness. Explaining how often minoritarian subjects have been compelled to perform for elite audiences, Muñoz further states: "The 'burden' of liveness affords the minoritarian subject an extremely circumscribed temporality. To be only in 'the live' means that one is denied history and futurity" (Muñoz 1999: 189). Indeed, advertisements urged their viewers to see Afong Moy as a fleeting presence, a live show that would quickly disappear. For example, an 1835 advertisement in the Philadelphia newspaper the *American Sentinel* exclaimed that this would be the "LAST DAY" to see "THE CHINESE LADY," noting "POSITIVELY CLOSING THIS DAY. Unprecedented Novelty! THE CHINESE LADY Afong Moy, accompanied by her Attendant and Interpreter, Acong." Such advertisements invested in Afong Moy and Atung's liveness, while denying them history and futurity. As Suh suggests, because sensational advertisements make up a large part of all that remains in documenting the lives of Afong Moy and Atung, there are significant challenges to grasping a sense of their lives before or after the exhibitions.

The Chinese Lady responds to these elisions within such advertisements and ephemera by making these gaps spectacularly visible. In the beginning of the play, Atung directly addresses the audience and states, "You do not need to know who I am or where I come from, or how it came to be that I speak both languages with such practical and occasional poetic fluency. Only that I will assist Afong Moy, The Chinese Lady, during all exhibition hours" (23). While nineteenth-century advertisements often simply referred to Atung or Acong as Afong Moy's "Attendant and Interpreter," here Atung directs the audience's attention to the fact that they know so little of his past, including how he learned to speak English and Chinese and how he came to be Afong Moy's translator. This act of laying bare this unknowing links into Lisa Lowe's efforts to explain the "*politics of our lack of knowledge*" and the "economy of affirmation and forgetting that characterizes liberal humanist understanding" (2015: 39).[5] How, we might ask, have these exhibition ephemera invited us *to forget to delve* into Atung's past or his hopes for the future? In Scene 3, after Atung reminds Afong Moy that the audience is still watching her live performance, Suh extricates Atung from the exhibition and its compulsory performances. Instead, Atung takes time to express his dreams. He explains how he dreams of China and his childhood and family. He dreams, too, of being the central attraction in the Room, making Afong Moy his translator and lover. As the curtain momentarily closes on Afong Moy, and the live spectacle fades into the background, this scene refuses the temporal circumscription of the "burden of liveness." Atung's theatrical dreamworld slowly and carefully conjures his own history and hopes.

Significantly, *The Chinese Lady* responds to the silences and elisions surrounding Afong Moy's life and exhibition. Newspaper advertisements hawked her "novelty" as they encouraged audiences to catch this show while they could. In these advertisements, Afong Moy appeared as an unchanging, singular representative of China; she was "the Chinese Lady." In the play, however, Afong Moy is aware that both she and the world around her are constantly changing. She notes that her English improves over time. She further explains: "[W]ith each passing hour I am less and less Chinese. Less and less Chinese, but more and more old, and therefore closer and closer to the inevitable day when you will stop looking at me altogether" (40). While advertisements invested in a frozen and fleeting portrait of Afong Moy's exotic otherness, Suh suggests that Afong Moy herself might have been eminently aware of the passage of time and its effect on her exhibition. Even as Suh is extremely careful to note how the real Afong Moy is unknowable, he floats the possibility that she might be aware of how the "success" of the show rested on her exotic novelty, and implicitly, her youth.[6] But while advertisements highlighted the limited runs of the exhibitions to drum up attendance, Suh focuses attention not only on Afong Moy's live presence, but also the costs of that presence. Her presence here entails an aching absence from her home and family. Afong Moy states:

> I can't remember
> I can't remember their faces
> I can't remember my mother
> I have not heard from
> for you see, The Carnes Brothers
> I gave them a letter
> to send
> in 1836
> a letter to send in 1837
> and of course they never sent it
> 1838
> why would they
> 1839
> so many years (48)

Advertisements may have presented the exhibition as fleeting, but here Suh suggests that Afong Moy may have experienced the exhibitions as painfully long. Invested in her live performance, the exhibition managers fail to care about her connection to her past in China and her family there. Suh gives Afong Moy broken, repetitive statements to reflect the slowly dissipating hope of ever reconnecting with her family. He gives her time to grieve.

Earlier in the play, Afong Moy had carefully structured the histories and stories she told to the exhibition audiences, explaining, for example, the history of tea. However, as Suh follows her as she falls out of the spotlight (and is replaced by Pwan Ye-Koo, a younger Chinese woman who also had bound feet), he again traces her more unstructured trains of thought. For example, Afong Moy states:

Forgive me I remember something now.
I remember a girl
In Guangzhou
Where was I
at a picnic I think
by the river
I think I was twelve
perhaps thirteen
I dropped my handkerchief
on accident I think
but who remembers
and she picked it up
and she looked at me
and she smiled

I wonder what she's doing now
Why am I talking about this?
What am I talking about? (49–50)

Suh carves out time for minor moments that might seem to have no relevance to the exhibition and its audiences. Within Afong Moy's hesitant, repetitive statements of "I remember" and "I think," we might hear a refusal of the temporal logic and structure of the exhibition. Challenging the exhibition advertisements of sensationally short runs, Afong Moy's small, quiet memory (and the process of trying to remember) presents itself as also vitally important and worthy of the audience's time and attention. As she asks, "Why am I talking about this? What am I talking about?" (in direct contradistinction to a younger Afong Moy's ability to assume narrative control and declare an item's relevance), the audience might also wonder why this memory might indeed matter. Thinking with Lisa Lowe's work on the "economy of affirmation and forgetting," they might wonder why they are able to know so little about the thoughts and memories of an aging Afong Moy as she is replaced in the exhibition. They might wonder why broadsides crowned Pwan Ye-Koo as "The Chinese Lady" while forgetting Afong Moy. What would it mean to remember Afong Moy by trying to conjure her memories?

In this moment of the play, Afong Moy's fragmented memory, per Walter Benjamin, offers a way to see history not as a continuum of events (in which Afong Moy is simply replaced by Pwan Ye-Koo), but instead to seize "hold of a memory as it flashes up at a moment of danger" (1968: 255). Afong Moy's memory of this girl in Canton Province gestures to a mode of seeing that is radically different from her present exotification in the exhibition. Just as she is being replaced in an exhibition invested in exotic novelty, this memory surfaces and presents another way of seeing her. The girl's act of picking up the handkerchief requires a type of attention and care that is distinct from the exhibition managers' and audience members' vision of her as sensational attraction and as expendable or an object of consumption. Whereas Afong Moy's exhibitions simultaneously served to display and sell Chinese goods, here an object serves to create a moment of human connection rooted in care. The girl picks up the handkerchief, looks at Afong Moy, and actually sees her. Suh spotlights this flash of a memory to gesture to Afong Moy's past and to earlier and alternative ways of being seen and relating to others. What if she had remained in China or if she had been able to find community and friendship? How might she have been seen and understood differently?

Historians often argue that Afong Moy was the first known Chinese woman to set foot in the United States. Yet whereas advertisements highlighted Afong Moy's novelty and exceptional nature, Suh suggests how isolated and alone Afong Moy may have felt in her firstness. In the play, Afong Moy wonders if she will ever be able to connect with a Chinese community again. In one scene, as she plans to leave the Room to look for the Chinese people who came during the California Gold Rush in 1849, she states: "I'm curious what Chinese people look like, and talk like. What the Chinese do. What they eat. How they walk. What they think about when they think about the future" (45). The statement alludes to the type of spectatorship that she has been subjected to, but now the shape of this vision has transformed. Curiosity is not propelled by the effort to reiterate Orientalism and ideas of otherness, but by a wish to create a community. Furthermore, this statement revises the temporal logic of the exhibition. In an earlier scene in the play, when Atung reminds Afong Moy that it is time for her to walk, she exclaims: "[H]ow irresponsible of me. Thinking ahead to the future when I have tasks in the now" (29). While the exhibition might have sought to regiment Afong Moy's time and thoughts and to force her to bear the burden of liveness, her own desire to see Chinese people works in tandem with her desire to understand their hopes and dreams. Even as the exhibition faces its closing day and the historical record loses the traces of these Chinese subjects, *The Chinese Lady* takes time to consider their futures. Indeed, although Afong Moy falls out of the historical record in the 1850s, Suh does not accede to her erasure in historiography at that point. He asks audiences to wonder how she might have faced the future and grieved to see the increasing anti-Asian violence and hostile, exclusionary legislation.

Towards the end of the play, Afong Moy states: "It is a beautiful thing to look at something long enough to really understand it. But it is so much more beautiful to be looked at long enough to be understood" (54). The play takes time to look at Afong Moy. And more importantly, it takes time to consider what she might have felt as audiences looked at her. In the end, Afong Moy asks contemporary audiences if they might really look at each other. This scene repeats a routine of looking from the beginning of the play. But it also offers the contemporary audience a way to depart from the nineteenth-century audiences with whom they have been combined the whole evening. Rather than catching a glimpse of exotic difference, the audience might take the time to see differently.

Notes

1 In a November 25, 2019, *Mochi Magazine* interview, Suh discusses the origins of the play and explains that it does not so much seek to recover the actual history of Afong Moy, so much as it seeks to "conjure" what might have been.

2 In this way, Suh's work aligns with Saidiya Hartman's "Venus in Two Acts," which explains the concept of "critical fabulation" as an act of writing with and against archival limits.
3 For more information on the routes of the exhibition, see Nancy Davis's *The Chinese Lady: Afong Moy in Early America*.
4 Linda Kimiko August wonders whether Afong Moy may have ended up in a poorhouse in the United States, and notes PT Barnum's reputation for exploiting performers and refusing to offer them adequate support. August further explains that it is unlikely that Afong Moy was able to return to China.
5 See Christine Mok's "Raiding the Bull in a China Shop" for an astute reading of how *The Chinese Lady* challenges the reparative capacities of "representational agency." Mok notes that the play, instead, stays with an exploration of the conditions of objecthood.
6 In speaking of crafting the performance of Afong Moy in *The Chinese Lady*, Shannon Tyo explains that she begins with a high-pitched voice, which shifts over the course of the play. The choice to begin this way highlights Afong Moy's great youth when she first arrives in the United States. Tyo uses her voice to tenderly spotlight Afong Moy's specific youthfulness and naivete, which then transition over time, rather than presenting Afong Moy as frozen in time, without a past or a future.

References

Advertisement in the Philadelphia newspaper the *American Sentinel*, February 17, 1835.
August, Linda Kimiko. "Remembering Afong Moy" The Library Company of Philadelphia. February 1, 2021. https://librarycompany.org/2021/02/01/remembering-afong-moy. Accessed 8 Feb. 2024.
Benjamin, Walter, "Theses on the Philosophy of History." In *Illuminations: Essays and Reflections*. Edited by Hannah Arendt. Translated by Harry Zohn. New York: Schocken, 1968.
Davis, Nancy. *The Chinese Lady: Afong Moy in Early America*. New York: Oxford University Press, 2019.
Duan, Virginia. "The Unknowable You: An Interview with Playwright Lloyd Suh" *Mochi Magazine*. November 25, 2019. www.mochimag.com/arts-culture/the-unknowable-you-aninterview-with-playwright-lloyd-suh/. Accessed 10 Aug. 2021.
Hartman, Saidiya. "Venus in Two Acts" *Small Axe*, 12 no. 2 (2008): 1–14.
Lowe, Lisa. *The Intimacies of Four Continents*. Durham: Duke University Press, 2015.
Mok, Christine. "Raiding the Bull in a China Shop" *Theatre Journal* 74, no. 3 (2022): 303–322.
Muñoz, José Esteban. *Disidentifications: Queers of Color and the Performance of Politics*. Minneapolis: University of Minnesota Press, 1999.
Said, Edward. *Orientalism*. New York: Vintage Books, 1979.
Tyo, Shannon. "THE CHINESE LADY Ma-Yi Production Shannon Tyo" Vimeo. November 4, 2018. https://vimeo.com/298921790. Accessed 10 May 2024.

The Chinese Lady premiered as a co-production by Barrington Stage Company (Julianne Boyd, Artistic Director; Branden Huldeen, Artistic Producer) and Ma-Yi Theater Company (Ralph B. Peña, Artistic Director). The co-world premiere was first presented at Barrington Stage, Pittsfield, MA, opening on July 26, 2018; and then in New York City at the Beckett Theater at Theater Row, opening on November 10, 2018. The cast was as follows:

Afong Moy   Shannon Tyo
Atung   Daniel K. Isaac

Director   Ralph B. Peña
Scenic and Costume Designer   Junghyun Georgia Lee
Lighting Designer   Oliver Wason
Music and Sound Designer   Fabian Obispo
Production Stage Manager   Geoff Boronda

The Chinese Lady was commissioned by Ma-Yi Theater Company and developed with the support of the Roe Green Award at Cleveland Play House.

Additional thanks to Claudia Alick, Christine Bruno, Nancy E. Davis, Loretta Greco, Sonia Fernandez, Andrea Hiebler, Laura Kepley, Peter Kim, Kimber Lee, Rachel Lerner-Ley, Teresa Avia Lim, Gregg Mozgala, A. Rey Pamatmat, Haleh Roshan Stillwell, and Krista Williams, all of whom contributed in essential ways to the development of this play.

Characters

Afong Moy, female, from 14 years old to advanced age.
Atung, male, older than Afong Moy.

Setting

The United States, beginning in 1834.

Notes

The characters should be played by Asian or Asian American performers. They should speak in their natural and organic speaking voice, with no affected dialect or accent (the lone exception is in Scene 3, when Atung performs multiple voices). Otherwise, the characters should simply talk the way the actors talk.

While acknowledging that there is a distinction between the historical practice of foot binding and a contemporary model of Disability culture, the relationship of audiences to Afong Moy's feet was certainly influenced by historical perceptions of disabled bodies. In an ideal circumstance, the role of Afong Moy would be played by a performer with a similar physicality to the historical Afong Moy. While further acknowledging that feet like Afong Moy's no longer exist, I encourage producers to seek out and consider performers with physical or mobility disabilities.

The text of the play acknowledges that the performers' bodies are not the bodies of their historical counterparts. The production should as well. Regardless of whether or not the performers have physical disabilities, at no point should they pretend to have a type of mobility that they do not possess. In some cases, of course, this may mean that certain physical actions described in the play may not occur literally. As with their speaking voices, the characters should simply move the way the actors move.

1.

> *Lights up on* **Afong Moy**, *14 years old, in her Room. The Room is a box placed in the center of the larger stage. Outside the box, the stage is unadorned. Inside the box, it is ornate, decorated with various types of Chinoiserie. Watercolor paintings, vases, curtains, silks, furniture, etc. She wears a traditional Chinese gown, and jade or lacquered jewelry in her hair.*
>
> *She begins the scene seated.*
>
> **Atung** *sits on a plain-looking chair, downstage of the Room.*

Afong   Hello. My name is Afong Moy.

It is the year 1834.

I am fourteen years old, and newly arrived in America.

I was born in Guangzhou in 1820. I am one of seven children, the youngest. My family has sold me for two years of service to Misters Nathaniel and Frederick Carnes, traders of Far East Oriental imports to New York. I will be on display here at Peale's Museum, for your education and entertainment, at a price of 25 cents adults, 10 cents children.

Thank you for coming to see me.

She bows.

Atung   I am Atung. I am

Afong   Atung is irrelevant.

Atung   I am irrelevant, that's what I was going to say, I was going to say I am irrelevant.

Afong   Atung has been in service to Misters Nathaniel and Frederick Carnes as a manservant and translator of Chinese to English and back again. He is now assigned to me.

Atung   You do not need to know who I am or where I come from, or how it came to be that I speak both languages with such practical and occasionally poetic fluency. Only that I will assist Afong Moy, The Chinese Lady, during all exhibition hours.

Afong   We will not be needing Atung's translation services for the time being, for I am not speaking. It would of course seem that I am speaking, as my mouth is moving and my thoughts are becoming articulated through sound, but this is not in fact what is happening. What is happening is a performance. For my entire life is a performance. These words that you hear are not my own. These clothes that I wear are not my own. This body that I occupy is not my own. This Room in which I am seated is intended to be representative of China, just as I am intended to be representative of The Chinese Lady: the first woman from the Orient ever to set foot in America, and yet this Room is unlike any room in China, and I am unlike any lady to ever live.

And yet here we are. You and I.

Atung   And Atung.

Afong   And Atung, who is irrelevant. Seated in this Room in this museum, in this exhibition hall advertising The Chinese Lady.

I shall assume that you have paid your 25 cents, 10 cents for children, because you are curious about China. Curious about what a Chinese lady might look like or act like. I have not been in this country long enough to know the ways in which I might differ from other ladies you have encountered, or what your particular curiosities might be. But I have been told to highlight certain features that I possess, as they may seem exotic and foreign and unusual to you.

I understand it is my duty to show you things that are exotic, and foreign, and unusual.

At the start of every hour, I sit down and stay seated. I watch the customers enter the exhibition hall. I do not move. Some customers stand quietly and expectantly, while some come directly towards the Room and examine its contents. They look at the furniture. The vases. The silks and the paintings. They talk to each other. Oh look at that. I've never seen such a thing. It reminds me of. I wonder if. What do you think it feels like? And they look at me. They look at my eyes. They look at my hands. At my clothes. At my hair. At my face.

They say things to each other. Do you think she . . . I wonder if she . . . And my goodness look at her feet.

Allow me to explain my feet.

In many parts of China, it is considered a sign of elevated social status and cultural refinement for women and young girls to have tiny feet.

When I was four years old, my feet were placed into a hot mixture of herbs and animal blood to soften the skin and muscles. My toenails were clipped to their smallest possible size. Both feet were then deeply massaged and oiled before the toes were broken by hand and bound flat against the soles, into triangles. My arches were bent, then bound in silk ribbons. These ribbons were wound in a figure-eight motion, multiple times, pulling the ball of the foot and heel together, and pressing the toes underneath the sole.

This continued for about a year, every few weeks, the bones broken, then set, then broken again.

And for this part of the exhibition, I walk. In one revolution around the Room, to illustrate and demonstrate the form and function of my feet.

She walks.

Atung Typically, during this part of the show I am the one who describes the process of foot binding to the audience. But I do not need to do that now.

Afong Because I already did.

Atung Because she already did.

Afong Moy *finishes her long revolution around the Room and sits.*

Atung And now I will bring her food.

Atung *exits.*

Afong Next, I will eat, and you will watch me. Atung will bring to me plates of steamed shrimp and Chinese vegetables, along with a pot of tea which I will pour and drink in a ritualistic way so as to demonstrate its importance in my culture.

Atung *enters with a tray of food and tea.*

Atung Shrimp and Chinese vegetables. Pot of tea.

Afong I will eat these foods with chopsticks.

She displays the chopsticks with a flourish.

She takes a bite.

Since arriving in America I have been living in a small room in the home of Mrs. Augusta Obear, wife of the ship's captain who brought me here. It is a lovely home with details quite peculiar and novel to my experience. The foods I have been eating there take some getting used to. There is much bread. There is much corn. There is much potatoes. I am unaccustomed to such foods. As is my digestive system.

Perhaps she burps.

The room in Mrs. Obear's house is quite different than this Room, though the Obears have added a few artifacts from China to the decor, presumably to make me feel more at home. These accents are comforting despite their inauthenticity, but I am even more appreciative and fascinated by the differences. I have been sleeping on a bed that is elevated some three feet above the floor. I hope I do not fall off of it!

Also, everyone wears their shoes inside the house! A curious phenomenon.

I am ambivalent about the fork. I have seen it in use and I understand its functionality; it seems a useful tool for the stabbing of food, but ultimately I feel it lacks grace. Chopsticks are elegant and poetic. Forks are violent and easy.

She has finished her food.

I am finished, Atung.

Atung Very well.

Atung *takes the food, leaves the tea, and exits.*

Afong Now I will pour the tea.

She does.

In China, tea is of the utmost importance. There are many kinds of teas, for various uses; it is as much for pleasure and entertainment as it is for health and medicine.

The story goes that over 4,000 years ago, the Chinese Emperor Shennong would boil his water before he drank it so that he could be sure it was not contaminated. One day, while traveling outdoors, a leaf from a wild bush fell into the water and steeped itself in the cup. He did not notice this leaf, and to his surprise he drank the very first cup of Chinese tea.

I like this story because it tells us that history is an accident.

The accident of tea has changed the course of history, and without it I would perhaps not be here with you today.

Let me put it this way.

It is human nature to be curious. Curiosity is evolution. We migrate, from the trees, through the jungle, across oceans and rivers, we are constantly searching. This is what sent the Carnes brothers to China. This is what brings me here. We want to see. It is the same impulse that brought you here, to this room, to me. You want to look at me. You want to understand more about the world. You want to understand more. More. More.

I will discuss the history of tea in greater detail at a later time.

For now, thank you for attending this presentation of The Chinese Lady.

I am very pleased to be here in this great country. I am very pleased to represent my homeland, my family, my culture, and my history to you in hopes that this may lead to greater understanding and goodwill between China and America, and between all the peoples of the world!

Atung *enters and draws a curtain across the room.*

2.

> **Atung** *opens the curtain across the room.*
> **Afong Moy** *sits, as before.*

Afong   Hello. My name is Afong Moy.

I came to America in 1834, when I was fourteen years old.

It is the year 1836, and I am sixteen years old.

The price of admission to Peale's Museum has increased, and I am grateful that you have deemed me worthy of such an honorable price as 50 cents adults, 25 cents children. I hope that I can entertain and educate you well enough to justify such a luxurious amount.

The agreement between the Carnes brothers and my father was that I would spend two years here, in exchange for a fee.

Those two years have now expired, yet here I am.

Why am I still here?

This is a complicated question.

I have only recently come to understand the magnitude of my presence here. So far in the history of America, there have been a very small number of Chinese men, who have migrated in pursuit of work in merchant or mining trades. Some have been granted less strenuous labor. Like Atung.

Atung   I do alright.

Afong   But there has never been anyone like me.

I am the first Chinese woman you have ever seen.

I am the first Chinese from nobility, the first educated Chinese, the first with bound feet, the first the first the first.

And so you see, this gives me a great responsibility.

This exhibition has become the most popular attraction in the history of Peale's Museum, and I am delighted to share with you the news that starting next week, we will begin a forty-week tour of the Eastern United States, in some fifteen different cities, where I will be on display for people all across this great land.

I will be in Boston. Philadelphia. Baltimore. Such a nice name. Baltimore. Washington, DC, named for your first emperor, George Washington. I delight in this. I will go to Providence, Cincinnati, Pittsburgh. How I long to see Pittsburgh.

How strange it is that I will now learn far more about America than I ever knew about my homeland.

Perhaps when I return, I will travel China as well. In much this same way. Perhaps I can travel to various cities there, and impart to the villagers all the lessons I have learned in America.

But no, perhaps what I should do . . . ah yes! I just had a wonderful idea. Perhaps I should hire a fourteen year old white American girl to come with me to China, and display her in a room with a raised bed, shoes on her feet in the home, eating with a fork! Perhaps I can tour her throughout the country and let the Chinese look at her and study her, put her on display for the education and edification of the Chinese curiosity!

And then I could be like Atung. Ha! Couldn't I?

Atung   Or I could.

Afong   Oh. Yes, I suppose that's true, Atung, you could serve the same function to the white girl.

Atung   I would like to return, someday, to China.

Afong   How long have you been in America, Atung?

Atung   A long time.

Afong   This is unspecific, Atung, how long?

Atung   I suppose since I was . . . oh, fourteen?

Afong   And how old are you now?

Atung   I am as old as the wind.

Afong   What?

Atung   I am as old as the hills.

Afong   Atung no you're not.

Atung   I am as old as the rain.

Afong   The rain is eternal.

Atung   Exactly.

Afong   Atung don't talk nonsense. Aren't you excited to travel the country? To see Philadelphia?

Atung   Sure.

Afong   To see Baltimore?

Atung   Baltimore, yes.

Afong   To see Pittsburgh?

Atung   No, not Pittsburgh.

Afong   Why not Pittsburgh?

Atung   I have been there before.

Afong   Nonsense again! When were you in Pittsburgh?

Atung   I was there . . . a long time ago.

Afong   Again with your non-specificity. Honestly, Atung, I must learn to accelerate my English studies so that I won't need you anymore.

Atung   You will always need me.

Afong   We'll see about that.

Atung   You will always need me.

Silence.

Afong   Anyway, yes, I am pleased to report I am learning English and I am doing quite well.

Atung   She's not doing well.

Afong   I am a remarkable student.

Atung   She is hopeless.

Afong   Soon I will be as fluent as I am in this performance.

Atung   No.

Afong   Right now I can only speak in simple terms, and I fear this makes people think I am stupid. When a white person asks me a complex question, such as "Are you excited to tour the country?", I can say only "Yes" or "Oh yes sir very much", and while this might convey some enthusiasm, it cannot convey the poetry of it. If I had the words in English I would say that I cherish the opportunity like a flower cherishes sunlight, that the thought of seeing the whole of America roots in me like a jewel that has lodged inside my eyes and colors every part of my vision.

Atung   When she says things like this, I translate them as: "She says yes, she is excited."

Afong   And so these white people they think I am simple. I must not allow that. I must express my voice. This is my obligation to America. This is my obligation to the world.

Atung   Afong Moy, it is time for you to walk.

Afong   Oh! Dear yes, my goodness, how irresponsible of me. Thinking ahead to the future when I have tasks in the now.

She walks.

I have noticed that my feet are a source of constant fascination. Most Americans consider it barbaric. Of course, in China, there are many who feel the same way, but it is tradition, and so there is hesitancy to alter it. Personally, I don't consider it barbaric. I like my feet.

I have noticed there are traditions in the American identity that are similarly entrenched, despite some controversy about them among the populace. Such as corsets. Or the Transatlantic Slave Trade.

Perhaps this is the way of tradition. We set systems in place so that we can provide a structure. So that we can feel secure. And then, at some point, as we evolve, these systems become unnecessary. But before we can move on to a new set of traditions, we must live in a slow dismantling of the old ways. It may take time. But it is useful work.

She completes her revolution around the room.

Atung   And now, I will bring her food.

Atung *exits.*

Afong   Every evening for two and a half years, I have eaten the same dinner with slight variations. A bowl of rice and a plate of shrimp or chicken or fish, and a pot of tea.

At lunchtime, however, I eat American food. Oh it is good. I get to eat beef. And mashed potatoes. And corn. And bread. When I tour the countryside, I wonder what new and exotic foods I might have the opportunity to try.

Atung *enters with the food and tea.*

Atung   Remember to watch your portion control. They pay to see a delicate girl.

Afong *eats.*

Afong   I wonder if they use forks in Pittsburgh. Perhaps they use something else entirely. I wonder what other instruments might exist for the consumption of food around the world. I hope there are so many that one could not possibly try them all in a single lifetime. I hope that each city in America is as different as Guangzhou is to New York. I hope that once we travel the eastern United States I have an opportunity to travel the west too. I have heard much of St. Louis. Of Utah and Montana, and oh man oh man San Francisco California. Has there ever been a name so beautiful as San Francisco California?

I hope that I can see it all, and beyond. See what types of foods they eat and what color their people are. What sort of rooms they live in.

Perhaps she burps.

Forgive me.

I should clarify. Because while I very much romanticize the differences between people and cultures, I am even more appreciative and fascinated by the similarities.

In order to illustrate what I mean, let us further discuss the history of tea.

Atung *takes the tray of food, now finished, and exits.*

He leaves the tea, which **Afong** *pours.*

Tea is Chinese. It is ancient and traditional and ours. In London, the British existed for hundreds of years without it. And yet when they encountered our Chinese tea in the year 1615, it quickly became so important to them that they started wars over it. They shifted the rituals of their day to include a tea time that has now become a deeply entrenched English cultural tradition as integral to their identity as William Shakespeare or the River Thames.

Is this not comforting? It is, right? That one culture can be so moved by another that it simply cannot resist the urge to appropriate it for themselves?

Atung *enters.*

Atung   Hrmpf.

Afong   What?

Atung   What?

Afong   What?

Atung   What?

Afong   Did you say something?

Atung   No.

Afong   Yes you did, you made a noise.

Atung   Oh. That. A noise, yes, I did.

Afong   What does such a noise represent?

Atung   It's just . . . well, I think it may be a little more complicated than you're making it sound.

Afong   Atung, you cannot possibly object to such a beautiful example of cultural sharing, for is this not our very purpose in America?

Atung   There is a difference, Afong Moy. Between sharing, and taking.

Afong   Why Atung, are you expressing a personal opinion about something?

Atung   Never mind.

Afong   I've never heard you speak this way.

Atung   What way.

Afong   Like there is something in this world that you care about.

Atung   There isn't.

Afong   Oh come now, Atung. Don't you care about the hopeful exchange of ideas and practices around the globe?

Atung   Just doing my job.

Afong   Don't you care about representing your people and your homeland?

Atung   I'm only here to translate.

Afong   Don't you care about me?

Atung Please just drink your tea.

She does.

Afong Would you like some?

Atung What?

Afong Yeah. It's sooooooo good.

Atung No thank you.

Afong Are you sure?

She slurps.

Atung Yes, Afong Moy. I require nothing.

She finishes her tea.

Afong All gone.

Atung Very well.

Atung *draws the curtain across the room.*

3.

> **Atung** *opens the curtain across the room.*
> **Afong Moy** *sits, as before.*

Afong   Hello. My name is Afong Moy.

I came to America in 1834, when I was fourteen years old.

It is the year 1837, and I am seventeen years old.

So much has happened and I can't wait to tell you all about it. I will save the biggest and most exciting news for last, so please be patient.

You probably cannot even tell, but this room has been dismantled and carried by carriage all across the United States, reassembled in museums and fairgrounds in your most renowned cities. We have been to Boston. We have been to Buffalo. We have not been to Pittsburgh, but we have been to Baltimore, and it was as lovely as it sounds.

In Philadelphia I saw the Liberty Bell! They say it is the bell that rang upon the signing of the Declaration of Independence in 1776, when you overthrew the Dynasty of George III. Atung has informed me that this is not a true story, and that the bell was created *after* your independence day, but I support the telling of the story as it was told to me, for it is better and more beautiful than the truth.

Atung   If you say so.

Afong   I do. I do say so. For what kind of a story would it be, if the bell lacked such relevance? Never mind what kind of a story, what kind of a *bell* would it be without the story? It would be insignificant, and eventually forgotten and discarded altogether. Atung, let the story live!

Atung   I disapprove of this.

Afong   No one cares.

Atung   I know.

Afong   Also, did you know that the bell is cracked?

Atung   I do know that.

Afong   I wasn't talking to you, I was talking to them.

Atung   Okay.

Afong   The crack in the bell appeared after the very first time it was rung. I think this is such a beautiful detail, isn't it? A beautiful poem, for it tells us that liberty is fragile. The crack is growing, as well. Even though the bell no longer rings, the crack continues to grow. Simply through the passage of time. This is another poem. It tells us that liberty has a cost. And an expiration.

Atung   Or it just means that it was badly made.

Afong   Atung why are you so cross? Is it not a beautiful day?

Atung How would I know? I haven't been outside at all, but stuck in here with you.

Afong And I've been stuck in here with you, yet still I feel so extraordinarily blessed. For it's now time to share the most exciting news about our trip.

Atung Alright.

Afong Guess where we are?

Atung Washington DC.

Afong NOT YOU ATUNG, I WAS TALKING TO THEM!

Atung Sorry.

Afong You've spoiled the surprise! I wanted to be the one to say it, and I also wanted to hear what guesses they might have before telling them. It was going to be fun, but now it's not fun. Oh Atung you ruined my delivery.

Atung So sorry.

Afong And yet you will not ruin my mood! For yes, we are in Washington DC, your national capital! And please do not be jealous, but here is the best part: I have just returned from a private meeting with your emperor, Andrew Jackson. It was just the two of us!

Atung And me.

Afong Oh yes, the two of us and Atung. Speaking of Atung, Atung is

Atung I'm irrelevant.

Afong I wasn't going to say you're irrelevant.

Atung Oh.

Afong I was going to say you could be of great use at the moment. For I have had an idea!

Atung Uh-oh.

Afong Why uh-oh?

Atung I do not like your ideas.

Afong I have extraordinary and wonderful ideas!

Atung You have dangerous and incomprehensible ideas.

Afong No I never.

Atung It was your idea to go swimming in the Susquehanna River.

Afong That was amazing!

Atung It resulted in pneumonia.

Afong And memories.

Atung And two cancelled performances.

Afong Well this idea is splendid, and shall delight us both. For in order to illustrate the extraordinary conversation I had with Emperor Jackson, a simple description will not suffice; Atung as you were there, let us . . . recreate the dialogue together!

Atung Wait what?

Afong We shall play-act the conversation. I will speak what I spoke, and you will speak what he spoke.

Atung What about what I spoke?

Afong But you merely spoke what he spoke and I spoke.

Atung Oh. Right.

Silence.

Afong Wait a moment. Atung. You did, right? You did not mistranslate any of our words, did you?

Atung Of course not.

Afong Atung.

Atung It's just that there are sometimes words or phrases which do not directly translate from Guangzhou Cantonese to American English, so the act of translation is more like . . . interpretation than direct recreation.

Afong What?

Atung Yes. Even as we play-act our roles, this is but an interpretation. For this is not then. I can present to you a memory of someone, but it will only be a performance. The words you hear will not be theirs. The clothes I wear will not be theirs. The body that I occupy will not be theirs. Like cracks in a bell or a story of when it first rang, we can only simulate the past, not in pursuit of the literal truth but some other less tangible truth about ourselves and the nature of truth itself. Mmm.

Afong Oh so now you like the story of the bell.

Atung I didn't say I like it, I'm just saying it's similar to the act of translation; it's a fact whether I like it or not.

Afong Very well then, you can play act your own self and the Emperor.

Atung President.

Afong What?

Atung Forget it.

Afong Come up here with me.

Atung Wait what?

Afong I said come up here with me.

Atung Up there?

Afong Yes.

Atung But. That . . . oh no. I don't think I should, that is not my place.

Afong Please, Atung. I need you.

Silence.

Atung Do I have to

Afong I need you.

Silence.

Atung Very well.

Atung *sits.*

He is remarkably comfortable in this play-acting—he performs both himself and Jackson with conviction.

Afong It is my humblest and most treasured privilege to meet you, most esteemed Emperor Jackson your highness.

Atung It is pleasure to meet President sir.

Atung as Jackson Marvelous!

Atung Good!

Afong It has been my great honor to be a guest in your most powerful and benevolent nation, and it is my hope that my presence here can lead to greater understanding between the peoples of China and America.

Atung Thank you much for let me be inside America. I hope Americans will like Chinese.

Atung as Jackson I do like Chinese yes, in fact I've often found Oriental people to be quite winsomely exotic.

Atung I admire the Chinese people very much for their many fine qualities.

Afong And I admire the American people for their boundless curiosity and fierce individuality.

Atung American people also good I think.

Afong I have had the great privilege of seeing so much of America, and have been performing to sizable crowds the very same performance I have shown to you today.

Atung I am so happy. Many Americans see me.

Afong While I am extremely pleased to be admired in this way, I cannot help but wonder if there is more I can do to bring our cultures closer together.

Atung   Maybe I can do better.

Afong   I feel my fame has provided me a tremendous opportunity to share more about who we are; not simply on the surface levels of clothing and adornments, but a deeper, more lasting intimacy.

Atung   I am famous. I want you to know who I am.

Afong   Through such proximity and visibility, we might be able to share the very best parts of Chinese culture and American culture with one another, in pursuit of greater empathy and commonality.

Atung   Become close . . . um, yes. We become close. We become more the same.

Afong   I wonder if your highness may have ideas on how to utilize this platform in more ambitious ways?

Atung   Does President Jackson think performance is good or can maybe be better?

Atung as Jackson   Oh I think the performance is marvelous.

Atung   He thinks the performance is good.

Atung as Jackson   I wouldn't change a thing.

Atung   He would not change a thing.

Atung as Jackson   I would like to touch your feet.

Atung   He would like to touch your feet.

Silence.

Afong   What?

Atung   It is not so typical for such a thing.

Atung as Jackson   I am not a typical person.

Atung   He says he is . . . strange man.

Afong *offers a foot.*

Atung as Jackson *is delicate.*

Atung as Jackson   It is at once disgusting and mesmerizing.

Atung   You are beautiful in your ugliness.

He releases her foot.

Atung as Jackson   I would like to visit China one day.

Atung   I wish to go to China.

Afong   I am so pleased to hear you say this.

Atung   Happy for you go to China.

Atung as Jackson Alas I probably won't have the chance, not for some time. The British are on the verge of war with China. Opium War, they call it. Dirty business, and no it's not our war but we do have interests. I have no love of the British obviously, but there's money in opium, money in tea. The trade routes are lucrative and so it behooves us, you understand.

Atung Um. Please to say again, more slow?

Atung as Jackson Ah, never mind, it's over your heads of course.

Atung So sorry I no can understand.

Afong Atung, what is he saying?

Atung as Jackson This was a marvelous diversion. I've always adored carnivals and freakshows. As a boy I would delight in them, and it's been a long time since I've recaptured the memory. I must take my leave now, and turn my attention to more important matters.

Silence, as Jackson leaves.

Afong Atung, what did he say?

Silence.

Atung He said . . . He said that. You, Afong Moy, are a special and most outstanding person, and your work in this country is an important step in the fruitful exchange of cultures and in the promotion of world peace.

Afong He said that?!

Atung He did.

Afong It did not seem that he was saying such things.

Atung Well he did. He did say them. I only . . . you see, I only hesitated because he spoke with such beautiful prose, a type of elevated lyricism that I could not so promptly translate. I needed a moment, to best consider how to articulate his most excellent message of hope and gratitude for all that you are, Afong Moy.

Afong Oh wow.

Atung *stands, and then takes his place in his regular chair downstage of the Room.*

Afong Yes it was a most marvelous meeting.

Silence.

Afong Atung, are we not behind schedule?

Atung Oh. Yes, of course.

Afong What's wrong with you today, Atung?

Atung Nothing. It is time for you to walk.

Afong Yes! It is time for me to walk.

She stands. Begins to walk.

While I walk, let us continue our discussion on the history of tea.

In our last episode, we discussed the British appropriation of tea. British Imperial rule in the Mughal Empire allowed for the

She stops.

Atung?

Atung   Yes?

Afong   Is there something you are not telling me?

Atung   No.

Silence.

Afong   Okay.

She starts to walk again.

Where was I. Oh yes. Britain conquered what is now India, giving them access to fields and fields and fields of opium. The British eventually weaponized this opium, distributing it throughout China, which ravaged the countryside. This led to the first of the Opium Wars, which led to the Treaty of Nanking. At least economically, the British Empire took over China as well.

She is finished walking, but does not sit.

Atung there is something you are not telling me and I would like to know why.

Atung   It is none of your concern.

Afong   Why is it none of my concern?

Atung   Knowing why it is none of your concern is also none of your concern.

Afong   Is it not appropriate for me to decide what is my concern and what is not?

Atung *stands.*

Atung   Time to eat.

Atung *exits.*

Afong *sits.*

Afong   The reason Britain *wanted* to conquer China was, of course, trade routes. And the most important reason to control trade routes, of course, is the price of tea.

Of course, I do not know any of this. At least not right now, in 1837, when the Opium Wars are beginning, when I am only 17 years old and so shielded from news of the world. I do not know that I do not know this, either. All I know is that you are looking at me, that I am presenting this image, that I have so much hope and so little reality, that the China of my mind is more and more distant every day, that the hope I hope is more and more hopeless, and with each passing hour I am less and less Chinese. Less and less Chinese, but more and more old, and therefore closer and closer to the inevitable day when you will stop looking at me altogether.

He brings a plate and some tea, places them before her.

Afong   Atung what is this?

Atung   Pork.

Atung *sits.*

Afong *picks at the pork but does not eat.*

Afong   In Cincinnati, we went to a zoo. They had many animals on display at this zoo.

I did not think very much about what the animals were thinking. If they had dreams or ambitions, or what they hoped to achieve in their lives behind glass. I admired them for the way they moved, their hair, their eyes.

If I am in a cage, what sort of animal am I?

Times I feel I am a swan or a peacock, with adornments to be admired.

Times I feel I am an ox, or a donkey, or some other beast of burden.

Times I feel I am a sheep.

Times I feel I am a tiger.

But I am none of these things, am I?

I am a human being.

She pushes the food away.

Afong   What are we doing here, Atung?

Atung   I don't know what you mean.

Afong   Is it good? What we are doing? Does it matter?

Atung   I do not think about that.

Afong   What do they see when they see me?

Atung   You cannot think about that.

Afong   What if it is not good, Atung?

Atung   You have had a long and remarkable day, Afong Moy, and you should rest.

Afong   Because I am thinking that perhaps . . . perhaps it is not good.

Atung   Please, Afong Moy.

Afong   What if we simply do not belong here?

Atung Whether we belong here or not . . . we are here. Whether it is good or not, Afong Moy . . . you. You are good. And you are tired. You must not worry yourself with things you cannot control. It is time to rest.

Afong NO.

Atung Afong Moy, please.

They are watching.

Perhaps he whispers this. Perhaps he takes hold of her head, by the chin, as if to show her the eyes of the audience.

And with that, she is silent. Perhaps she forces a smile.

He then moves to comfort her. Simple, and gentle. If she wears a headdress, perhaps he removes it for her. If her hair is tied, perhaps he loosens it.

This can take time.

She closes her eyes and rests.

Atung *tiptoes towards the plate of food.*

He eats. Voraciously. Heaps and heaps of food into his mouth at once.

He closes the curtain.

Lights shift a little—not much, but a little:

We are now in **Atung***'s Dream.*

He stands and speaks with his mouth full.

Atung Sometimes when I dream, I dream of China. I dream of my childhood, of sky and streams of memory, of earth that bore me and mother and father that look like me. Sometimes when I dream, I dream of ocean, and the ship that carried me to all of these new worlds.

But most of the time, when I dream, I dream of the Room.

I dream that it is *my* Room. My dress. And when the people come to look, everyone looks at *me*.

In the dream, Afong Moy is my translator.
I know it is a dream because she cannot speak for me.
No one can speak for me. In a dream or otherwise.
I speak for myself, and my voice is beautiful.

It is so beautiful that when I discover that the Carnes Brothers are charging now, all over the country, 75 cents adults and 50 cents children, I demand that we are paid as well. I demand that Afong Moy is paid, for her translation services, but I demand that I am paid more.

In this dream, my demands are met.

Also in the dream, Afong Moy is my lover.

I know it is a dream because I have no physical desire for Afong Moy. But I also know the dream is real because I see how men look at her. I see how women look at her too, and I see the difference. When I see the way that men look at Afong Moy, I am filled with a desire to protect her. From the dangerous eyes of men, and the thoughts that arise from a gaze of that kind.

As if she can be protected from a gaze! Her life depends on that gaze.

My dream ends with the physical act of love, between me and Afong Moy.

I will tell you a secret. I like to look at the white women. The white women with their white dresses and flowery hats, their parasols and lace. When I look at them in real life, I imagine tearing off those dresses and tossing their hats in the sea, I dream of breaking their parasols into fractions and ripping their lace from their bodies with such wild abandon it causes these women to moan in delight.

I also like to look at the white men. The white men with their ridiculous mustaches and too-tall top hats, their booming voices and splotchy skin. When I look at them, I dream of biting their flesh to watch as it reddens, I dream of burying my face in the jungle of their woven hair, I dream of overpowering their maddening power with a power they've never imagined, making them submit to my charms until the volume of their voices subside in soft, supple whispers of breath, like a caress.

I know what these daydreams mean.

I have an appetite for what I cannot have.
And because I cannot have anything-
In this life, you see . . . I cannot have anything.

So it is natural that what I want. Is always that which is *most* forbidden.

What is most forbidden to me is not the white women. It is not the white men.

The physical act of love that occurs between me and Afong Moy . . . *That* is what is most forbidden. For it comes from a different impulse and a different emotion. It comes from the desire to possess. I know I can never possess a spirit like the spirit of Afong Moy. She is like a wisp, a memory, an idea, a poem. A poem about the sadness one feels after a brief fall of rain, so slight it leaves only a hint of dampness on the earth, and soon the roaming sun will evaporate completely any evidence that such a beautiful rain ever existed.

This is not something one can possess.
One can only try to enjoy it while it lasts.

In order to illustrate this point, you will not see us again for many years.

This has been my dream. Or at least, the part of my dream I am willing to tell you.

Lights.

4.

> **Atung** *opens the curtain.* **Afong Moy** *sits, as before.*
>
> *Perhaps the contents of the room are sparser. Perhaps her costume is altered somewhat, in an attempt to increase the costume's appeal to men.*

Afong   Hello. My name is Afong Moy.

I came to America in 1834, when I was fourteen years old.

It is the year 1849, and I am twenty-nine years old.

Silence.

Perhaps she crosses her legs.

Before I start describing my various daily ills and the general tedium of repetitious life inside a box, allow me to fill you in on what has happened in the twelve years or so since we last spoke. Since Washington, DC, and my triumphant tour of the United States, and my most memorable meeting with President Andrew Jackson.

First of all, yes I now know the difference between a President and an Emperor.

Which is to say, my English is better than it was. You see, I am speaking English now. So what you are hearing me say is perhaps closer to what I truly sound like.

Unfortunately, however, I am starting to lose my understanding of Cantonese. I have little occasion to use the language, except with Atung. And Atung doesn't speak very much these days anymore.

Atung *shrugs.*

Also, I am back in New York. Or I should say, *we* are back in New York. The three of us: Me, Atung, and of course, The Room.

We are no longer employed by the Carnes Brothers, who have retired from the trade of Far East Oriental Imports. Peale's Museum has been sold to our new employer, Mr. P.T. Barnum, a theatrical impresario and purveyor of exotic entertainments for the viewing pleasure of all ages. There is no longer a separate fee for viewing me in my Room, for we are but one part of a larger attraction now, and the cost of general admission to P.T. Barnum's American Museum grants each attendee access to our exhibition.

Crowds have been light, in other words.

Part of this is due to the fact that Chinese people are becoming more common in America. The Opium Wars have led to widespread hardship and instability in the Qing Dynasty, and the promise of gold has brought waves of Chinese men to California. Eager to work for lower wages than their white American counterparts.

We'll see how that turns out.

She stands.

For the sake of changing tastes, it has become necessary to change certain aspects of my regular performance. But one part that has not changed is this: the part where I walk.

She begins to walk.

Speaking of walking, speaking of gold, and speaking of mass migration, here's something I learned about Andrew Jackson.

You might already know this, but when Europeans first arrived in America in 1492, there were lots of people who were already here. For the sake of clarity, let's call them Americans, and let's call people like Andrew Jackson oh let's say . . . European-Americans.

Since 1492, European-Americans colonized these lands, constructed a liberty bell, and rang that bell for their freedom. The Americans, meanwhile, were slowly forced to leave their native lands, and fight for their survival.

Here's where the gold comes in. Because the European-Americans discovered that the mountains of Georgia had gold in them. Andrew Jackson said hey let's take their land so that we can better access the gold.

So Andrew Jackson decreed that all Americans east of the Mississippi River had to resettle in the West.

How did they get there?

They walked.

She sits.

Usually, at this point in the performance as you might remember, I would eat. We cut that.

Food is too expensive and Mr. Barnum insists I manage my weight.

So I just demonstrate the use of chopsticks by grasping at the air.

She takes a pair of chopsticks out of her hair and uses them to grasp at the air.

Yes.

She puts the chopsticks back in her hair.

I have no further insights on the subject of tea.

She looks around to make sure no one can see, before removing a bottle of whiskey and a glass tumbler she has concealed.

Nowadays it's all about gold.

She pours herself a drink.

Which brings me to one other thing I should mention before we jump ahead in time a little bit once more.

I've decided to retire from the entertainment business.

She knocks back her drink.

Yep. See, 1849's gonna change the whole world and me right there with it. They're calling it the California Gold Rush, so I'm pulling up stakes and heading west.

She removes a cigarette and a match.

Here's the secret though, see: I'm not going in search of gold. I'm going in search of more Chinese in America. I'm curious what Chinese people look like, and talk like. What the Chinese do. What they eat. How they walk. What they think about when they think about the future.

She lights the cigarette, and takes a long slow drag.

Don't tell anyone, okay? It's probably best if I just sneak out, less trouble that way. I'll see you when I get there.

Until then, thank you for coming to P.T. Barnum's American Museum.

Atung *draws the curtain across the room.*

5.

> **Atung** *opens the curtain across the room.*
> **Afong Moy** *sits, as before.*

Afong   Hello. My name is Afong Moy.

I came to America in 1834, when I was fourteen years old.

It is the year 1864, and I am forty-four years old.

Perhaps you are surprised to see me still here.

Perhaps you had the delightful expectation that for this scene, once Atung pulled the curtain back, I would be in San Francisco California, on a mountain high up in the Sierras, feeling the wide wild western wind in my hair, great autumn sunset behind me and the expansive liberty of America at my feet?

No, you knew that wouldn't happen, didn't you? You knew it all along. Silly me, silly Afong Moy, for hoping it might happen.

Yeah, I'm still here.

But not for long.

To which you say: Ah there she goes again! She still thinks she can escape!

But no, I'm not talking about escape. I'm talking about being replaced. Betrayed. Discarded.

This morning I have learned that Mr. P.T. Barnum has made arrangements for the importation of a young woman by the name of Pwan Ye Koo from Peking. She is fourteen years old, her feet have been bound half an inch smaller than mine, she plays the erhu and performs improbable Chinese acrobatics, sings like a trained chorus of nightingales and arrives in New York Harbor later this afternoon.

I am to make immediate arrangements for my departure from P.T. Barnum's American Museum.

Silence.

Atung   Afong Moy. It has been the honor of my life to work beside you these thirty years. I have little to show for my life. I have no money, I have no friends, I have no family, I have an aging body that will not see many days beyond this one. I have spent my life in aid to you, and it was a privilege to do so. I have watched you from the time you were fourteen years old, a beautiful ray of too warm sunshine cutting across my hardened cheek; since that time you have experienced great disappointment in the face of your most earnest good hope. And yet you have endured. You will endure. I know this because I know you, Afong Moy. It is possible I know nothing else about this world, except that it would be a much better world if it were more like you.

Silence.

Afong   Oh Atung. What shall we do now?

Atung   What do you mean?

Afong Where can we go?

Atung Oh. Perhaps I was unclear.

Afong What?

Atung I am staying.

Silence.

Afong Oh.

Atung I am paid nothing. I am already here. There is no sense for P.T. Barnum to hire another to translate for Pwan Ye Koo.

Afong Oh.

Atung It makes no difference how old I grow, how irrelevant. I am not the one they are looking at.

Afong Oh.

Silence.

Atung I

Afong Please leave me.

Atung Afong M—

Afong Please.

Atung I wish I

Afong LEAVE ME.

Atung *hesitates, but then*

He bows a deep, sincere, and honorific bow

Before slowly exiting.

Silence.

She is alone.

Afong I would like to share with you
I would like
some further details on the subject of
updates since last we spoke
on the subject of gold.

Gold, yes, but also
the subject of
the subject of Liberty.

Beginning last year, in 1863, work on the Transcontinental Railroad began. It is one of the most ambitious projects ever undertaken in the history of American ingenuity, and it will join East and West together.

Excuse me, I meant to say East and West *America* together not East and West, ha.

This railroad is being constructed primarily by Chinese laborers. Many of these Chinese arrived on the western shores in pursuit of gold. They arrived with such earnest hope, but none would find their fortune. There is only so much gold in America. It does not matter if our hope is boundless. Fortune is finite.

In the absence of fortune, to the rails they go.

Oh yeah I should mention, at this point, it is still only men.

I wonder what they would have thought of my show.

I should also mention
I have not heard
in over thirty years I have not heard
my father, you see
I sent a letter
1836 1837
when I was
1839
1841
fourteen years old
youngest of seven children
I can't remember
I can't remember their faces
I can't remember my mother
I have not heard from
for you see, The Carnes Brothers
I gave them a letter
to send
in 1836
a letter to send in 1837
and of course they never sent it
1838
why would they
1839
so many years

There are many jobs required to complete a project so vast as the Transcontinental Railroad. The Chinese were ideal for the most dangerous duties, such as clearing the terrain, leveling trees, or blasting through ancient rock and mountain formations with pickaxe and dynamite.

They needed a level field to lay down their tracks.

Building tunnels.
With gunpowder, yes, but with newer industry as well,
Nitroglycerine, mixed on site,

Creating holes in the mountains for trains to pass.
Sometimes the mountains fought back.

But they bent the earth to their will.

Apologies.
Not their will.
Someone else's design, of course.
Someone else's map.
Someone else's vision.
But they executed that vision,
even as that vision executed . . .
the vision was executed
executed

The vision of course
Was Manifest Destiny
For you see
All you see
It is yours
The vision was about
more more more

I should also mention however
Simultaneous to this
As you know
There is Civil War
There is fracture
Some land you claim, but
Some land breaks away
And thus you battle
To understand the proper shape of yourself

And perhaps this is always the way.
You grow bigger
And yet you grow smaller.

Forgive me I remember something now.
I remember a girl
in Guangzhou
Where was I
at a picnic I think
by the river
I think I was twelve
perhaps thirteen
I dropped my handkerchief
on accident I think
but who remembers

and she picked it up
and she looked at me
and she smiled

I wonder what she's doing now

Why am I talking about this?

What am I talking about?

I don't suppose there's a carriage?
I don't suppose I could have

Never mind

Atung?

Atung are you there?

No

In the Gettysburg Address, delivered last year by President Abraham Lincoln, he says this nation was conceived in Liberty.
The world will little note, nor long remember.
It is for the living, rather, to be dedicated here to the unfinished work.
The great task remaining before us.

I will take my leave of P.T. Barnum
I will take my leave of the Room

And you may say
But you have no skills
And you may say
But your feet
And you may say
But you have nothing
But you have no one
But you've never
and you grow old
you have lost
you are done
you are irrelevant
Afong Moy
But I will walk
to Philadelphia
where I will ring the Liberty Bell
I will walk
to Gettysburg
to Pittsburgh
where I will forge steel
I will walk

to and from Cincinnati
I will build my own carriage
I will build my own train
and from St. Louis Union Station
I will ride the Transcontinental Railroad to
San Francisco California
and from there
maybe further
maybe China
maybe the edge of the world,
but I'll decide.

You may say
such a thing
it has never happened

And I say
I will be the first.

She exits the Room.

She closes the curtain from the outside.

She exits the stage.

52   Once in the Countryside

6.

> *The curtain drawn.* **Afong Moy** *opens it herself, from behind.*
>
> **Atung** *is not there, but his chair might remain.*

Afong   Hello. My name is Afong Moy.

I came to America in 1834, when I was fourteen years old.

It is the year 1882, and I am sixty-two years old.

As you can see, I am still here.

But where is here? This is not an exhibition. This is a different space entirely, though you will please indulge me as I allow the details of where I am to remain a mystery for the time being.

In this year, 1882, Congress passes the Chinese Exclusion Act, banning Chinese migration to the United States for 10 years. Those Chinese already here are forced to find refuge in new spaces, their own improvised spaces, separate spaces, safe spaces.

Like this one.

This Room was built with a hope, that it might serve as a platform for understanding, for learning, for sharing.

Just as I, Afong Moy, was built with hope for understanding, for learning, for sharing.

But just as the Room did not fulfill its purpose, I offer to you, my friends, my deepest and most sincere apology. For I too did not fulfill mine.

In the year 1871, a mob of 500 Californians descend upon the residents of Los Angeles' Chinatown. 52 Chinese Americans are injured, while 20 are tortured, lynched, and displayed along the town's borders in exhibition.

Perhaps if I had done things differently.

It is the year 1885, and I am sixty-five years old. One of these safe spaces, in Sweetwater County, Wyoming, is burned to the ground by a mob of 150 white men, resulting in the mutilation, decapitation, and castration of 50 Chinese American miners, many of whom are burned alive or left to die along the river as they fled.

It is the year 1887, and I am sixty-seven years old. The Snake River Massacre in Hells Canyon, Oregon, results in the death and torture of 34 Chinese Americans, stripped of their gold, their bodies dumped in the river; many will not be discovered for years.

Perhaps if I had been more worthy of the task. If I had shown you more of myself. If I had walked differently. Eaten differently, provided more clarity on the metaphysical metaphor of tea, perhaps . . .

It is the year 1892, and I am seventy-two years old. The Chinese Exclusion Act is renewed for another 10 years.

If only I could have shown you how we are so alike in many beautiful ways. And how we are so different in beautiful ways as well.

It is the year 1902, and I am eighty-two years old. The Chinese Exclusion Act is made permanent.

I am so so sorry.

We are pushed further and further away, and so we make our own space. Separate space.

Like this one.

Let me tell you about this space.

It is the year 20__ and I am _____ years old.[1]

Thank you for coming to see me.

I have been waiting for you for so long.

Waiting. Preparing. For this chance to try again. I hope I am worthy of the opportunity.

In anticipation of your visit, you see, I have rented this room, searched for and purchased identical versions of each artifact that was contained in the original Room, and have renovated this space to represent all of the Room's features.

It was the best I could do. It is but a replica, a performance. This is not my voice, for it was never recorded; these are not my clothes, for they were not kept; this is not my body, for it no longer exists.

And yet, I hope I have been able to convey the . . . relevance.

I know it is human nature to forget. To think about the future more than the past. I thank you for indulging me in listening to my past; it is all that is left of me.

I have shared it with you in hopes that you might see what it means for the present, and how it might shape the future. I have shared it in the hope that you might recognize some part of it as your own.

But mostly I share it because I don't want you to forget me.

This is the part of the show where I walk.

Afong *stands and begins to walk.*

I walk but I am not going anywhere. I walk in a circle.

I stop when I arrive at the place I began.

She completes her revolution around the room.

---

1 The year and age here should directly correspond to the timing of performance.

The place I began was a place of endless possibility and earnest good hope. It was a place of aspiration and empathy, where we could all look upon something we've never seen before and recognize that the world is so much more vast and varied than we could ever have imagined. But if we take the time to really look at each other. To really look at each other. Then we might see, through all that vastness and variance, something true and real and wonderful.

It is a beautiful thing to look at something long enough to really understand it.

But it is so much more beautiful to be looked at long enough to be understood.

She sits.

At the start of every hour, I sit down and stay seated. I watch the customers enter the exhibition hall. I do not move.

They talk to each other. Oh look at that. I've never seen such a thing. It reminds me of. I wonder if. What do you think it feels like? And they look at me.

So let's do that.

Let's look at each other.

I'm looking at you.

Are you looking at me?

Perhaps the lights begin to fade.

Perhaps the frame of the Room is like a picture frame.

Perhaps the lights continue to fade, until she is barely seen.

Can you see me?

End of play.

Postscript

In Performance

Shannon Tyo

Being part of this play changed my life.

Between 2018 and 2022, I played Afong in four iterations of the show, all directed by Ralph B. Peña. The world premiere was at Barrington Stage in Pittsfield, MA, followed shortly after by a quick run at Theater Row in New York City (both co-productions with Ma-Yi Theater Company). After that, we were at Long Wharf Theatre in New Haven, CT, and finally back in New York City, this time at The Public Theater and again with Ma-Yi.

In late 2017, I came across a short documentary about a group of Chinese Americans who had lived and worked in Mississippi for generations. My world opened up a little more as I listened to their thick Delta accents tell tales of their family grocery stores and lives in the segregated south. It made me insatiably curious about what else I didn't know about the history of Asians in America. Having been educated in America in the 90's and early aughts, there was little to no mention of this history. I happily fell down a rabbit hole of research. Learning about the likes of Fred Korematsu and Grace Lee Boggs filled me with a feeling I couldn't quite put to words, but would soon find again when, in the spring of 2018, I received an audition for Lloyd Suh's *The Chinese Lady*.

I remember standing in a friend's kitchen relaying every detail, incandescent about this incredible play, this playwright who said all the things I felt, more cleverly and eloquently than I could have ever hoped to. I described the crushing scene where Afong Moy apologizes for failing future generations, how she linked her perceived failings as an ambassador of China directly to the violent, systemic racism that followed. It's a gut-wrenching sequence, the anachronistic presence of our collective AAPI ancestor witnessing death and destruction through time and space, apologizing that her suffering did not eliminate our suffering.

After the elation of being cast wore off, I felt the responsibility of Afong's mission settle onto my shoulders: "My job is to sit there and *feel*, fully, in front of an audience —particularly a white audience—and show them what it's like to live in my body. In *our* bodies. If I feel enough pain, surely that will be enough to reach them. And if I fail, it will be because I have not suffered enough." With those misguided principles quietly tucked into my pocket, I launched myself headfirst into the process. The journey from rehearsal room to stage was supportive and collaborative, buoyed by Daniel K. Isaac, the consummate professional and extraordinary human playing Atung, along with the generosity and genius of Ralph and Lloyd. But I still chose to push and punish myself. I frayed my nerves to the breaking point. If I bungled a line, if I was late on a cue, if the audience did not collectively sigh and ascend to their feet in one roaring cheer at curtain call, I had failed entirely. And I failed often.

The meta-theatrics wormed their way into my brain and body: I was an Asian woman in America trying to explain both an entire culture and her complicated emotions to a predominantly white audience, playing an Asian woman in America trying to explain both an entire culture and her complicated emotions to a predominantly white audience. By the end of that first run at Barrington, I was so exhausted I collapsed in the chair in the final blackout before pulling it together just enough to bow. And for all that labor, the reception was mixed. We all believed in our show, especially after the response we got from our brief run at Theater Row, and after the last performance, I instinctively held onto my impossibly marked-up script.

A year and a half later, on Friday the 13th, March of 2020, *The Chinese Lady* at Long Wharf Theater reached its first day of tech but would never see the second. The following day, public gathering spaces were shut down across the country, and our show was put into storage with the promise to continue if and when we could. By the time we were cleared to continue, it was the fall of 2021, and the phrase "Stop Asian Hate" was scrawled on poster boards and scrolling across Instagram. It was a vulnerable time just to step outside. I was terrified of sitting entirely exposed to a room full of strangers in the dark. It was always scary doing this show, like white-knuckling the steering wheel while driving late at night, the threat that highway hypnosis would catch you complacent and send you careening into the abyss always present, but what a treat to be scared for such a hashtaggable new reason.

We were moved from the black box to a much larger amphitheater-style space so the audience could be spread out for social distancing. It felt cavernous and removed, sparsely attended even on our fullest houses. I took this removedness as a challenge to be even more consistent and professional. I remember feeling so pleased that a tear was dropping out of my left eye at the same point every show, just before it slowly, slowly dawned on me that, probably similar to the real-life Afong, the last thing I wanted to do was cry in front of these people who made me afraid. It was also a much stronger acting choice for her to fight and lose than to let her wallow. The Long Wharf run gave me the time and space to finally understand that.

By the spring of 2022, when rehearsals began at The Public Theater in New York City, it felt, at least to me, like the height of the violence against the AAPI community. In 2018, when we tried to explain that Asian people had withstood a history full of violence directly connected to structural racism in America, the response felt tepid, the history distant. Now, with the political landscape raging around us, the cast and crew taking three rapids and a PCR test a week, and the racial reckoning of the summer of 2020 crackling like static in a dry office building, the audience was primed to receive Lloyd's words. I felt different, too. I was still driving cross-country in the middle of the night, but now I was a long-haul trucker: experienced, relaxed, alert.

It was the slightest of adjustments, but this time around, the final line, *"Can you see me?"*, was no longer a plea. It felt like defiance. And after living all day, every day in my body, getting spit on twice, hyper-vigilant on the train, pepper spray clutched in a sweaty fist every time I stepped out the door, I was spent on suffering. My job was *not*, actually, to suffer so much that it changed hearts and minds. My job was to show up on time and perform the version of this beautiful play that the team had agreed on creating, to be as kind and professional as possible, and then to go eat fries with my friends and feel grateful for a moment to recharge before tomorrow's performance. If the audience could see what we were trying to do, wonderful. If not, that's okay, we did our best. Pass the ketchup.

To any actor reading this who is about to perform the show, please allow my anachronistic presence to say to you what I wish I could have said to Afong: This is a hard show to perform. It asks a lot of you, emotionally, spiritually, and mentally. Do your best, work hard, but don't punish yourself in the process. Your suffering will not eliminate our suffering. Please live well, inside and outside this show.

The Far Country

Preface

Almost Invisible: Paper Families, Ghostly Poems, and the Archives of Chinese Exclusion

Ju Yon Kim

In *The Far Country,* two kinds of inscriptions converge to tell the stories of Chinese migrants at a time when their entry into the United States was severely restricted and often required long, arduous interrogations. Before leaving China for the United States, Moon Gyet reassures Gee, the man he must claim as his father, that he understands what the endeavor requires: "I know I must study and memorize documents. A biography. A map. Exacting details that you will provide of the person I am to be . . . I know that I must recount these details perfectly, to men on the other side of the world, who will test me with their utmost power" (85). In the papers that Moon Gyet studies and in the transcripts of the interrogations that test his memory, the unremarkable shapes of everyday life, whether the color and the number of steps, or the build and the feet of family members, become the grounds upon which his new identity—and the passage that it promises—can be claimed and rejected. Losing hope as months pass and his entry is repeatedly denied, Moon Gyet discovers a reflection of his despair in the poems written on the walls of the Angel Island Immigration Station, where he is detained. Faintly drawn on or etched into the wood, these poems offer a different archive of Chinese immigration, one that insists on the injustices suffered and rejects the reduction of their authors to the stony assessments of bureaucratic documentation. Gradually illuminated in the walls behind Moon Gyet in the Atlantic Theater Company's 2022 production of *The Far Country*, the poems project the voices of Chinese migrants across the stage as light and shadow—ghostly yet indelible presences.

The Far Country's depiction of a Chinese American "paper family" formed by the exigences of racial exclusion draws deeply from the multiple archives of Chinese immigration in the late nineteenth and early twentieth centuries. As scholars have shown, the regulation of Chinese immigration in this period marked the emergence of modern systems of US and global border control.[1] Following laws passed in 1862 and 1875 to combat the so-called "coolie trade" and the entry of women (primarily Chinese) suspected of being prostitutes, the Chinese Exclusion Act of 1882 explicitly made nationality a condition for assessing prospective immigrants. The act was renewed in the decades that followed, and immigration restrictions expanded in the early 20th century to encompass applicants from Asia and southern and eastern parts of Europe. Reflecting the particularly intense hostility directed at Chinese workers, who were vilified as threats to American labor and vectors of disease and cultural degradation, the exclusion act allowed entry to those of Chinese descent engaging in studies, tourism, or business, and to those who were US citizens or their spouses or children. Importantly, in 1898, the Supreme Court case *United States v. Wong Kim Ark* affirmed the birthright citizenship of US-born children of immigrants, thus ensuring the possibility of continued passage for these latter groups.

These restrictions and accompanying exemptions necessitated new procedures for evaluating those who sought to enter the United States. These responsibilities moved from customs officials to the Bureau of Immigration at the turn of the century, and by the first decade of the twentieth century, an established bureaucratic apparatus had emerged. 1910 also saw the opening of the immigration station at Angel Island, which allowed officials to assess those who arrived by ship before they were allowed to land in San Francisco.[2] Despite the strict barriers set against Chinese laborers, those seeking to migrate were able to take advantage of exemptions, especially after the 1906 San Francisco earthquake and subsequent fires eradicated many of the paper trails used to verify identities. When Gee, in 1909, applies for a "Preinvestigation of Status," he seeks not only to facilitate his re-entry, but also to lay the groundwork for securing the future passage of others, such as Moon Gyet, whom he might claim as family members. Inspector Harriwell's "Yes, this is not uncommon" (73), in response to Gee's explanation that the earthquake destroyed his personal records becomes a kind of refrain, dryly registering the duplication of accounts as potential duplicity.

As immigration officials scrutinized Chinese applicants who claimed exemptions for merchants, US citizens, and family members, complex systems developed on each side to curtail and to facilitate entry, respectively. At the crux of this system were the interrogations of applicants and witnesses, and the sprawling network of files on applicants, including transcripts of lengthy interviews. When inspectors asked questions about the details of a village or a family, they were not comparing applicants' answers to any actual knowledge of places and people, but rather comparing them against all the other answers collected in their interviews of witnesses and family members connected to the case.[3] Interrogations grew longer and more exhaustive while strategies to gain admittance, such as the circulation of coaching papers, grew more elaborate.[4] Furthermore, suspicion was directed not only at applicants and those who supported their cases, but also at government employees working on Angel Island, who were investigated for and found guilty of corruption.[5]

Interpreters, like Yip in the first scene of *The Far Country*, were particularly scrutinized, especially if they were of Chinese descent, and would sometimes be switched in the middle of interrogations.[6] Tackling the challenge of conveying these multilingual conversations solely in English, *The Far Country* immediately establishes a device where translation is heard in repetition as well as the nuances of accent. Yip's translation of Harriwell's words initially unfolds as an echo, a small adjustment for succinctness adding the only notable variation. This scene thus offers a dramatization of such exchanges that diverges from that presented in *The Chinese Lady*, where the translation of a conversation between Afong Moy and President Andrew Jackson by Atung, Afong's interpreter, instead highlights gaps and distortions. The comparatively smooth rendering of translation in *The Far Country*, however, ultimately serves an important purpose. Namely, its seamlessness brings into sharper relief a key moment in which Yip, rather than translate Harriwell's words, uses the moment to offer Gee crucial advice. When Harriwell asks Gee to identify a witness to help confirm that his mother was a prostitute (which, he suggests, would make it easier to accept Gee's claim that he was born in the United States), Yip tells Gee, "If you can find someone who would be willing to tell them such things are true, it will help. It should be someone who has never testified here before, someone you trust, to say what you want them to say" (77).

In this moment, the play recasts Yip from neutral facilitator to someone whose position affords him opportunities to trouble the system set up to enforce Chinese exclusion.

When Moon Gyet is detained on Angel Island in 1911, the Chinese interpreter is replaced with a white one, just one indication of how his interrogation will differ from that of Gee. The clutter of paperwork on the set accentuates the increasing importance of documents in these interactions, as the Inspector engages as much with existing records as with the applicant. The truth about an applicant's identity, the system insisted, would be found by cross-checking responses across ever-proliferating transcripts and forms, searching for inconsistencies that would reveal the ruse. Every facet of social life, anything that could be known or experienced by two people involved in a case, became a possible point for questioning. Recognizing an obvious objection to this process, the Inspector acknowledges, "You might presume that this story represents a failure of the system; how could anyone possibly know how many steps there are in so many flights of stairs? But no, that is not what you should take away from this. What you should take away, knowing that they do, always, they always know how many steps ... Is that they are lying" (97). These remarks point to a contradiction that emerged as the interrogations grew ever more elaborate: what if the applicant who could not answer the questions or gave incorrect ones was actually the truthful one, whereas the one who answered too well was the imposter?[7] Some inspectors accepted this situation and came to see the interrogations as tests of recall rather than identity: one reported, "In the above test it must be admitted in justice to the applicant that he has acquitted himself well. No doubt the applicant was prepared for the test."[8] Yet others, much like the Inspector in *The Far Country*, regarded the commonness of the "good" test as evidence of rampant duplicity. In dismissing the potential complaint that the interrogations exemplify "a failure of the system," however, the Inspector obscures the intimate connection between the expanding scope of questions and the necessity of preparing for these interrogations, whether or not an applicant was claiming another identity.

Whether regarded as tests of rote memory or identity, these lengthy interrogations exacted a heavy toll from applicants. *The Far Country* captures their impact in a striking second act that shifts sharply from realism. Moon Gyet, stuck on Angel Island, contemplates the kinds of topics covered by the interrogations:

> Houses. Doors, and the directions they face. Names and faces of people, and their physical build. Distance. Snowfall and rainfall, the quality of the sunlight, whether animals come out at night, the sound of the wind, the color of trees, the texture of dust. How people live and where they are buried. Gossip and innuendo. Sex. Money. Religion. The detailed rules of all our children's games. Politics. Pottery. Parsnips. The practice of farming, the names of our mules, whether we look at the stars, and what names we use for both the bright ones and the dim. What we dream about. (93)

Beginning with the houses, doors, names, and distances that were frequent subjects of questions, Moon Gyet's list seeps into more unlikely areas of examination. It thus captures the expansiveness of the interrogations and their infiltration of every aspect of life, while also acquiring a poetic quality that lends these topics a double meaning.

Separated from family and home, Moon Gyet might be rehearsing both a list that he must memorize for a test and a list that indexes the life he left behind. To move through the immigration process as a Chinese man in this period is an experience of both multiplication and loss, the injunction to remember that comes from the inspector competing with nostalgia's inclination to remember what one has left behind.

The Far Country further dramatizes the deep and contradictory impact of the interrogations when Moon Gyet and four Chinese applicants identified only as "One," "Two," "Three," and "Four" speak in turn about their experiences of immigration and detention. After One relates, ". . . you make your way down a creaking, narrow staircase toward your bunk below," Moon Gyet follows by noting, "There are seventeen steps" (96). The practice of preparing for the interrogations permeates Moon Gyet's most mundane experiences, reshaping his relationship to space: stairs that one might take up or down without a thought become estranged, the number of steps and the color suddenly features important enough to commit to memory. Although the men's examination of the walls in their barracks at Angel Island reflect the torturous boredom and emptiness of their detention, it also aligns with this new attention to qualities and objects that usually remain unattended. Two shares, "But you look closely at the walls and see the light outline of black ink on the gray walls; in delicate calligraphy indicating hundreds of hands, you discover careful volumes of almost invisible poetry" (98). The black ink and the gray walls recall the repeated attention paid to the monochromatic palette of steps in the interrogations. Yet here, black and gray are more than answers on a test; they "contain the hearts and minds of those detained here" (98), or exactly what the transcripts of interrogations refuses to record. The *almost* invisibility of the poetry and its authors reflects the power of erasure and, ultimately, its partiality and failure. Describing how, after detainees began carving their poems, the characters were first filled with putty then painted over, One remarks, "So that not only are the words erased, but the eraser too" (Act 2 TBC). And yet, the gradual shrinking of the putty and the preserving effects of the paint together ensure the rediscovery of the poems. Decades after Angel Island was closed, a park ranger walking through the barracks in 1970 noticed the carvings. Community activists advocated to preserve the station and the writings, and many of the poems were published by Him Mark Lai, Genny Lim, and Judy Yung in *Island: Poetry and History of Chinese Immigrants on Angel Island, 1910–1940.*[9]

In *The Far Country*, the poems are the living and the dead. Moon Gyet mourns, "You were buried beneath clay and earth" (102), while One explains, "You trace your fingers over the gray paint, as if to tell the words hidden beneath that although they're unseen they are not forgotten" (99). Buried like bodies, the poems prompt physical solace and connection: the gray walls are like gravestones, inadequate yet vital surrogates for the dead poems.

Despite the grim, punitive conditions that awaited them, Chinese migrants managed to gain entry and developed expansive networks of "paper families" that enabled further crossings. As exemplified by Gee and Moon Gyet, an individual with US citizenship could facilitate the immigration of a "paper son." Alternate kinship formations thus proliferated, as did new identities. When Moon Gyet marries Yuen, they, and their children, carry on Gee's name. Because of the surveillance of Chinese immigrants, and the obdurate suspicion directed at them, these identities and networks had to be guarded carefully. Yuen's reflections on what should be shared with her children while taking care of Gee highlight how these systems blurred the lines between "blood" and "paper" families, and bestowed a complicated set of familial responsibilities and inheritances.

The Far Country imagines uncanny resonances between Gee and Moon Gyet, echoes of the familiar that generate a sense of the familial. The interrogation featured in the first scene ends with Gee's declaration that he is the hardworking, never-complaining, always grateful immigrant: "I work hard. Never make no trouble. I no want take from America, I want give. Give America. I am so happy be in America. So happy for . . . for work here, so beautiful. Beautiful life. So Lucky Chinaman I am" (79). Yet when speaking with Low, Moon Gyet's mother, Gee offers a divergent understanding of what drives his life in the United States: "And yet I am *done* with being humiliated! I am trying to build something" (84). He reframes his efforts not as expressions of gratitude, but as attempts to restore a sense of purpose and dignity in the face of demeaning circumstances. When Moon Gyet visits Low, he echoes Gee, "What I endured. On that rock, the shame is all over me and always will be, but this is my revenge. To live with dignity, to make something of this name I've been given, to thrive, yes thrive within the life that's been thrust upon me" (111). Witnessed with sadness by Low, Moon Gyet has become Gee's son in more than name during his time in the United States: a part of his paper inheritance is a shared determination to counter his sense of degradation by reshaping the arc of his life.

As Act Two ends, the pounding of fists on chests by Moon Gyet, One, and Two suggests the beating of war drums, and anticipates Moon Gyet's oath to exact revenge. Yet the scenes that follow, even as they include his expressions of bitterness, are not defined by conflict. Instead, in the meetings between Moon Gyet and Low, then Moon Gyet and Yuen, and finally, Yuen and Gee, a quieter mood prevails. Mother and son catch up and share a mediocre bowl of millet. A young man makes a proposal to a clever young woman. A woman cares for her sick (paper) father-in-law. If the revenge promised by Moon Gyet, or the triumph claimed by Gee, finds dramatic realization, it is in the hints of a business and a family that continue, very undramatically, to grow.

Central to these scenes are the Chinese women who might seem to occupy the peripheries of the history of Chinese immigration during the era of exclusion. *The Far Country* insists that efforts to preserve and pass on the stories of Chinese immigrants in this time must include not only the men crowded in the Angel Island barracks, but also the women who were integral to these transnational networks of migration, whether the vast majority who stayed in China, or the few who made the crossing to the United States. Recovery (the "digging" Gee describes in the last scene) is continuous and multilayered.

By centering Low and Yuen, *The Far Country* shifts away from the narratives of vengeful triumph over humiliation articulated by Gee and Moon Gyet. Instead, it ultimately leaves the audience with a story about *continuing* as a powerful choice given a painful history. As Yuen feeds Gee soup in the play's concluding scene, she assuages his fears about forgetting by asserting the body's ability to remember: "Even if you forget for a moment, you cannot long forget the pain, because the body remembers . . . . if I know anything from motherhood I know this, that everything we are, *everything,* it passes down; we will carry it, as a family should" (125). After intense arguments among the other characters about the importance of names and the difference between blood and paper identities, Yuen offers, with characteristic clarity, that the body transmits more than the lineages of blood, that the shared inheritances of their paper family will endure. She asks Gee, nonetheless, to "continue to dig," and the play closes as "*She continues to feed him. He continues to eat. Linger*" (125). In this strikingly undramatic conclusion, histories and memories are carried not only in bureaucratic files and etchings on walls, but also in bodies that linger, and continue, together.

Notes

1. See, for example, Erika Lee, *At America's Gates: Chinese Immigration During the Exclusion Era, 1882–1943* (Chapel Hill, NC: University of North Carolina Press, 2003), 10, and Adam McKeown, "Ritualization of Regulation: The Enforcement of Chinese Exclusion in the United States and China," *The American Historical Review* 108.2 (Apr. 2003): 378.
2. Lee, *Gates*, 11.
3. Reflecting on the importance of ensuring consistency across files, McKeown contends, "The effect was not to find out who the applicant really was but to make sure that he was properly enmeshed into the cross-referenced web of surveillance. Investigators were most concerned to obtain answers that fit the preestablished pattern of previous testimony." (McKeown, "Ritualization," 395.)
4. Estelle Lau notes that by 1905, files became more standardized and questions become more detailed (87); by 1915, the files included standard forms to be completed about applicants (88); and by the 1920s, "not only were the various forms completely developed, but coordination between immigration offices and the exchange of information were readily apparent through the requests and exchanges of files" (89). Lau, *Paper Families: Identity, Immigration, Administration, and Chinese Exclusion* (Durham: Duke University Press, 2006).
5. One such investigation, led by John B. Densmore in 1917, cited numerous instances of graft among employees and fraud by applicants. Densmore Investigation Files (1914–1918), Records of the Immigration and Naturalization Service, San Francisco District, RG 85, National Archives, Pacific Region, San Bruno, California.
6. On the suspicion directed at interpreters, particularly Chinese interpreters, see E. Lee, *Gates*, 58–63, and Mae Ngai, "'A Slight Knowledge of the Barbarian Language': Chinese Interpreters in Late-Nineteenth and Early-Twentieth-Century America," *Journal of American Ethnic History* 30. 2 (Winter 2011): 5–32.
7. McKeown notes that some officials worried that an applicant claiming a false identity who had been coached would have a better chance of landing than someone who had not prepared for the interview because they were who they claimed to be. (McKeown, "Ritualization," 394.)
8. In re Dong Moon, report by Inspector Theiss, 11 May 1916, file 15220/8–24, box 1031, Records of the Immigration and Naturalization Service, San Francisco District, RG 85, Immigration Arrival Investigation Case Files, National Archives, Pacific Region, San Bruno, California.
9. Him Mark Lai, Genny Lim, and Judy Yung, *Island: Poetry and History of Chinese Immigrants on Angel Island, 1910–1940*, 2nd edition, (Seattle: University of Washington Press, 2014).

References

Densmore Investigation Files (1914–1918), Records of the Immigration and Naturalization Service, San Francisco District, RG 85, National Archives, Pacific Region, San Bruno, California.

In re Dong Moon, report by Inspector Theiss, 11 May 1916, file 15220/8–24, box 1031, Records of the Immigration and Naturalization Service, San Francisco District, RG 85, Immigration Arrival Investigation Case Files, National Archives, Pacific Region, San Bruno, California.

Lai, Mark Him, Genny Lim, and Judy Yung, eds. 2nd Edition. *Island: Poetry and History of Chinese Immigrants on Angel Island.* Seattle: University of Washington Press, 2014.

Lau, Estelle. *Paper Families: Identity, Immigration, Administration, and Chinese Exclusion.* Durham: Duke University Press, 2006.

Lee, Erika. *At America's Gates: Chinese Immigration During the Exclusion Era, 1882–1943.* Chapel Hill, NC: University of North Carolina Press, 2003.

McKeown, Adam. "Ritualization of Regulation: The Enforcement of Chinese Exclusion in the United States and China," *The American Historical Review* 108, no. 2 (April 2003): 377–403.

Ngai, Mae. "'A Slight Knowledge of the Barbarian Language': Chinese Interpreters in Late-Nineteenth and Early-Twentieth-Century America," *Journal of American Ethnic History* 30, no. 2 (Winter 2011): 5–32.

The Far Country received its World Premiere at the Atlantic Theater Company (Neil Pepe, Artistic Director; Jeffory Lawson, Managing Director) in the Linda Gross Theater from November 17, 2022, to January 1, 2023. The cast was as follows:

Moon Gyet	Eric Yang
Yuen	Shannon Tyo
Gee/Two	Jinn S. Kim
Low	Amy Kim Waschke
Yip/One	Whit K. Lee
Harriwell/Interpreter	Christopher Liam Moore
Dean/Inspector	Ben Chase
Director	Eric Ting
Set Designer	Clint Ramos
Costume Designer	Junghyun Georgia Lee
Lighting Designer	Jiyoun Chang
Music and Sound Designer	Fan Zhang
Dramaturg	Christine Mok
Production Stage Manager	Alyssa K. Howard

The Bay Area premiere was produced at Berkeley Repertory Theatre (Johanna Pfaelzer, Artistic Director; Tom Parrish, Managing Director) from March 8 to April 14, 2024. The cast was as follows:

Moon Gyet	Tommy Bo
Yuen/Four	Sharon Shao
Gee/Three	Feodor Chin
Low/Two	Tess Lina
Yip/One	Whit K. Lee
Harriwell/Interpreter	Aaron Wilton
Dean/Inspector	John Keabler
Director	Jennifer Chang
Set Designer	Wilson Chin
Costume Designer	Helen Q. Huang
Lighting Designer	Minjoo Kim
Music and Sound Designer	Fan Zhang
Projection Designer	Hsuan-Kuang Hsieh
Movement Director	Erika Chong Shuch
Dialect Coach	Joy Lanceta Coronel
Production Stage Manager	Alyssa K. Howard
Assistant Director	Rebs Chan

The Far Country was commissioned by the Atlantic Theater Company.

The Far Country includes published and copyrighted material from *Island: Poetry and History of Chinese Immigrants on Angel Island, 1910–1940,* by Him Mark Lai, Genny Lim, and Judy Yung, University of Washington Press, 2014, which was an essential and primary source in the research of the play.

Characters

Gee 朱
Harriwell
Dean
Yip 葉
Low 羅
Moon Gyet 文傑
Inspector
Interpreter
One
Two
Three
Four
Yuen 元

Setting

San Francisco, USA, and Taishan, China
1909–1930

Notes

The region of Guangdong referred to here is officially recognized as *Taishan*. At the time of the events depicted in the play, it was more commonly referred to by US officials as *Toisan*. While a variety of dialects were in regular usage within the region, one common pronunciation of the name by residents would have sounded more like *Hoisan*. All three variations are used in this text, depending on the context.

Act One.

1.

> *1909. An interrogation room in a nondescript office building. San Francisco.*
>
> **Gee** *sits at a table with two empty chairs. A smaller table with a stenograph machine is to the side, with an additional empty chair.*
>
> *Three people enter.* **Harriwell** *takes a seat across from* **Gee**, *as* **Dean** *sits at the stenograph machine.* **Yip** *sits between* **Harriwell** *and* **Dean**.
>
> **Text marked with an asterisk is heard in English but understood to be translated. When speaking English,* **Yip** *may speak with a moderate accent.*

Harriwell Mr. Gee. Thank you for your patience.

Everyone settles.

Ready?

He looks at **Dean**, *and* **Yip**, *who nod their readiness.*

Harriwell This is a board inquiry of the U.S. Department of Labor, Bureau of Immigration and Naturalization Services, Form 430 Application of Alleged American Born Chinese for Preinvestigation of Status in the matter of Han Sang Gee, to ascertain the validity of his claim to birthright citizenship in these United States of America. The date is February 1, 1909. I am Chief Inspector Thomas P. Harriwell, presiding. Present is the claimant, Han Sang Gee, Clerk Francis Dean, and Interpreter H.P. Yip.

Yip *This is a board inquiry of the U.S. Department of Labor, Bureau of Immigration and Naturalization Services, Form 430 Application of Alleged American Born Chinese for Preinvestigation of Status in the matter of Han Sang Gee, in his claim to birthright citizenship in the United States of America. The date is February 1, 1909. He is Chief Inspector Thomas P. Harriwell, with Clerk Francis Dean.

Yip *I am Interpreter H. P. Yip. I am available to translate as much or as little as you may require.

Gee *I understand, thank you.
I have some English, little bit. But yes perhaps

Yip Just in case.

Gee   Ha, yes just in case, sometime it is words I know but brain ha ha, sometimes too slow you know?

Harriwell   Yes, this is not uncommon. Please ensure the claimant understands he is under oath, and any false testimony shall be subject to severe penalty under the law, including but not limited to imprisonment or deportation.

Yip   *You promise to tell the truth, and any false testimony could lead to imprisonment or deportation.

Gee   I understand, yes ha. Whoa talk fast big word!, but yes I understand.

Harriwell   Claimant, please state your name.

Gee   My name Han Sang 漢生 Gee 朱. Gee Han Sang. Han Sang Gee.

Harriwell   Han Sang Gee.

Gee   Yes, thank you for start with easy question, ha!

Harriwell   Please confirm your date of birth.

Gee   October 4, 1867.
*According to American reckoning.

Yip   According to the American reckoning.

Harriwell   Please state your place of birth.

Gee   Yes, born America. Proud of born America!

Harriwell   More specifically.

Yip   *More specifically.

Gee   Yes, San Francisco, also proud of born San Francisco!

Harriwell   More specifically.

Yip   *More specifically please.

Gee   Yes, yes.
*I was born at home.
741 Sacramento Street. San Francisco, California.
*In my family's apartment. Directly above a meat packing business, where my father was employed.

Yip   A home birth, where his parents lived above a meat packing business, where his father was employed.

Harriwell   How did you come to learn the little amount of English you have?

Gee   For two years I go American school. I am eight, nine years. Little bit learn.

Harriwell   Why did you stop going to an American school?

Gee   Because two years, I can come. And then, no more they let me. Um. They say Chinese can go no more. Go Chinatown school after.

Harriwell   Do you have any brothers or sisters?

The Far Country 73

Gee   No, no.

Harriwell   Have you ever been married?

Gee   Marry, yes.

Harriwell   Please describe the circumstances under which you were married.

Gee   1893, I go China. I am 25 years. Hope for find wife.
*I had lived as a bachelor for so long, you know there are so few Chinese women in San Francisco.

Yip   I had lived as a bachelor for so long, there are so few Chinese women in San Francisco.

Gee   In Hoisan, I meet wife.

Harriwell   What is her name?

Gee   Her name Sok Ying 淑英.

Harriwell   When were you married?

Gee   Yes, we marry after six month, so . . . November. 1894.

Harriwell   And do you have any children?

Gee   Two boy, one girl.

Harriwell   And what are their ages?

Gee   Yes, ah oldest boy, he born 1895, daughter born two year after. Youngest boy, born same as year I come back, so 1899.

Harriwell   You returned in 1899.

Gee   Yes, yes.

Harriwell   Do you recall the specific date of disembarkation?

Yip   *Do you recall the specific date of disembarkation?

Gee   No, but. Winter. December, I think, yes December 1899.

Harriwell   So you don't have documentation to show proof of departure or disembarkation?

Yip   *Do you have any documentation to prove departure or disembarkation?

Gee   *I am sad to say that no, all of my papers were destroyed in the earthquake.

Yip   He is sad to say that no, his papers were destroyed in the earthquake.

Harriwell   Yes this is not uncommon. Is it safe to assume then that any documentation that might corroborate the claimant's assertion of his birth in San Francisco have also been destroyed?

Yip   *Yes this is not uncommon. Is it safe to assume then that any documentation that might corroborate your assertion of birth in San Francisco have also been destroyed?

Gee Yes, yes. Everything gone.

Harriwell And so you must be aware that the earthquake also destroyed all existing government files, including those within this Bureau pertaining to birth records and any other potential corroborating or contradicting documents, correct?

Yip *Are you aware that the earthquake also destroyed government files, including birth records and any other potential corroborating or contradicting documents?

Gee Oh! No . . . but I hear this maybe true. I don't know it is true, but I hear something, some people are say.

Harriwell Can the claimant explain why he makes this petition now?

Yip *Why do you make this petition now?

Gee Why?

Harriwell Why now?

Gee Yes. Because I wish to visit to China. Again, soon. See my family. See my family. Um . . . I know . . .
Chinese Exclusion Act,
*I know that now it is permanent.

Yip I know that the Chinese Exclusion Act is now permanent.

Gee I remember this. Make very difficult. To travel China, yes? To come home again. I want to be . . . To be responsible. Last time when I come home, 1899, this also Exclusion time. I remember was important I show proof, yes? Prove I am Gee.

Harriwell According to your claim, you are employed as a laundryman, correct?

Gee Yes, laundry.

Harriwell Upon your return from China, do you have any intention of attempting to bring your children or your wife to the United States to accompany you?

Yip *When you return from China, do you have any intention of attempting to bring your children or your wife to the United States to accompany you?

Gee Ah, my wife no.

Dean *chuckles.*

No, I wish so! But no, not because, ha! No, is because she happy in China, so I send money back, for children. Very hard in China but she cannot leave mother.

Harriwell And what about your children, do you plan to bring any of them with you?

Gee Oh, I don't know. Maybe oldest boy if he want. I hope so, yes? He can help, with laundry, help father. Maybe old enough now.

Harriwell Mm-hm.

Harriwell and **Dean** *exchange a look.*

The reason I have to ask, you see, is that the current circumstance, even under Exclusion law, has been and continues to be plagued with a preponderance of fraudulent claims to U.S. birth by Chinese currently residing in California.

Yip   *The reason I ask is that the current circumstance, even under Exclusion law—

Harriwell   It is therefore incumbent on this Bureau to take special and sometimes unusual precaution in cases such as these,

Yip   *There has been a preponderance of fraudulent claims—

Harriwell   in order to ferret out deception and protect the interests of the United States against the abuse of its immigration law.

Yip   *So the Bureau has been forced to take extra precautions—

Harriwell   In other words, I'm going to be very frank with you, and I expect you to be very frank with me. Yes?

Gee   I understand. I understand.
Yes. I want be very very honest. Tell you truth.

Silence.

Harriwell   Good. So then. Tell me about your father.

Gee   My father.

Harriwell   Where was your father born?

Gee   My father born Hoisan.

Harriwell   And what was his name?

Gee   Name Gee Gyen Go. 建國

Harriwell   Is he still living?

Gee   No.

Harriwell   When did he die?

Gee   Die at earthquake.

Harriwell   Which one?

Gee   Which? Big one. 1906, yes, big one.

Harriwell   Was he employed at the time of his death?

Gee   Yes, same as now I do. Laundry.

Harriwell   And how did he come to be in America?

Gee   Come to America for build railroad. What year, I don't know, he no say, you know how is father no want to talk about, ha, painful time so he no to talk about.

Harriwell   And how did he come to be in San Francisco?

Gee Yes. This he tell. After railroad finish, no work for Chinese. Look for work but nothing. Most of Chinaman go San Francisco, he say very lucky, have friend help for get job meat packing. Factory. Hard work. But my father, yes, he have so many friend, everybody they like my father, he is how say, he is funny guy, yes? Everyone like funny guy, I do this too!, I am funny guy, everybody know, funny Gee they are say, so funny Gee! You, maybe you see how funny am I too?, but no no no, this is serious today, have to stay serious for serious meeting with serious man, so no funny Gee today, serious Gee!, okay!, but anyway my father, he so funny guy so no problem he can get job meat packing.

Harriwell When did he begin working at the laundry?

Gee When he meet my mother. Hope for want something different. He and friend in meat packing, they save many money, together can make laundry shop. They see laundry so success business, even white people come for Chinese laundry, yes? Best laundry! You come my laundry, you see, best work! I give discount!, but don't tell to anyone okay, so many good customer I never give discount gonna make mad. But for you discount. You will see so good work!

Harriwell Tell me about your mother.

Gee My mother?

Harriwell Is your mother alive or dead?

Gee Yes, dead, she is die.

Harriwell How did she die?

Gee When I was only small. I no remember many.

Harriwell Yes, but how did she die?

Gee She get sick, she die. Fever. Bad fever, no doctor. So she die.

Harriwell And how did your mother come to be in America?

Gee I—I don't know.

Harriwell You don't know?

Gee So young I was, I don't know and never they talk about this, I don't know.

Silence.

Harriwell Try to remember.

Gee I don't . . . what?

Harriwell I said I would be frank with you, so let me be frank. There are very few Chinese women in the United States. Even fewer in the year you were born. Based on the number of Chinese males submitting claims to birthright citizenship, we've calculated that if all such claims were truthful, every Chinese woman in America would have had to give birth to more than 20 boys, each. Now I know your race tends to breed prodigiously, but that still seems to me quite a stretch. So if you expect us to take your claim seriously, Mr. Gee, you're going to have to tell me about your mother.

Yip   He says that

Gee   I understand. I understand.

Silence.

Harriwell   Was your mother a prostitute?

Silence.

Do you know this word, prostitute?

Yip   *Was your mother a prostitute?

Gee   I know this word.

Harriwell   Perhaps you are aware that a sizable portion of the female Chinese population in the time period described were brought to this country as prostitutes?

Gee   Yes.

Harriwell   Yes, you are aware? Or yes she was a prostitute, please be specific.

Gee   Some have say. Yes that she was, but I don't know what is true.

Harriwell   Can you be more specific about who you've heard this from?

Gee   Oh, I don't—I don't know.

Harriwell   If you can identify someone who can confirm that they have knowledge your mother was a prostitute, that your father had a child with a prostitute, and that you are the child of this prostitute, then you have a witness who can testify that you were born in the United States. And if we can determine the validity of that person's testimony, it will support your claim to birthright citizenship.

Silence.

Gee   What?

Yip   *If you can find someone who would be willing to tell them such things are true, it will help. It should be someone who has never testified here before, someone you trust, to say what you want them to say. But they will need to know details of your home, your business, your father, they will face difficult questions and even the smallest details must match yours exactly.

Silence.

Gee   I understand.

Silence.

Harriwell   So?

Gee   I must try to remember. Try to think.

Silence.

I am sorry. Because. Everything gone. When earthquake happen, all I have, gone. Just like you, paper gone, proof all gone, even we are gone. All Chinese taken, no allowed come back Chinatown, long time—they take us go Presidio, no allowed leave, many weeks. When finally return, all of things gone. People come and take things, all we Chinese have not get destroy, people take it. Steal. Yes, steal. So many people have nothing. Some die. My father, die. People who know my father, I see them no more. No one left who know.

Harriwell   In that case, how did you come to be employed at the current laundry?

Gee   Ha! This one – I make it myself!

Harriwell   Oh?

Gee   Yes, yes. Because: From my father, I learn everything about laundry business. *After the earthquake, the laundry shops were closed, everyone who did that labor was gone.

Yip   After the earthquake, the laundry shops were closed, everyone who did that labor was gone.

Gee   *But people still need a laundry shop. That doesn't stop. The dirt of the world doesn't stop, it always finds a way to mark us and we must always find a way to make ourselves clean again.

Yip   But people still need a laundry shop. That doesn't stop. The dirt of the world doesn't stop, it always finds a way to mark us and we must always find a way to make ourselves clean again.

Gee   Even white people, they come Chinatown, they know I do good work. *This I am proud of.

Yip   This I am proud of.

Harriwell   How did you obtain the capital necessary to start the business?

Yip   *How did you obtain the capital necessary to start the business?

Gee   *I did not need capital. I had my hands, I had a system, I had my pride. Wash clothes by hand, water from a well, soap from the rubble. Chinatown rebuilds. I save. One bucket, one load of laundry at a time. Until I can afford a steam boiler. And then an iron press. And then a storefront.

Yip   I did not need capital. I had my hands, I had a system, I had my pride. Wash clothes by hand, water from a well, soap from the rubble. Chinatown rebuilds. I save. One bucket, one load of laundry at a time. Until I can afford a steam boiler. And then an iron press. And then a storefront.

Harriwell   Can you provide names of anyone who could confirm this part of your story?

Gee   This, yes, many can say. Sacramento Street, I am there long time.

Harriwell Please provide names and addresses, that we might consult them.

Gee Mok 麥 Hung Fat 鴻發, have grocery 830 Sacramento, he know me many years.

Ha 夏 Gun At 君達, work same store.

Chin 陳 Chek Wa 卓華, of course you know Chin Chek Wa!

Silence.

Heh? How you not know Chin Chek Wa!, he is most great man Chinatown, 965 Clay Street, he is long ago time know me there. Ask, ask. All of everyone. They will say Gee, he do good work. He is funny guy too, ha!, yes they say this too, but most important they say Gee he do good work.

Harriwell Are there any white people who could speak on your behalf?

Silence.

Gee White people

Harriwell You mentioned you have some white patrons, keep in mind that white testimony could be especially compelling.

Yip *If you can find a white man to speak for you, this will be enough.

Gee Ah, but this is – how?

Harriwell Of course, I know it's unlikely, but I have to ask. With respect to the individuals whose names you've provided, we will gather testimony from each of them to corroborate the information you've given, and such testimony will be considered against your petition. Now:

Gee Wait.

Silence.

I want to say.

Harriwell Yes?

Gee Something I say now. To you. To all you.
Because I.
I am honest person. Yes. Simple person. I want . . . just to live, yes? Go China, see my family. I miss my family. Children, they are grow up now already, so much time I am away, miss so much their life. My two son. I don't know what kind of man are they. My daughter, last I see my daughter just little girl, I don't know anymore what she is look like. Just I want to see. For small time. And then, I come home. I work hard. Never make no trouble. I no want take from America, I want give. Give America. I am so happy be in America. So happy for . . . for work here, so beautiful. Beautiful life. So Lucky Chinaman I am.
And so. What I say. What I want say.
Thank you. Yes?
I say thank you.

Lights.

2.

> *Inside a home in Taishan.*
>
> **Low** *sits, and* **Gee** *stands.*
>
> *The furnishings are spare. It is a farming community, and it is unlikely there's anything in the space that isn't functional and related to the life and practice of farming.*
>
> *It is late summer, 1910.*

Low You told them you were born in America?

Gee Yes.

Low And they believed this?

Gee When you tell a man what he wants to hear, he will believe you.

Low Even the white man.

Gee Even he.

Silence.

Low I wonder what your father would think of this.

Gee It doesn't matter.

Low Or your mother.

Gee This matters even less.

Low I remember you. You would not remember me, of course. Your family was quite prominent here, yes? This was before the worst befell our village, before the floods, before your mother left for Shanghai and your father went north to fight and die in one of those preposterous rebellions. I remember your father, he was notorious in the village; he was always the tallest, the loudest.

Gee Well

Low But never the kindest.

Gee He's not my father anymore.

Silence.

Low Yes. Well, I can see how true that is.
Look at you. An American. Yes?

Gee Yes.

Low A citizen?

Gee Yes, full American citizen.

Low Full?

Gee Yes.

Low Hm.

Silence.

Gee So: The cost, based on fair market value, is $100 for every year of age. You say your son is 15, and will be 16 upon crossing, so the price shall be $1,600. To be paid ten percent now and the rest I will recoup from his wages until the debt is fully paid.

Low So he'll be indentured.

Gee He'll carry a balance on a reasonable loan.

Low Indentured, on Gold Mountain, in the land of the free.

Gee He'll owe the balance to me, to a Chinese from Hoisan. I will give him work, food, clothes, shelter. I will not simply call him my son, I will treat him as such; I will give him purpose and I will give him my name.

Silence.

Low Why us?

Gee What?

Low Why do you make this offer to us, and not some other?

Gee I should be clear, there is no "us," this is for Moon Gyet. And Moon Gyet alone.

Low I am not an idiot.

Gee I don't care.

Low Do not assume that everyone wants to go to America; some of us have pride in where we come from, pride in our names, we do not sell them to strangers or trade them for another, some of us find dignity in knowing we will be buried in the same ground we were born from.

Gee If you don't have interest I can easily find another.

Low So then why us.

Gee Because you come from the same village as the man who was once my father. Because you know the land and your son can describe the terrain. Because the story he will have to memorize is complex, so his foreknowledge of such details is valuable. Because he is the right age to match the description in these papers, and because your neighbors tell me you're desperate.

Low The neighbors overstate.

Gee They know your circumstance.

Low We all have the same circumstance.

Gee They say yours is worse.

Low Who said that?, tell me their name and I will ensure theirs becomes worser still.

Gee From what I hear of your circumstance, that would take some doing.

Silence.

Low Well in that case what makes you think I can afford this this what is it, $160 as advance?

Gee I know you can't, but I can connect you to a moneylender here, for the advance plus the cost of passage

Low A moneylender! To charge me extraordinary interest

Gee That is not my concern

Low So I should take a loan from a gangster in order to *give you my son*

Gee To give him a better life

Low To let you take his name

Gee He will send home a hundred times what you owe the gangster.

Silence.

Low How much?

Gee That depends on him. He's a strong worker?

Low As strong as you will ever find.

Gee It's just the two of you here? On a farm this size?

Low We manage to work beyond what is typical.

Gee Has it always been just the two of you?

Low Of late.

Gee No brothers, sisters? Husband?

Low But this is not your business, is it? So. How much will you garnish from his wages, and how soon will he send money back?

Gee To start I will pay $1 per day, this will increase as business increases. Twenty cents will go to room and board, the rest I will garnish until his debt to me is paid; however, I will allow his sending 10 percent to you for repayment of advance costs, this can start as soon as he's landed.

Low Which is how long

Gee Once he's prepared to take the trip, the boat is on average three weeks, processing is unpredictable, it can be done in just a matter of days if he studies the biography I will provide him, and studies it well enough to avoid suspicion.

Low Oh, he can study it well.

Gee Yes. That's what I've heard about him. They also say he is ideal for the work I have in mind.

Low And what work is it?

Gee Laundry. Hot press, large machines. Long days, high temperatures. Stamina. Strength.

Low Laundry is woman's work.

Gee But then, there is more strenuous work. The work of being Chinese in America. This takes patience. Focus. A serious mind and. Well, a necessary grace.

Low Hm. And these are qualities you possess yourself?

Gee I believe I do, yes.

A clatter from just outside the door.

Moon Gyet (*off*) Ow.

Low *moves to investigate.*

Low Moon Gyet!

Moon Gyet (*off*) I wasn't listening!

Low Go back to the field.

Moon Gyet (*off*) What? I can't hear—I'm not listening, I can't – I can't -

Low Shut up and go back to the field.

Moon Gyet (*off*) Yes, mother.

Gee How much do you think he heard?

Low I would have noticed if he entered mid-conversation, he has heard everything.

Gee Good. That's good, perhaps we should ask him to join us?

Low Absolutely not.

Gee He's the one who needs to convey the information upon landing, so it's good for him to know everything.

Low He will know what I'll have him know, until I decide what's going to happen.

Gee We both know what's going to happen. And so does he.

Silence.

Low You talk like an American.

Gee I am an American.

Low Is that what you believe?

Silence.

84 Once in the Countryside

No. You know you are but a fake American, only a citizen because of embarassing lies. Because they would never take you as you really are. So you have to pretend, yes? And this is what you will make of my son.

Gee I will make him money.

Low At what cost?

Gee At the cost of $1,600 and the price of passage.

Low And his name.

Gee Yes, that too.

Low And once he has his new name, what do you imagine? He should break his back at woman's work, apply his grace in the face of mistreatment, and then what? Once his debt to you is paid, once he is of an age to claim a pretended son of his own, would you advise he sell that false name to others, return here in the years to come, bleed dry the most impoverished souls he can find and garnish the wages of another?

Gee If he is lucky.

Low And how long should that cycle continue?

Gee As long as it is possible. As long as it is lucrative.

Low This, yes at last this is the most American thing you've said.

Gee America has been good to me, and it can be good to your son.

She spits on the ground.

Low There is no part of the ill we're facing that isn't caused by America, there is no good here that America can claim that was not preceded by depths of evil and mistreatment, you cannot commend a beast for gently carrying his prey if he is the one who has wounded it.

Gee Perhaps, but

Low America forced commerce upon us until we depended on such commerce, then they took that commerce away; they did the same with opium, *opium!*; the Treaty of Nanking, my god you have me talking now of the Treaty of Nanking

Gee The Manchus are as much to blame for

Low The Manchus the *Manchus* he brings up the Manchus

Gee And the French, and the British

Low The French and the British it's all the same, and any weakness of the Manchus comes directly from decades of western humiliatiion

Gee And yet I am *done* with being humiliated!

I am trying to build something. I am done with being humiliated. Whether by the Manchus or the Americans or the weather or the world. Because I am crossing oceans. I am building a life. I am working toward the future and no I don't give a damn for who is to blame, because I am not intersted in blame, only in building. This is what I can give to your son. If you do not accept then you are a fool and I will be on my way; if you do accept then at long last quiet your tongue, woman, and bring the boy to me.

Moon Gyet *enters.*

Moon Gyet   I am here.

Low   Go back to the field, we're not finished yet.

Moon Gyet   I'm finished in the field.

Gee   And we are finished here. Do you know who I am?

Moon Gyet   You are my father.

Silence.

Gee   Yes. I am. And do you know what you must do?

Moon Gyet   I know I must study and memorize documents. A biography. A map. Exacting details that you will provide of the person I am to be, and that I must internalize them all without error, so they are as familiar to me as my memories, my feelings, and my dreams. I know that I must recount these details perfectly, to men on the other side of the world, who will test me with their utmost power. I know that I will never again be the person I was before, that I will be in debt to you until that debt is paid. I know that if I fail it will lead to my family's ruin.

Gee   Good.

Moon Gyet   I know I must hope and strive and struggle with every part of my being for the opportunity to live among people who consider me less than human. I know that I sacrifice all I have ever known in hopes of entering a country that does not want me.

Silence.

Low   And you will find a way to do so with dignity, and grace.

Moon Gyet   Yes, mother.

Low   I'm not your mother anymore, child.

Moon Gyet   Yes, madam.

Low *looks straight into* **Gee**'s *eyes.*

Low   You told me you have such a grace too. Please see that you show it more effectively than you have with me today. Lest you teach your son those manners.

Gee   Yes, madam.

Low   No matter where in the world he lives, he shall respect a woman like me. Whether he lives in America or China or the bottom of the damned ocean, you will not allow him to forget where he comes from. He will behave as Chinese behave, with Chinese honor and Chinese discipline, do you understand? Even if your passions are high, even if you are right and she is wrong, you will respect a woman like me. Respect her position and don't raise your voice when she asks for reassurance. She raised your son. Do not forget that.

Gee I promise, I will not.

She turns to **Moon Gyet**. *Places her hand on his cheek.*

Low Do not forget me.

Moon Gyet I promise, I will not.

Lights.

3.

> *A different interrogation room, this one at the Angel Island Detention Center. 1911.*
>
> *A table with three chairs.*
>
> *The **Inspector** sits along with an **Interpreter**. Both are white males. The **Inspector** has piles of papers before him, which he is busy reviewing.*
>
> ***Moon Gyet** sits in the empty chair across from the **Inspector**, with the **Interpreter** between them.*

Inspector   This is 5359586, Gee Lip Lun 立倫. This is his sixth testimony, sixty-third day since arrival on Angel Island. Gee Lip Lun?

Moon Gyet   Yes.

Inspector   Very well, let's begin.

*The **Inspector** reviews his paperwork.*

*The **Interpreter** repeats everything they say, exactly word for word.*

Inspector   During your third testimony, you spoke of your first home, the home where you and your brother and sister were born, before you moved to the home further east.

Moon Gyet   Yes.

Inspector   How many rooms did that home have?

Moon Gyet   Three.

Inspector   How many beds were there?

Moon Gyet   Four.

Inspector   Did you and your siblings ever share a bed?

Moon Gyet   No. We each had our own bed.

Inspector   Were there any stairs leading to the house?

Moon Gyet   Yes.

Inspector   How many steps?

Moon Gyet   Three steps.

Inspector   Of what material were the steps made?

Moon Gyet   Of stone.

Inspector   What color were they?

Moon Gyet   Gray, dark gray.

Inspector   Dark gray. Of a solid gray color, or was it speckled? With different colors?

Moon Gyet   No, it wasn't speckled, but a solid dark gray.

Inspector   How dark?

Moon Gyet   Um. Dark, like -

Inspector   Darker than the walls in this room?

Moon Gyet   Yes, darker.

Inspector   But not dark enough that a reasonable person could mistake it for black?

Moon Gyet   No, not for a reasonable person.

Silence.

Inspector   Were there other homes nearby?

Moon Gyet   Yes, there were homes on either side.

Inspector   What were the names of your neighbors?

Moon Gyet   The Chin 陳 family to the south, the Moy 梅 family to the north.

Inspector   Did either the Chins or the Moys have any children?

Moon Gyet   The Chins had many children. It was so long ago, I cannot recall everyone.

Inspector   And the Moys?

Moon Gyet   No, there were no children living there, but they were an older couple, so it's possible their children were away.

Inspector   Did the Moys home have steps leading to the house?

Moon Gyet   I don't—I can't remember this detail.

Inspector   Did the Chins home have steps leading to the house?

Silence.

Moon Gyet   It seems likely, but I can't say for sure.

The **Inspector** *makes notes, studies his papers.*

Inspector   Tell me about your mother.

Moon Gyet   My mother.

Inspector   What is your mother's name?

Moon Gyet   Sok Ying.

Inspector   What is her date of birth?

Moon Gyet   In American reckoning, it is June 14, 1872.

Silence.

Inspector   Do you always calculate based on the American calendar?

Moon Gyet No, I typically use the Chinese calendar.

Inspector How is it that you've calculated your mother's date of birth according to the American calendar?

Moon Gyet I wanted to know, so I calculated the date in American reckoning.

Inspector Is it because you've learned the date based on coaching papers?

Moon Gyet No.

Inspector You just happened to be curious.

Moon Gyet I anticipated that you might ask me questions about my family, so I calculated the American reckoning. I had hoped it would be helpful to you.

Silence.

Inspector Is your mother tall or short?

Moon Gyet She is of average height.

Inspector Is she taller or shorter than you?

Moon Gyet Shorter.

Inspector Is she of slender or thick build?

Moon Gyet She has the build of a woman who has been a farmer all her life.

Inspector So . . . thick?

Moon Gyet I will say athletic.

Inspector So then, you'd say your mother does a significant amount of the physical labor on your family's farm?

Moon Gyet Well . . . I suppose, um. I suppose I shouldn't say she does a *significant* amount

Inspector You have siblings, yes, and it says here you also have cousins who do much of the labor?

Moon Gyet Yes.

Inspector So your mother, she can focus instead on less strenuous domestic tasks, correct?

Moon Gyet That is correct.

Inspector But prior to your arrival here, as the eldest son, *you* would have performed a significant amount of the labor required for the maintenance of the farm, yes?

Moon Gyet Yes.

Inspector So in your absence, there is now a void.

Silence.

Moon Gyet Yes.

Inspector How does your mother feel about that?

Silence.

Moon Gyet She is pleased.

Inspector Your mother is pleased that her eldest son, who performed significant responsibility in the maintenance of the family farm, has left?

Moon Gyet Well yes, because she understands . . . she understands that the farm, the farm is not – it is not enough, even at its best we are able to grow barely more than we need to consume, and whatever surplus we have, well . . . there are so few buyers, so the opportunity here in America is worth the . . . it is worth the burden.

Inspector But she'll probably need to work harder, won't she? On the farm? Without you there?

Silence.

Moon Gyet I suppose.

Inspector What does your mother think of America?

Silence.

Moon Gyet She adores America.

Inspector Can you describe the ways in which she adores America?

Moon Gyet She adores it as the homeland of her husband, as a place where he can maintain a successful trade, where I can now work with him, in a such a way that she need not worry herself with the void left on our family's farm, for its value is insignificant to what we can accomplish together, here in the beautiful country.

Silence.

Inspector Okay.
Are her ears pierced?

Moon Gyet No.

Inspector Does she have bound feet?

Moon Gyet No.

Inspector Are your sister's ears pierced?

Moon Gyet No.

Inspector Does your sister have bound feet?

Moon Gyet No.

Inspector How old were you when your family moved to its current home?

Moon Gyet Current home? Eight. Or—nine years old.

Inspector   Can you take a moment to calculate which, eight or nine?

Moon Gyet   I was . . . yes, let's see. I was in primary school, so. When was that? Nine. Yes, I was nine.

Inspector   Can you let us understand what you were thinking just now, how it was that you were able to calculate that you were nine?

Moon Gyet   I thought about things that happened when we first moved, and I remember a friend who visited the home when it was still very empty. I recall that although I knew him before, we did not become close friends until I was nine years old.

Inspector   Did you attend the same primary school before and after you moved homes?

Moon Gyet   Yes.

Inspector   At this second home, were there stairs leading up to the front door?

Moon Gyet   I'm sorry, could you repeat the question?

Inspector   At this second home, were there stairs leading up to the front door?

Moon Gyet   Second home, stairs . . . yes. One step, just one step.

Inspector   Of what material was it made?

Moon Gyet   Of stone.

Inspector   What color was it?

Moon Gyet   Light gray.

Inspector   How light?

Moon Gyet   Lighter than the walls in this room, but not light enough for a reasonable person to mistake it for white.

Silence.

Inspector   Did you attend the same primary school before and after you moved homes?

Moon Gyet   Did I attend the same . . . Yes, I did. Did you ask that already?

Inspector   I will often repeat a line of questioning in order to ensure your answers are consistent. Were there stairs leading to the main entrance of the primary school you attended?

Moon Gyet   Yes.

Inspector   Does your sister have bound feet?

Moon Gyet   No.

Inspector   What does your mother think of America?

Moon Gyet   She adores it.

Inspector   Were there stairs leading to the main entrance of the primary school you attended?

Moon Gyet   Yes.

Inspector   How many steps?

Moon Gyet   Eight.

Inspector   There were eight steps?

Moon Gyet   Yes, eight steps.

Silence.

Inspector   Did you count them?

Moon Gyet   Yes, I counted them.

Inspector   When did you count them? While you were a student there, or recently?

Silence.

Moon Gyet   Both.

Inspector   Both?

Moon Gyet   I had remembered eight stairs, because sometimes—we would sometimes learn counting on the stairs, or play games on the stairs that involved counting. They were very large stairs, wide—

Inspector   Of what substance were they made?

Moon Gyet   Stone.

Inspector   When you say both, do you mean you recently recounted the stairs?

Moon Gyet   Yes.

Inspector   You went, physically went to your old primary school and counted the number of steps despite already remembering their number from counting games as a child?

Moon Gyet   Yes, because

Inspector   Or did you recently revisit the question of how many stairs there were because you came across the number in coaching papers?

Moon Gyet   I physically went to my old primary school and recounted the stairs because I was told that I might be asked such details

Inspector   Details about stairs

Moon Gyet   Yes

Inspector   You were told that you might be asked details about stairs

Moon Gyet   Yes

Inspector   So then you were coached

Moon Gyet   No

Inspector   Who told you I might ask about stairs?

Moon Gyet   My father.

Inspector   Your father?

Moon Gyet   And others.

Inspector   I've reviewed the transcripts of your father's testimony—your supposed father's testimony—and he has never been questioned about stairs

Moon Gyet   Others, who have told my father, and told me, of the sorts of things people are asked

Inspector   And they said I would ask about stairs.

Moon Gyet   Not just stairs.

Inspector   What else?

Moon Gyet   Houses. Doors, and the directions they face. Names and faces of people, and their physical build. Distance. Snowfall and rainfall, the quality of the sunlight, whether animals come out at night, the sound of the wind, the color of trees, the texture of dust. How people live and where they are buried. Gossip and innuendo. Sex. Money. Religion. The detailed rules of all our children's games. Politics. Pottery. Parsnips. The practice of farming, the names of our mules, whether we look at the stars, and what names we use for both the bright ones and the dim. What we dream about. What we decipher those dreams to mean. Which of those dreams we share with others, and which ones we keep to ourselves, unspoken. They said we would be asked about everything.

Silence.

Inspector   Do animals come out at night?

Moon Gyet   Yes. Rabbits. And field mice, mostly. And so many birds.

Inspector   Where is your grandmother buried?

Moon Gyet   In a field by a hill seven li east of home.

Inspector   Your friend, who visited your house when you were nine, what was the name of his family's mule?

Moon Gyet   His mule was called Little Ox.

Inspector   What names do you have for the stars?

Moon Gyet   As a child I would lie with my brother and my sister atop the hill at night, and we would choose stars for ourselves. We would call them by our own names, and yet we were often changing our minds about which ones to claim. We changed so often that we must have claimed each star in the sky at least once; their names are our names.

Inspector Tell me your dreams.

Moon Gyet What?

Inspector What do you intend to do, should you be granted passage into San Francisco?

Silence.

Moon Gyet I will weep.

Inspector Will they be tears of joy, or tears of sorrow?

Silence.

Moon Gyet I've been here, in this prison, waiting, for more than two months.

Inspector Will they be tears of joy, or tears of sorrow?

Moon Gyet I don't know if you believe me or not. I don't know what you intend. I don't know how many more days it will be until I'm released, either to San Francisco or on a slow boat back to China, or how many days I'll have to wait until my next chance to be interrogated. So it doesn't matter. If there is a difference between joy and sorrow, at this point I cannot tell. They will be both, or neither. They will be tears of relief.

Inspector Is this the sort of dream you share, or the sort you keep to yourself?

Moon Gyet I share everything now, I have nothing to myself.

Inspector The second home, after you moved, were there stairs leading to the front door?

Moon Gyet Yes.

Inspector How many steps?

Silence.

Moon Gyet Just one.

Inspector That will be all for today.

Lights.

End of Act One.

Act Two.

A liminal space.

One   毋忘此日君登岸.

Interpreter   You are allowed one hour of outdoor time per day.

One   愁人獨坐倚窗邊

Inspector   Your number is 5359586.

Interpreter   Angel Island Immigration Station was opened in 1910 to detain incoming Chinese for inspection and interrogation in enforcement of the Chinese Exclusion Act, passed in 1882.

Two   People are housed in one of four rooms.

One   The southernmost room on the second floor is for men; it can hold as many as 144 men, but often holds more than that, typically all Chinese, all men.

Two   There is a small room on the second floor facing north that holds women, as many as 50 women at a time, from various countries.

One   The men's barracks on the first floor can also hold up to 144; it too typically holds more than that, also all Chinese, all men.

Two   There is one lavatory.

One   You are led to the second floor barracks and assigned a bed and a number.

Moon Gyet   There are thirteen steps.

Two   In the men's barracks there are twelve poles, with twelve beds attached to each pole.

One   Seventeen inches of space between each bed and the bed above and beneath it.

Two   Four beds below, four beds in the middle, four beds on the top.

Moon Gyet   There are one hundred and forty-four beds.

One   Your bed is at the bottom left corner of the middle pole on the northernmost side.

Moon Gyet   From the second floor barracks to the recreation area, there are twelve steps.

Two   The outdoor recreation area is enclosed by barbed wire fencing.

One   Armed sentries are posted at guard towers on either side.

Two   Why do they need armed sentries? Even if someone escapes, there's nowhere to go; it's an island.

One   Well, if they shoot you, they don't have to look for you.

Three This is how they got me.

Silence.

One I brought an English/Chinese phrase book. A gift from a relative who came here, to Gold Mountain, years before. I share it with my bunkmates.

Two Commonly Used English phrases for Chinese in America.

Three Such as: He cheated me out of my wages.

Two He was choked to death with a lasso by a robber.

Three Please help, I need a doctor.

Two I will do whatever you ask.

One We study these phrases diligently.

Two We know they'll come in handy.

Three We've all heard the stories.

Two Of the wild west.

One When you left home, you carried with you one small knapsack, three days of clothes, twelve dollars, and the uncertain hope of a faraway future.

Two You came to Hong Kong from Hoisan by foot, a twelve hour walk, with an $80 steerage class ticket to board the U.S.S. William McKinley.

One On board, you are among over a hundred other hopeful Chinese of various ages, nearly all men; you make your way down a creaking, narrow staircase toward your bunk below.

Moon Gyet There are seventeen steps.

One The boat is three weeks, close quarters, wooden bunks, unusual food, men elbow to elbow in the bowels of a ship, no way to clean, no clothes to change.

Two You all carry coaching papers but never speak to each other of their contents; you wouldn't want to confuse another's paper history with your own.

One You are advised to throw your coaching papers into the sea, for if you're caught with them it's immediate deportation.

Two This is how they got me. I was caught with my papers in the lining of my jacket.

Three When you arrive at Angel Island, your suitcase is taken separately to a storage facility.

Moon Gyet From the docking area to the Administration Building there are forty-two steps.

One You are led to the medical center and ordered to remove your clothes.

Moon Gyet From the Administration Building to the medical center there are ninety-nine steps.

Two There are twenty of you in this room at a time.

Three The doctor examines you for hookworm.

Moon Gyet From the Medical Center to the Immigration Station there are seventy-five steps.

One Some are immediately led back to the boat.

Three This is how they got me.

Moon Gyet The stairs are white.

Two Detainees are strictly segregated by nationality.

One A room on the second floor holds Koreans, Japanese, and the occasional Sikh.

Three A more spacious room is for the Russians.

Two There are not many Russians.

Three And they never stay long.

One Sometimes they have parties. You can hear the music and the laughter through the walls.

Two I've heard that the staff at the Immigration Station, they sometimes go and join these parties.

Interpreter They throw pretty good parties.

Inspector One day my children were playing on the front stairs of our house. I asked them to close their eyes and tell me how many steps there are. We have lived at this house all our lives. My oldest said six steps. My youngest said eight.

Moon Gyet There are five steps.

Inspector You might presume that this story represents a failure of the system; how could anyone possibly know how many steps there are in so many flights of stairs? But no, that is not what you should take away from this. What you should take away, knowing that they *do*, always, they *always* know how many steps . . . Is that they are lying.

Interpreter Breakfast 7:15am.

Inspector They are always lying.

Three Lunch 1:00pm.

Two During my first few interrogations, the translator was himself Chinese.

Inspector Dinner 4:15pm.

Interpreter After one year, the Bureau determined it was dangerous to employ Chinese translators, and that only white translators would be permitted in those rooms.

Three This is why we wait.

One   There are not enough white translators to process detainees quickly.

Two   Lights out 9:00pm.

Inspector   Absolutely no noise is permitted.

Two   If you break a rule, even a minor one, you can be deported.

One   This is how they got me, I argued with a guard.

Two   This is how they got me, I was caught stealing.

Three   This is how they got me, in a fit of rage I threw a rock through a window.

One   You try to calculate how many days you have been here in your head.

Three   So you consider scratching out marks on the walls.

One   Not just to help with the counting but to see how the gathered marks grow and collect, each mark representing a day of uncertainty.

Two   But you look closely at the walls and see the light outline of black ink on the gray walls; in delicate calligraphy indicating hundreds of hands, you discover careful volumes of almost invisible poetry.

Silence.

Moon Gyet   What can one sad person say to another?[1]

Silence.

One   Written in sorrow, in fatigue, in boredom and regret.

Two   These are not walls to mark numbers onto.

Three   Not walls to mark the counting of days.

One   The walls of the second floor men's barracks at Angel Island Immigration Station are sacred.

Two   They contain the hearts and minds of those detained there.

Moon Gyet   I write my wild words to let those after me know.[2]

Silence.

One   In your third month on Angel Island, you return from breakfast to find that the poems on the walls have been painted over.

Three   Erased.

Moon Gyet   Splendor fades with the turn of an eye.[3]

---

1 Poem 38 in Lai, Him Mark, Genny Lim, and Judy Yung, eds. *Island: Poetry and History of Chinese Immigrants on Angel Island, 1910–1940* (Seattle: University of Washington Press, 2014), 76.
2 Poem 96, *Island*, 128.
3 Poem 127, *Island*, 154.

Two   But even after the poems are erased, you go to the walls every day and try to recall what had been written there.

One   You trace your fingers over the gray paint, as if to tell the words hidden beneath

Two   That although they're unseen, they are not forgotten.

Silence.

One   Until you do forget.

Two   For after your sixth interrogation, you resolve that you will think of nothing but your biography, your paper history, which must occupy every corner of your memory, there is no room now for poetry.

One   There is a rumor that a woman couldn't handle the waiting, she took a chopstick and pushed it into her brain, through her ear.

Three   I was there, the story is true.

Inspector   She made a mistake in her testimony.

Two   This is how they got me.

Three   She knew she would be deported, she knew it.

Two   But they made her wait.

One   They want this. When you are sent home, they want you to speak of how difficult it is, they want you to fear the journey.

Inspector   So you don't try again.

Silence.

One   After your eighth interrogation, you are so overcome with a sense of hopelessness and desperation that you return to the walls and attempt to conjure the poetry again.

Two   It is then that you see that they are once again dressed with invisible poetry.

One   But not in ink—now the verse has been carved into the wood, so lightly that each character is still the same color as the wood, imperceptible to any eye that does not look for it.

Two   These poems cover every wall, from ceiling to floor.

Three   Verses and verses.

Moon Gyet   Feeding on wind and sleeping on dew.[4]

One   But it hurts you to read them.

Three   It confuses you too.

---

4   Poem 114, *Island*, 144.

Two   For the poems, they seep into you.

Moon Gyet   A thousand sorrows and a ten-thousand-fold hatred burn between my brows.[5]

One   To read them is to know them.

Two   This worries you; you must not confuse another's circumstance with your own.

Three   Another's pain with your own.

One   And so sometimes, you read only one line, one character at a time.

Moon Gyet   Drifting[6]

Two   Until your pain is the same.

Moon Gyet   Like[7]

Three   Your circumstance the same

Moon Gyet   Duckweed[8]

One   You read them in secret.

Two   And when you do it is with panic

Three   For you can be punished for anything

One   Perhaps even for reading a poem

Two   Perhaps especially for writing one

One   Perhaps they will see you by the walls and suspect it is you who has done the carving.

Two   Perhaps even this does not matter, perhaps they will yet find some other reason.

One   Perhaps even absent a reason, they will invent one, any reason at all to finally, at long last, expel you from this place.

Silence.

Moon Gyet   This is how they got me.

Silence.

One   In your seventh month on Angel Island, you finally receive your ruling.

Interpreter   On on August 11, 1912, Gee Lip Lun is officially denied entry to the United States based on a determination that he is "likely to become a public charge," as evidenced by the fact he carries with him only $12 cash.

---

5   Poem 110, *Island*, 138.
6   Poem 133, *Island*, 160.
7   Poem 133, *Island*, 160.
8   Poem 133, *Island*, 160.

Moon Gyet   I am like pear blossoms already fallen.[9]

Inspector   Once a detainee has officially been denied entry, he has ten days to appeal the decision to the Board of Immigration and Naturalization Services.

Interpreter   The filing fee for a writ of habeas corpus is $100.

Two   You appeal the decision.

Inspector   An appeal can take an average of two months.

One   In your case, it takes three.

Silence.

Inspector   The Board of Immigration and Naturalization Services upholds the original ruling of deportation.

Interpreter   You have five days to file an appeal to the Secretary of Commerce and Labor.

Two   It is not until your thirteenth month before you add your own verse to the walls.

Inspector   This appeal to the Secretary can take two months more.

One   When you first encountered these poems, you did not think you had the right to share your thoughts on these walls, did not dare to think your sorrow could compete with those who had suffered so much more, who had been here longer.

Two   They seemed insane to you, with a madness you could only fear and respect.

Three   But now you look at the poems and find their sorrow is small compared to what you have endured.

Inspector   The Secretary of Commerce and Labor upholds the decision for deportation.

Silence.

Interpreter   A legal appeal to the Federal District Court can last up to three months more.

Two   Beyond the Federal District Court, there are no avenues of appeal; this is the final step.

One   And so you wait.

Silence.

Two   Two years after you leave Angel Island, the poems on the walls are covered once again.

One   This time with a wood putty that fills each groove of each character in each verse.

---

9   Poem 57, *Island*, 92.

Three   The putty erasing the words, and then another coat of gray paint covering the putty.

One   Not only are the words erased, but the eraser too.

Two   The walls, once again, seem unmarked.

Three   This history.

One   This truth.

Two   This verse.

Three   Eradicated.

Moon Gyet   You were buried beneath clay and earth.[10]

Silence.

Inspector *and* **Interpreter** *now sweep all remaining files from the table onto the floor.*

One   Thirty years after the closing of Angel Island Immigration Station, this putty that covers the poems begins to shrink.

Two   With each passing year, it grows smaller. And weaker.

Three   Somehow the putty and the paint taken together acts as a sealant.

One   And as it dissipates, it gradually reveals the markings underneath.

Poems are revealed, slowly, along the walls.

Two   All these poems.

Three   All these poems.

Two   All these poems, preserved by the very materials that attempted to erase them.

Still slowly, poems are revealed. Until every part of every wall is covered in illuminated poetry.

One   毋忘此日君登岸.

Four   Do not forget this day when you land ashore.[11]

Moon Gyet   What is my poem?

One   愁人獨坐倚窗邊

Four   The sad person sits alone, leaning by a window.[12]

Moon Gyet   I'm hungry
But this isn't my hunger, it's his

---

10 Poem 112, *Island*, 140.
11 Poem 10, *Island*, 54.
12 Poem 24 by Yee of Toishan, *Island*, 66.

One 悲苦相連天相遣

Four Grief and bitterness entwined are heaven sent.[13]

Moon Gyet I'm frightened
But this isn't my fright, it's his

One 芳草幽蘭怨凋落

Four The scented grass and hidden orchids complain of withering and falling.[14]

Moon Gyet I'm scared to dream at night
Because the dreams that come, they're his

One 那時方得任升騰

Four When may I be allowed to soar at my own pleasing?[15]

Moon Gyet Like the dream where he dreams he's some other boy
And wakes up at sea
So far asea and
afraid to remember
which one is he

One 浪大如山頻駭客，

Four Waves as big as mountains.[16]

Moon Gyet All I have
Are the things we share
He and I
We share this waiting

One 政苛似虎倍嘗蠻

Four Laws as harsh as tigers.[17]

Moon Gyet This waiting is a rock
This waiting is a gray rock and
We share confusion
This confusion is a smell
A smell like fish rot and ashes
And we share a wound

One 雲霧潺潺也暗天

Four The floating clouds, the fog, darken the sky.[18]

---

13 Poem 24 by Yee of Toishan, *Island,* 66.
14 Poem 41 by Lee Gengbo of Toishan, *Island,* 80.
15 Poem 41 by Lee Gengbo of Toishan, *Island,* 80.
16 Poem 10, *Island,* 54.
17 Poem 10, *Island,* 54.
18 Poem 24 by Yee of Toishan, *Island,* 66.

Moon Gyet   This wound
It is a weapon
A cold gray weapon
It smells like anger
We share this anger
And at last this anger
Is something we can hold in our hands
He and I
Its hilt is long
So we can hold it together
And when we leave this place
Either out the door or
Through the ceiling in some more ghostly state of freedom
We will stay holding it together
And we will never let go and
Never forget
Who put this weapon in our hands
And what it is for.

He makes a fist.

He beats his fist to his chest in a slow steady rhythm.

One   精衛唧砂填夙恨

Four   The zingwai bird carries gravel to fill its old grudge.[19]

Moon Gyet   And when we are free
We will remember each other
And all the things we buried
All these words painted over
All these memories erased
All this pain, hidden with the gray paste of their fear
Will endure
Because time shrinks them
Like this paste over our poems

One   毋忘此日君登岸.

Four   Do not forget this day when you land ashore.[20]

The beating stops.

Moon Gyet   And time?
I have time
So I will wait.

End of Act Two.

---

19 Poem 41 by Lee Gengbo of Toishan, Lai, Lim and Yung, *Island,* 80.
20 Poem 10 in Lai, Lim and Yung, *Island,* 54.

Act Three.

1.

>*1920.*
>
>**Low**'s *home. The furnishings are exactly the same as before.* **Low** *holds a broom; she cleans the space as lights rise.*
>
>*After a moment, a knock at the door.*
>
>**Moon Gyet** *opens the door and stands in the doorway.*
>
>*There is a long silence as they stare at each other, still.*
>
>*Until* **Low** *drops her broom on the ground and moves quickly towards him.*
>
>*She places her hand on his cheek.*

Low   How is it that you're here?

Moon Gyet   I would have written but it was sudden. I didn't know if I could make my way to the boat I took, and in not knowing I didn't want to say it, to put it in writing if it might not come true.

Low   How is it that I'm looking at you?

Moon Gyet   By the time I was on the boat I knew I would make it here even before a letter ever could, and by then I was already looking forward to this, this moment.

Low   Tell me everything.

Moon Gyet   Wait. Let's just stay like this a moment longer first.

They stay like that, hand on cheek, a moment longer.

Low   You said you couldn't visit.

Moon Gyet   I couldn't before. Every moment away from the laundry is money lost, and debts unpaid.

Low   So how long can you stay?

Moon Gyet   I don't know. But at least long enough to make the passing worthwhile.

Low   It's already worthwhile.

Moon Gyet   I'll need to go back as soon as my work here is finished.

Low   What work?

Moon Gyet   I brought you something.

He takes an envelope from his knapsack.

Low What is this?

Moon Gyet There are two things inside. Money, and . . . a remembrance.

Low What sort of remembrance?

Moon Gyet Open it and see.

She does, inside is a stack of about five bills, and a drawing.

Of course I can't spare the expense of a photograph, but I met a man with a talent for drawing likenesses, and he did this in exchange for laundry; Gee allowed it without garnishing my wage.

Low It's beautiful. It's nothing compared to the reality of you, yet still, it's truly beautiful.

Moon Gyet I'm no illustrator but before I leave I should sit and study you awhile, try to make one in your likeness, to carry with me.

Low Have I changed much?

Moon Gyet You, no. The house, no. The village though, the people, this land I can't recognize.

Low I told you how it changed, in my letters.

Moon Gyet It's all exactly as you described, I didn't know if you might be understating or exaggerating, but you weren't.

Low I always tell the truth.

Silence.

Moon Gyet I know.

Silence.

Low This is too much money.

Moon Gyet It's not enough money.

Low It's too much for me, not enough for most perhaps but too much of your own money to give an aging woman living all alone. You need this money.

Moon Gyet No, I'll be fine for money.

Low Then you can stay longer.

Silence.

Low (Cont'd) Yes? If you don't need money then you don't need to rush back to America, you can stay longer and we can have many days together.

Moon Gyet I'll be fine for money so long as I leave.

Silence.

Low What work do you have?

Moon Gyet You know the work I do.

Low You said you have work in Hoisan, what is it?

Moon Gyet Let's eat first. It's been too long, will you make something? Anything, I've gone too long and dreamt too much about mother's cooking.

Silence.

Low You call me mother?

Moon Gyet Today, here, I call you mother.

Silence.

Low It's all terrible past days and meals you dream about, I can't remember ever cooking anything for you beyond the most meager millet, the occasional rice.

Moon Gyet It's not the ingredients I missed, but the way you made them.

Silence.

Low I will boil us a chicken!

Moon Gyet No, save the chicken.

Low I have two chickens! All thanks to you, you deserve it.

Moon Gyet Save them both. I'm craving millet.

Low No one craves millet.

Moon Gyet I do. I crave remembering.

Silence.

Low Then I will make millet.

She begins to prepare a meal of millet.

Silence.

Low Did you understate, or exaggerate?

Moon Gyet About what?

Low In your letters. Did you understate, or exaggerate?

Moon Gyet I probably understated some things, exaggerated others. But occasionally I do tell the truth.

Low For your mother, I hope you would.

Silence.

So then Gee, he is good to you?

Moon Gyet He is good in many ways.

Low But not so good in others?

Moon Gyet He is acceptable in others.

Low   Business is good?

Moon Gyet   Business is acceptable.

Low   So you and Gee, you are able to live well?

Moon Gyet   We are able to live.

Silence.

Low   What work do you have in Hoisan?

Moon Gyet   Let's not talk about work today, I'm busy remembering.

Low   And yet you have me do the work of preparing millet. If it's past days you wish to remember then you must remember how to be dutiful and answer my questions; what work do you have in Hoisan?

Silence.

Moon Gyet   There is one thing I misrepresented. In my letters. At the beginning, I misrepresented my days on Angel Island.

Low   How so?

Moon Gyet   I was not there for three months.

Low   You were not?

Moon Gyet   I was there for seventeen months.

Silence.

Low   Oh, Moon Gyet.

Silence.

Moon Gyet   I haven't heard that name in . . .

I haven't heard that name.

Low   I'm sorry.

Moon Gyet   It's okay. It's okay. I.

I was on Angel Island for seventeen months with no expectation of landing in San Francisco. In order to have me landed, Gee was forced to pay for an attorney, as well as two timely and carefully orchestrated bribes to officials in order to expedite my case, and only because of these very unexpected and very large additional expenses was I able to finally set foot in San Francisco. Only at the additional cost of $1,075 was I able to begin working at his laundry and repaying my debt.

Low   He cannot expect

Moon Gyet   It is my duty and responsibility to pay it back.

Low   But

Moon Gyet   In the nine years since landing I have nearly repaid a third.

Low   Yet in those same nine years I have repaid far more of what I owe the moneylenders, what is wrong with you? Why do you still send me money, why do you give me this envelope?

Moon Gyet   These small bills and what I send you are meaningless. To try and fill my debt with this amount is like trying to calm an ocean with tears; it makes no difference in the shape of it.

Low   So

Moon Gyet   I don't have a choice.

Low   What do you intend?

Moon Gyet   I am here to sell my name.

Silence.

Mother, I have no choice. I'm here to bring someone with me to America, I'm here to sell my name.

Silence.

Low   A false name. And false promises.

Moon Gyet   My promises will not be false.

Low   But your name is.

Moon Gyet   All the easier to sell it then.

Low   You're too young to claim a grown son.

Moon Gyet   I don't need a son. I can take anyone, I could take a woman, someone to claim as a wife, I can take whoever is willing to pay.

Low   And what will you tell them? How they might stay in debt forever? Will you tell them they too will be forced into the type of indignity you show here now?

Moon Gyet   I will tell them the truth.

Low   And what is that?

Moon Gyet   That the crossing is maddening. That Angel Island is a prison built no better than for animals; that even in San Francisco Chinatown they will not find an end to the questioning, the interrogation; that most of America will always be forbidden to them, and their most fanciful dreams of Gold Mountain will never come true.

Low   You are a bad salesman.

Moon Gyet   And yet I will not have difficultly finding a buyer.

Low   Do you have no concern for that buyer's regret?

Silence.

Moon Gyet   Do you regret it?

Low Every day of my life. Every day of my life. But never so much as I do now. Looking at you here. Looking and seeing how much time I've lost, time I could have spent with you, as you were. Seeing what all of this has done to you. What *I've* done to you. What you've become.

Moon Gyet And what is that?

Low Desperate.

Moon Gyet Well

Low Dishonest.

Moon Gyet I'm not

Low Nameless.

Silence.

Do you not regret it?

Moon Gyet I do not.

I bless it. I cherish it.

Because this house still stands. You are still here. Ten years ago that seemed unthinkable. We are here together, in this home that hasn't changed even as the rest of the village beyond it burns. For everything I've endured, for all my toil, this to me, this moment right now makes it all worthwhile.

Low Oh child, this moment, right now? It's already over. What good does it do to cling to the past? I have no future. Without a name, you have none either, you only have rememberances and present day toil. When I had a son, I had a future. I dreamed it so clearly. Grandchildren, with faces like mine, names like mine, when I thought about my parents I could imagine them watching this family line stretching far into the future and way past our imaginations, even if we struggled we would be real, we would be family, we would be together. Not spending our days in hopes of recreating a moment already lost. I have no son anymore, he has sold his name and now he tells me he hopes to sell his marriage bed too?, what should my parents think of this?

Moon Gyet I will tell them what to think! I will tell them to think me brave, to think me so dutiful in what I'm prepared to sacrifice, for a dream of the future that yes, they could never imagine. I know my name even as I keep it unspoken. I am your son. You are my mother. And I do have a future if you will let me finish my work.

Low Your work is only about commerce.

Moon Gyet No, it's not

Low What then?

Moon Gyet It's about survival.

Low Survival, ha

Moon Gyet And at long last, mother, it is about revenge.

Silence.

What I endured. On that rock, the shame is all over me and always will be, but this is my revenge. To live with dignity, to make something of this name I've been given, to thrive, yes thrive within the life that's been thrust upon me.

I will have this diginity. I will earn it, and when I do, it will be worthy of all our sorrow.

Silence.

Low   Oh, my child.

Moon Gyet   Mother.

Low   This bitter boy. This is not the boy who was once so small I could hold him with just a hand, who could only fall asleep beside me well past the age a boy should sleep so, who cared not a moment when his brothers and sisters chided him for it, who would squeeze my hand when he held it, do you remember? Three soft squeezes, through all our family's loss, he maintained his tenderness even through the ravage of years, years that left us like this, just the two of us now. I can endure this, I have endured, even as I'm now here alone, but I don't know how to endure this bitterness in your heart.

Silence.

Moon Gyet   But I'm trying. I'm trying to . . . make something from it.

Low   Make what?

Moon Gyet   A future. Not for me, not for my children either, perhaps, but . . . but maybe. Maybe beyond that. Past what you or I can see. Because they say there is no more gold on Gold Mountain, but yes . . . Yes. There is. There is. And I will find it. This, this is the only path.

Low   It is a crooked path.

Moon Gyet   It is a path.

Silence.

Low   Your millet is ready.

Low *scoops the millet into a bowl and places it before him.*

Moon Gyet   Thank you.

He eats.

She watches him.

Low   There is a girl in Tung Sing Lay, by the name of Ah Yuen 阿元. She is 19 years old, her family is in dire need, they have already sent a son to America with false papers but he was sent back, the cost of his failure is enormous and I know they are desperate for an opportunity to try again.

Silence.

Moon Gyet I will look for her.

Low How is the millet.

Moon Gyet It's terrible.

Low It's millet.

Moon Gyet Have some with me.

Low If it's remembering you wish to do, then we should do as we did then. You eat. I do not.

Silence.

He eats.

Moon Gyet I thought you didn't wish to dwell in the past.

She sits across from him.

Low Perhaps for just a moment.

He eats and she watches him.

She places her hand on the table.

He grasps it, and gently squeezes three times.

Lights.

2.

> *A few days later.*
>
> **Yuen**'s *home.* **Moon Gyet** *sits across from her. They are alone. She is dressed meagerly, and he is dressed in a western suit.*

Yuen   I'm sorry I cannot offer you tea.

Moon Gyet   I don't need tea.

Yuen   Have you ever been to Stockton?

Moon Gyet   Stockton, no. But I have heard much about it.

Yuen   It's where my brother was supposed to go.

Moon Gyet   Mm.

Yuen   To labor on a fruit farm, as the son of a man named Lu. His name was to be Lu Wee Min 雷偉民. He was very excited about the possibility, but he never made it to Stockton.

Moon Gyet   I have heard.

Yuen   He never even made it to San Francisco. He sat on Angel Island for twelve weeks before coming back.

Moon Gyet   It is not an easy journey.

Yuen   He will not talk about it.

Moon Gyet   If you have questions, I will answer them honestly.

Yuen   He will not talk about anything, in fact; he's a broken person, it's been nearly a year since he returned and he sits around all day and stares at the walls, speaking little.

Moon Gyet   Perhaps he just wants to protect you from knowing.

Yuen   No, he knows I do not need protection. He is just a weak person.

Moon Gyet   Oh.

Yuen   He knows he is weak. And that's why he says nothing, it is because of the shame.

Moon Gyet   I see.

Yuen   My parents would perhaps be more confident in sending *me*, for they know I'm not so weak as he, but they might also be alarmed at the idea of my being in America as a woman; this has not been a common practice thus far, yes? Please explain.

Moon Gyet   Ah. Yes, well. There have naturally been changes . . . in the patterns of. Um, there are increasing numbers of Chinese men in California, but fewer jobs in the fields, on the fruit farms of Stockton for example—you know, this is perhaps not pertinent

Yuen I would think it's all very pertinent

Moon Gyet I wouldn't think you'd be interested in discussing trends in labor practice, demographic shifts of transnational migration

Yuen On the contrary I am very interested, please continue.

Moon Gyet Ah. Well. Then—immigrants have often performed the tasks that white Americans have been unwilling to perform, so

Yuen I know this part.

Moon Gyet Then in brief, we are being pushed into urban centers. Driven from spreading too far afield; we are more and more concentrated into Chinatown.

Yuen And so this necessitates women?

Moon Gyet Well, it facilitates it, in a way. Angel Island is filled with men, supposedly the women's barracks are less crowded, so perhaps it will be easier for you to cross than it was for your brother.

Yuen How long did you stay there?

Moon Gyet Seventeen months. But I was an early traveler, they wanted to set an example perhaps. Now with the overcrowding, they are speedier in their processes, and more casual with their deportations.

Yuen Seventeen months.

Moon Gyet Yes.

Yuen So then. It is clear that you are not a weak person.

Moon Gyet No. I am not.

Silence.

Yuen What would you expect of me?

Moon Gyet That depends.

Yuen On what.

Moon Gyet On your capacities.

Yuen My capacities are limitless.

Silence.

Perhaps that sounded boastful. Forgive me, it's probably not true; there is much I do not know. But lately I have been working hard to practice optimism.

Moon Gyet Ah.

Yuen You work at a laundry.

Moon Gyet Yes.

Yuen I can handle this work.

Moon Gyet This work can be very physical.

Yuen I routinely outperform my brother and father in the field.

Moon Gyet It can be mentally taxing, repetitive, unrewarding.

Yuen More so than the life of a farmer in Hoisan?

Moon Gyet Gee and I have a routine, and we are strong at performing what is necessary.

Yuen I am certain I could contribute. How would the money work?

Moon Gyet Yes, the money—is this . . . should we ask your father to join us for this part?

Yuen My father is a drunkard, you can talk to me.

Moon Gyet Very well. Um. The price is $100 for every year of age, typically the fee is a little less for women, so we can say $1,600. You'll need $160 as a down payment, plus the price of passage. You'll need to obtain these fees from a moneylender, I can connect you to one. You will earn $1 per day, twenty-five cents will go to room and board, ten cents you can send home for repayment of the advance costs; the rest will be garnished until your debt is paid.

Yuen What are the conditions of this room and board?

Moon Gyet The conditions?

Yuen Do you live in the workspace?

Moon Gyet Yes.

Yuen Where?

Moon Gyet In a room above the storefront.

Yuen Like an apartment?

Moon Gyet Apartment, attic . . .

Yuen So it is upstairs?

Moon Gyet Yes.

Yuen Is it just one room?

Moon Gyet Yes, with one small closet.

Yuen Is there a bathroom?

Moon Gyet The bathroom is downstairs.

Yuen Is there a kitchen?

Moon Gyet Also downstairs.

Yuen I see.

Moon Gyet There are twelve steps.

Yuen What?

Moon Gyet Never mind.

Yuen Who cooks, who cleans?

Moon Gyet Gee and I.

Yuen The food, is it good?

Moon Gyet No.

Yuen Is the apartment clean?

Moon Gyet No.

Yuen Will I be expected to do the cooking and the cleaning?

Moon Gyet Well, I wonder that you might find the food unacceptable and the lodging unsanitary, we are often tired at the end of the day and as bachelors have given way to an admitted indolence, so if you are motivated to improve our collective lives in either way we would be open to it, but if you don't mind our mess you are more than welcome to join us in our collective sloppiness.

Yuen So then yes, I am expected to do the cooking and the cleaning, understoood. So you and Gee share a room?

Moon Gyet Yes.

Yuen But not a bed?

Moon Gyet No, we have separate beds.

Yuen And for me?

Moon Gyet I hadn't yet considered

Yuen I need to fully understand your expectations.

Moon Gyet Right.

Yuen Because if I'm not mistaken, you are asking me to be your wife, yes?

Silence.

Moon Gyet Technically, well, yes.

Yuen And technically, in your expectation, does this involve sharing a bed?

Moon Gyet I haven't really thought that through yet

Yuen I find that hard to believe, you've come here after several weeks on a boat in preparation to bring back a wife, you haven't really thought that through yet?

Moon Gyet Well I might have thought about it, but. I don't want to make presumptions or assumptions about something that ultimately—um. I'm sorry, I'm feeling a little. Surprised? Unprepared.

Yuen Surprised by what?

Moon Gyet Not surprised, unprepared.

Yuen For what?

Moon Gyet I don't know.

Yuen For me?

Moon Gyet Well.

Yuen I'm not asking the kinds of questions you expected?

Moon Gyet I guess no? Or.

Yuen It's the way I'm asking?

Moon Gyet Maybe?

Yuen I've met your mother, surely you're familiar with a woman who speaks plainly.

Moon Gyet Familiar with, sure. Comfortable with, that's . . . different. I'm not

Yuen You're not used to talking to women. Plain-spoken or otherwise.

Moon Gyet That's true.

Yuen So it makes you uncomfortable when I ask about sexual matters?

Moon Gyet Yes wow. Very much so yes.

Yuen And yet you understand why I need to ask, of course?

Moon Gyet Yes. Yes, of course. But . . . I don't know how to answer, I uh. I mean it depends, right?

Yuen On what does it depend?

Moon Gyet Well I would think—alright, let's. Um. Because yes, I imagine that we—if we were to agree to terms on this, we would be entering into a sort of partnership. Yes? A partnership that would . . . that we would be . . . working together to come to some uh, common understanding of what the what this what the terms of the partnership are. So it's . . . negotiable?

Yuen Mm.

Silence.

Moon Gyet Because I mean, well—I mean, yeah why what do you think?

Silence.

Yuen Well, this is not how I imagined my marriage proposal would transpire.

Moon Gyet Yeah no me either.

Yuen And yet.

Moon Gyet Mm?

Yuen And yet since I was a very young girl, I had been prepared for the possibility that my father would try to marry me to Bo Ping 博平 from down the street, and although Bo Ping has a nice farm and a pleasant mother, he is of catastrophic hygiene and painfully boring to talk to; all things considered this arrangement does seem preferable.

Moon Gyet Wait what?

Yuen Then again you are a professed criminal, convincing me to pay you an exorbitant sum in the commission of international fraud, so I should perhaps not assume you're telling me the whole truth.

Moon Gyet I've tried to be very sincere in everything I've told you.

Yuen You're lucky in that I've been conditioned by life to have very low expectations.

Moon Gyet Ah.

Yuen But that said, you do seem like a favorable person.

Moon Gyet Oh good.

Yuen If I'm going to engage in such grossly illegal activities, the least I can hope is that the people are nice, right?

Silence.

Moon Gyet I promise. That I will do everything in my power to honor you.

Silence.

Yuen That—perhaps that is a bit too much.

Moon Gyet Yeah.

Silence.

Yuen What is it like?

Moon Gyet Pardon?

Yuen America. What is it like?

Silence.

Moon Gyet It is lonely.

Yuen Mm.

Moon Gyet It is vast but it feels crowded. The way we live, the way we . . . must live, it is crowded but it feels empty. The work is empty, there is a distance between the work and the world, there is a distance between the world and me, it is like . . . I am in a place but I am not really in that place.

Yuen   Where are you?

Moon Gyet   I don't know.

Silence.

Yuen   Do you think it's possible for that to . . . change?

Silence.

Moon Gyet   Yes.

Silence.

Yuen   Good. So then. Are we to share a bed?

Moon Gyet   Well, when we arrive you can uh look at the room and we can uh assess the most optimal arrangement, but for uh practical reasons I suspect

Yuen   Practical reasons aside, this is not an idle question. Do you hope to have children?

Silence.

Moon Gyet   Again, this is . . . negotiable, but

Yuen   Yes or no.

Moon Gyet   Yes.

Silence.

Yuen   Good.

Moon Gyet   Good?

Yuen   I have this hope as well.

Silence.

My grandfather, my mother's father, he was an amazing man. He came to Hoisan from Korea, in his youth, he was a sojourner, an explorer. He settled here after a massive mudslide destroyed the village, he was hired to help rebuild, for this was his practice, wandering the country, working at whatever he came across, whenever he could, which was often because his skills were considerable and everywhere there are people who need. He planned, long ago, to travel to Gold Mountain. During the gold rush, during the railroad era, he dreamed of it but he never had the chance; he lost a leg while unloading a steamship in one of his many odd jobs. Before he died I told him he was my favorite of everyone in our family, my favorite of everyone in the world in fact, and he told me I was his favorite too, not only because everyone else in our family was such a tragic failure, but because, he said, he could see that I might make of my life something akin to his vision of success; a life of exploration, of adventure. I'm glad to travel to Gold Mountain in his place, and don't worry; I do not presume that we will have any real adventure, as I said my expectations are realistic of what this life can offer. But this is why I insist on children. They need to do what he could not, what we cannot.

Moon Gyet Children it is then.

Yuen And everything else, we will figure out as we go.

Moon Gyet This is sensible.

Silence.

Yuen I accept your offer, Gee Lip Lun.

Yuen *holds out her hand to shake.*

Moon Gyet And I accept yours, Ah Yuen.

They shake hands cordially.

Lights.

3.

> *1930.*
>
> *At home,* **Gee** *sleeps, covered in white sheets.*
>
> **Yuen** *enters with a tray holding a pot of tea and a bowl of soup.*
>
> *She is visibly pregnant.*
>
> **Gee** *continues to sleep as she sets the tray down, replacing another tray which she takes away, out of the room.*
>
> *She returns and tidies up a little, and then opens a curtain to allow in streaks of morning sunlight.*
>
> **Gee** *wakes, slowly.*

Gee   Where am I?

Yuen   Uncle you're home.

He attempts to orient himself.

Gee   Is it morning?

Yuen   Almost afternoon.

Gee   No.

He tries to get up.

Yuen   Don't get up, you need to rest.

Gee   Almost afternoon, there is work to do.

Yuen   You have a fever, Uncle. The work is being handled.

Gee   Who is doing the work?

Yuen   Moon Gyet.

Gee   Alone?

Yuen   No, of course he is not alone, he's with the workers.

Silence.

Gee   The workers, of course. We have workers now.

She presents the tray and helps him to sit up.

Yuen   I made you some soup, and brought you some tea. You've had a fever for days, you should eat something. Get your strength back.

Gee   Days? What day is it? Tuesday.

Yuen   Today is Friday. You've been sick since Monday.

Gee   That can't be right.

Yuen   It doesn't matter the day. Try some soup, Uncle. You've eaten so little over too many days.

Gee   Friday? No. Something doesn't feel right.

Yuen   You must have had a bad dream.

Gee   It wasn't a dream.

Yuen   Well then it's the fever and you need to eat. Try the tea, it's a special tea, I got it from Dr. Yu and he says it will help.

Gee   Help with what?

Yuen   Help with the fever.

Gee   Help with my mind.

Yuen   Your mind is fine, it's just the fever.

Gee   No.
No.
I have moments of confusion, moments of forgetting, but I remember now: I remember forgetting things even before the fever.

Yuen   This is nonsense, Uncle.

He looks at her.

Gee   You are having a baby.

She laughs lightly.

Yuen   I know.

Gee   I know you are having a baby, you have four babies and this will be the fifth, you have four girls, of course I know this, but somehow just now when I looked at you I was surprised to see you're having a baby, why was I surprised?

Yuen   Again, this must be the fever. Which the soup can correct.

Gee   What will you name the baby?

Silence.

Yuen   We haven't decided.

Gee   You must decide.

Yuen   We have time still.

Gee   Names, names, names are important.

Yuen   I know, this is why we continue to carefully consider.

He remembers something.

Gee   Zingwai 精衛.

Yuen Yes.

Gee You've chosen the name, the name is Zingwai, this is a good name, I chose it. Did I choose it?

Yuen You did.

Gee Why did you pretend you hadn't chosen yet?

Yuen Because I knew you would remember.

Gee Zingwai is a good name, for it flies, it knows it is beautiful, it endures.

Yuen I agree.

Gee Names are important.

Yuen I know. You said that already.

Gee I cannot say it enough.

Yuen Of course, Uncle.

Silence.

Gee What's in this soup?

Yuen Taste it and see if you can guess.

Silence.

He doesn't taste the soup.

He closes his eyes.

Uncle?

Gee Shhhh.

Yuen What are you doing?

He opens his eyes.

Gee Please.

Yuen What's wrong?

Gee Promise me.

Yuen Promise what?

Gee Don't let me forget.

Yuen Forget what?

Gee Any of it. All of it. Please, Yuen, I don't want to forget things.

Yuen You won't.

Gee But I already do.

Yuen Only for a moment, only for a moment you forget, but you see you always remember again.

Gee I remember an ocean. I remember . . . a rock. A gray rock, but I forget where it comes from. And so I struggle to remember, I dig at it, my hands clenched, digging at the rock for what lies buried beneath it, I know I must remember because what am I if I forget? And when I have dug enough, I remember. But sometimes . . . sometimes the memory is more sad than the forgetting.

Yuen I understand.

Gee You do?

Yuen I do.

Gee Because I do not.

Yuen I understand remembering things that are better left forgotten.

Gee But that is all I have.

I have a memory of Tuesday, of days and days in accumulation like barrels of unclean laundry, and these I cannot forget even when it isn't Tuesday, it's Friday; but my memory of the ocean is the memory of *why*. If I cannot remember Hoisan, if I cannot remember my. If I cannot remember my. If I cannot remember my mother. If I cannot remember why I. why I . . . if I have to dig for it I dig only for the pain, is this what I should forget?

If this is what I forget then what am I?

Silence.

She takes a spoon and stirs the soup.

She draws out a spoonful of soup and, holding her other hand beneath it, draws the spoon to **Gee***'s mouth.*

Yuen This is what I tell the girls.

When they ask. Because they've started to ask. Not about the pain but about simple things, questions that should be easy to answer:

How did you and Daddy meet?

Tell me about your mother.
What is her name?
I tell them the truth.

I tell them the truth, and so far the truth is enough. But I know the questions will become more difficult. As they grow, for they will grow, as birds rise, because their names are deliberate, their names are their own, and they each have the names of birds. They will ask me questions and I will have to choose. How much will I tell them? How much do they need to know?

Mrs. Sun from the market, she has a daughter almost sixteen. The oldest of the children I know, the oldest of this new generation, and so I watch her to see how it begins. Mrs. Sun is resolved to tell her nothing. For to tell her would be a burden, she says, so she invents a history to tell her. A glorious history it is, for this is a skill we have mastered, isn't it?, the art of inventing a history of our selves that says to whoever listens yes, yes, we belong.

So far I tell the truth, but yes, I invent things too. Not a history, but a future. I invent a future for the girls, and I know this isn't fair, I want to allow them their own future, one that comes from their invention, not mine. But I cannot help but hope.

And in that hope, it is not a future of pretend. It is a future of truth. You cannot forget, Uncle. Even if you forget for a moment, you cannot long forget the pain, because the body remembers. Your body remembers, it is in your hands, your calloused hands, it is in your legs, your tired legs, it is in your back, your unbendable back grown uncommonly strong from all it has carried.

And it's in *their* bodies too. The pain is there, it's in their blood and in their hearts, it's in their memory too because it all passes down, if I know anything from motherhood I know this, that everything we are, *everything,* it passes down.

We will carry it. As a family should.

We cannot forget it away or deny it to them when they ask, or else somewhere in their future they will notice the pain, they will feel it, and if I do not tell them the truth now, then they will not understand where that pain comes from.

Better to tell it, I think.

Uncle, don't worry about the forgetting.

Okay?

I appreciate that you dig for it. I like that you dig for it.

Continue to dig, Uncle.

One day, it will rise.

She continues to feed him.

He continues to eat.

Linger.

End of play.

Special thanks to:

Genny Lim, who along with her colleagues Him Mark Lai and Judy Yung, made it their life's work to uncover and document and share this history. Their work, especially in *Island: Poetry and History of Chinese Immigrants on Angel Island, 1910–1940*, University of Washington Press, 2014, is an essential part of Asian American history. I want to publicly apologize to them, and to Genny in particular, for not including that acknowledgement during its two initial productions, and am deeply grateful for her permission not only to include excerpts from her translations in the text, but for the extraordinary work she has done to illuminate and share the history contained within this play;

Edward Tepporn and everyone at the Angel Island Immigration Station Foundation for their research and production support;

To Neil Pepe, Annie MacRae, Abby Katz and everyone at the Atlantic Theater Company for their extraordinary support in the development and production of the play;

To Daisy Yee and Dustin Chinn for their wisdom and assistance, especially with names and the spirit behind those names;

To Christine Mok, Kimber Lee, Andrea Hiebler, Krista Williams, Nissy Aya, Loretta Greco, and Beth Blickers, not only for their dramaturgical brilliance but for their care and advocacy;

To the poets of Angel Island for their legacy.

Bibliography

Jung, John. *Chinese Laundries: Tickets to Survival on Gold Mountain*. CA: Yin and Yang Press, 2011.

Lai, Him Mark, Genny Lim, and Judy Yung, eds. *Island: Poetry and History of Chinese Immigrants on Angel Island, 1910–1940*. Seattle: University of Washington Press, 2014.

Lee, Erika. *At America's Gates: Chinese Immigration During the Exclusion Era, 1882–1943*. Chapel Hill: University of North Carolina Press, 2003.

Lee, Erika and Judy Yung. *Angel Island: Immigrant Gateway to America*. NY: Oxford University Press, 2012.

Lowe, Felicia, director. *Carved in Silence*. Lowedown Productions, 1988. 46 min.

Yung, Judy. *The Chinese Exclusion Act and Angel Island: A Brief History with Documents*. NY: Bedford/St. Martin's, 2018.

Postscript

My Journey into *The Far Country*
Whit K. Lee

In 2022, I worked on a production of *The Chinese Lady* directed by Shannon Tyo, at Adirondack Theatre Festival. I remember Lloyd asking Sami Ma (Afong Moy) and I (Atung), "How do *you* feel doing it?" While I was only concerned with what impact the production was having on the audience, Lloyd was more interested in how these plays made us feel. Why? Because he wrote them for us.

Lloyd wrote *The Far Country* for us, the Toisanese people. He wrote it to honor our part in American history. If my great grandmother and grandfather hadn't been paper sons and daughters themselves, I would never have known. This American history was not taught to me in my schools and I know this to be true for many others. When I got the audition for the play, I was excited for the opportunity to help tell this story, our story.

The Audition

At the audition, Eric Ting's direction was to "talk to us." In *The Far Country*, several lines are directed at the audience: "Well, if they shoot you, they don't have to look for you." This directness, that connection to the audience can be jarring, sometimes comforting, even unpredictable. It is a vulnerable and powerful way to engage with you. It is part of the beauty of Lloyd's play.

When my manager Susan Campochiaro Confrey told me I got the job, I welled up with emotion. How incredible. I now had the opportunity to represent a person like my great grandpa and grandfather on stage. In the Atlantic Theater Company's world premiere production, I played two characters, Yip and One. Yip is a Chinese interpreter and One is a character who represents the many voices of Paper Children. Similar to Yip, my great-grandpa (mom's side) was a self-taught, highly educated, well spoken (with his perfect American accent) Chinese interpreter for the federal courts. My great-grandpa was of a higher class than Yip, but both were interpreters. My grandfather (dad's side) was like One, and all the people One speaks for. A Paper Son. A valiant survivor.

Rehearsal to Performances

An important part of the rehearsal process, especially doing a history play, is research. Christine Mok was instrumental in giving us historical context. In addition to her extensive list of resources, I turned to my family. I found an interview that I'd recorded for an elementary school assignment. On this cassette tape, a higher pitched me interviewed my aunt (dad's side) about my great-grandmother and grandfather's immigration through Angel Island: class struggle; starvation in China; little to no choices; horrific conditions; arrival at Angel Island; becoming a well-respected influential family in their community. For Yip, Mom and her 93-year-old mother, Grandma, were very helpful. The condensed story: A family of firsts in their fields. Visionaries.

While reading the script again, I gravitated towards the poems. I had a feeling I'd be asked to say them in Toisanese, which I did not speak. I reached out to my extended family, and my aunt found a friend, Grace, who spoke the dialect. Grace lives in Canada and sent me recordings of the poems. Listening to these recordings, I would imitate the tones and pronunciations. Working on these poems, like much of this play, was an act of uncovering, reclaiming, and honoring Chinese American heritage. Later in the process, the production hired someone to help us. Her Toisanese was different. Dialects, like people, are beautifully diverse.

Act II. The play shifts. Actors speak directly to the audience. You. Lloyd talked about the use of the word "you," and how "you" functions in a play where we speak directly to you. "In *your* seventh month on Angel Island, *you* finally receive *your* ruling." Working on this scene, Eric helped us hone in on how lines connected between actors to make a full thought, and how to dramatize historical facts by giving them meaningful staging. In performance, by the end of Act II, the character Two and I would step into a pool of water that surrounded the stage just as I spoke the poems in Toisanese, feeling the power of speaking my ancestral dialect, our fists beating our chests in unison as we looked into the audience. I felt the Toisanese poems reverberate in the theatre bringing to life the hearts and minds of those imprisoned at Angel Island. Blackout.

Watching the other scenes in the play made me think of my family and those families in the audience who might also have similar stories. Had our families, like Gee and later Moon Gyet, gone back to bring people over and continue the cycle? Had they endured the specificity and insanity of interrogation? The people who made it must have been quite intelligent. Three weeks in the bowels of a ship. The will to survive. Doing it for the next generation. Establishing our claim to belong in the United States.

Talkbacks

I wish there were talkbacks after every show, especially after a play that challenges, educates, and empowers the audience—you. *The Far Country* would stir questions and thoughts about immigration, the complex nature of survival, Chinese American history. Here are two questions that we would often get.

Question: What was behind the glass on the back wall?

Answer: Coaching papers made into flowers.

Response: Ooooh! Beautiful! (and other sounds of appreciation for Clint Ramos' set design)

Question: How did you feel doing the play?

Answer: Doing *The Far Country* and *The Chinese Lady* made me feel proud, fulfilled, and powerful. I hope others have the chance to do this play and feel the same. I hope that this play is read and discussed in schools, in book clubs, amongst friends and family. I hope it is produced often across the United States. This American story needs to be told and discussed.

In 2024, I also played Yip/One at Berkeley Rep. Berkeley Rep held many talkbacks, related community events before the show, and filmed one of our performances to be shown in local schools. To quote Gee and Yip from the first scene of the play, "This I am proud of."

I think the end of the process is how a story lives on after it is read or seen. Perhaps my postscript is like a talkback where I can offer you some questions.

Ask yourself. How did reading the play make me feel? What did I learn? What was surprising? How can I relate? What conversations will I have with others after reading it? What did I already know? What will I look into further?

Bina's Six Apples

Preface

Carrying History

Elizabeth W. Son

"*Wait, what's happening*," asks ten-year-old Bina of her father in Lloyd Suh's *Bina's Six Apples* as they stand in a clearing in their family's apple farm and orchard (143). "We have to leave," urgently responds her father who holds a worn cloth knapsack (143). It is the early fall of 1950, and the growing sounds of fighting that prompt the family's sudden departure are from encroaching North Korean troops that have pushed their way down the Peninsula since the start of the Korean War on June 25, 1950. After one city after another fell to North Korean troops, US-led UN forces set up and guarded what was called the Busan Perimeter, a defense line protecting an area in the southeastern part of the country that included Busan.[1] Shielding Busan was central to the war effort because it was a key port city for the transport of UN troops and military supplies.[2] Bina's bucolic family farm is located between Geochang and Busan and therefore close to the fighting near the perimeter. They have no choice but to flee to Busan. The embarking of this 70-mile journey by foot sets the action of the play into motion.

Each family member is tasked with carrying provisions; Bina carries six apples, one for each member of her family. When a bomb suddenly explodes, Bina gets separated from her family. As she makes her way to Busan in search of her family, she encounters a series of individuals—a mother who is searching for her lost daughter, a soldier who is trying to make his way back to his family, a boatperson who finds meaning in transporting people, a merchant who is just trying to make a living to survive, and a boy who is waiting for his kidnapped mother to return. Bina is on an atypical hero's journey. She does not overcome a challenge at every turn, but during each encounter she learns something about survival, community, family, and herself. As a child, she is an unlikely hero and yet she manages to complete her journey and even help others along the way.

Inheriting the Korean War

The Korean War holds an uneasy place in US national memory and in many Korean American families. "Despite the Korean War's being the condition of possibility for Korean diaspora, it is called the 'Forgotten War' in the US," explains sociologist Grace M. Cho. "The permanent state of war temporarily suspended continues to haunt Korean Americans for whom memory of the war is often erased or denied."[3] It was called the "Forgotten War" because news coverage of the conflict was censored at the time and "its memory decades later is often overshadowed by World War II and the Vietnam War."[4] The signing of the Armistice Agreement on July 27, 1953 formally ended the war, but the two countries are still technically at war and the division of the Korean Peninsula along the 38th parallel solidified the separation of millions of families. For Korean Americans who lived through the traumas of war, silences about their wartime experience have pervaded their homes and created a sense of transgenerational haunting for their children.[5] The nation-state, community, families, and individuals are implicated in the enforcing of these silences, observes psychologist Ramsey Liem, who conducted oral history interviews with Korean Americans about their memories of the war.[6] Artistic forms like *Bina's Six Apples* have the potential to become a critical site of remembering and reckoning with these historical traumas.[7]

The idea for *Bina's Six Apples* began with Suh's own family lore. Suh's father grew up on an apple orchard in the southeastern part of South Korea. When he was around five or six, the youngest of eleven children, in 1950, his family left behind their home for Busan. "They gave him a backpack and filled it with apples," explains Suh. "I remember him telling me it made him feel important and useful. It was a happy memory."[8] Suh's father is unlike many first-generation Korean Americans who experienced the war and decided not to talk about their experiences. Though war and displacement led to this experience, endowing a child with responsibility has colored Suh's father's remembrance as a happy one. While none of the characters in *Bina's Six Apples* are factually based on family members, the play could still be viewed as a performance of memory—a way for Suh to honor and remember his family's history of survival. The play also becomes an intergenerational commingling of perspectives. "I have three children, and my oldest is ten," explains Suh. "Somehow, I didn't realize I was doing this at the time, but looking back on it now, it seems obvious I was imagining what would happen if I put someone like my daughter into that moment of my father's history."[9] The intergenerational inheritance of wartime memory not only provides inspiration for Suh, but also becomes a framework for the play's storyline.

Framing this reimagining of a family story as a Theatre for Young Audiences (TYA) play focuses attention on the perspective of a child. "Seeing like a child," explains anthropologist Clara Han, is "to follow the childhood memory as a route into the child's world-in-the-making."[10] Suh invites audiences to look anew at this historical trauma and the world, through the eyes of a child because, at a fundamental level, when faced with war and displacement, one is like a child, trying to make sense of something that makes no sense. Returning to that frame of mind can be an illuminating first step towards understanding. *Bina's Six Apples* brings both adults and children into its world-in-the-making. "While writing this, it was useful to imagine my father and my daughter watching it together," explains Suh. "It was designed to be experienced multigenerationally."[11]

Bina's World

As Bina goes on two walks—one with her family and another by herself—the apples she carries are not only significant objects of value, but they also come to develop greater symbolic meaning. Apples in Korean culture are typically eaten for dessert after a meal or given in boxed sets as gifts. They are also put on display on special occasions: one-year doljanchi birthday celebrations and jesa rituals on the anniversary of the passing of loved ones and during Chuseok harvest festivals. They are woven into everyday life but also have status as special fruit for how they connote bounty. Apples also have a unique significance for Bina's family because the livelihood of two generations of her family has depended on apples. After her maternal grandfather passed away, her mother's family walked from Seoul to live with her uncle in Geochang. While walking, her mother muses that what she remembers the most from that time is that "we endured. We lived. We built a farm. A home. Had a family. An apple orchard. The best apple orchard in Geochang!" (150). For Bina to carry apples in her knapsack, she is not only carrying a food source for her family, but a tangible and symbolic connection to her family's legacy. It is this connection that gives her strength and hope during her journey when she also talks to the apples as if they were her travel companions. The apples also function as a tool of survival as she reluctantly relinquishes them, except for one, during her journey.

Bina's Six Apples also delicately balances contradictions and ambiguities, becoming a way for young audiences to expand their understanding of how different people navigate life in the face of devastation and loss. "Lloyd's play doesn't offer us easy answers," explains director Eric Ting, "there's no villain, there's no hero, only a little girl trying to make sense of a strange and terrifying world where everyone is a victim in their way just trying to get by."[12] Bina's first encounter puts two people desperately trying to find their way back to family into a moral quandary. Bina runs into a hungry mother who is heading north to look for her daughter. When asked if she has any food, Bina, responds, "I/ No," equivocating again after an apple is spotted by the mother before telling her, "I'm sorry I can't help you. I have to find my family" (154–155). In trying to convince Bina to hand over an apple and to join her, the mother cruelly tells Bina that her family must have purposely abandoned her because "they wanted one less mouth to feed" (155). They are both willing to deceive the other as a way to survive. "Help me find my daughter," swings the mother in one direction, as Bina swings in the other direction, "I have to find my family" (156). Bina runs away after the mother fails to convince her that she will not make it alone.

There are no clear lines between right and wrong, truth and lies, and oppressor and oppressed—all thrown into disarray because of the conditions of war and the necessity of survival. Bina's encounter with the soldier raises an important question about the justness of war and which side is in the right.

Bina   What side are you on?

Soldier   I'm with the good guys.

Bina   What does that mean.

Soldier   Okay, fair enough. I guess if you asked someone on the other side they'd say they're with the good guys too. No one thinks they're on the bad guys' side, right? Wait. You're not on the bad guys' side, right?

Bina   I don't think I'm on any side. (159)

Saying that he is on the side with the "good guys" has little meaning to Bina because it is not clear who is "good" during war, especially when the person in question is wearing a military uniform with a gun in his hands. The soldier concedes that who is considered the "good guys" versus the "bad guys" will vary wildly depending on who is asked. Contrary to his appearance, the soldier turns out to be the character who helps Bina the most. Though he steals an apple from her while she sleeps, he returns to help her learn how to read the constellations and warns her about Yongsan, a city that was decimated during prior bombings. In this tender vignette with the soldier, young audiences learn about moral ambiguity when it comes to war and that one should not be quick to judge in any circumstance, but especially during times of conflict.

The meetings with the boatperson and merchant teach Bina important lessons about the economic reality of survival, but her last encounter with the six-year-old boy invites her to practice kindness, arguably the most difficult posture to exercise in a situation like Bina's. "As a storyteller," explains Suh, "the most important things to me about this play are the ways in which it's about kindness, and about a particular kind of hope."[13] Sitting on a step that once belonged to a hut that no longer stands, the boy waits for his mother who was taken away by military men after they destroyed his village. Without hesitation for the first time, she hands him an apple, telling him, "I want you to eat this apple and stay strong and wait for your mother" (182). Except for her last apple, Bina gives him everything she has, her map and bag, so that he has something to help him stay alive while he waits. Because of what she has endured, Bina knows what the boy needs in that moment. "I think Bina's journey is an exercise in empathy," explains Suh. "I think the play itself is an exercise in empathy.[14]

When audiences saw the run of *Bina's Six Apple* in early spring of 2022 at Alliance Theatre, news coverage of the war in Ukraine dominated global news.[15] One can imagine how the play might have resonated with audiences and invited the adults and children to reflect on how they talk about the war, its impact on refugees, and the enduring need for kindness and empathy. *Bina's Six Apples* teaches us that war touches everyone across time and space and that we all have a choice in how we act. In Suh's performance of memory, he creates a world where generations together reflect on the senselessness of war through the eyes of a child and hope for a better world.

Notes

1 For more on the "drive on Pusan" at the beginning of the Korean War, see Bruce Cumings, *Korea's Place in the Sun: A Modern History* (New York and London: W. W. Norton & Company, 1997, 2005), 267-275.
2 Jill Frahm, *So Power Can Be Brought into Play: SIGINT and the Pusan Perimeter,* Series V, Volume 4 (Fort George G. Meade, Maryland, National Security Agency, 2000), 7-9.
3 Grace M. Cho, "Performing an Ethics of Entanglement in *Still Present Pasts*: Korean Americans and the 'Forgotten War,'" *Women & Performance: a journal of feminist theory* 16.2 (July 2006): 304.
4 Liam Stack, "Korean War, a 'Forgotten' Conflict That Shaped the Modern World," *The New York Times*, January 1, 2018, accessed on February 3, 2024, https://www.nytimes.com/2018/01/01/world/asia/korean-war-history.html.
5 For more on how the Korean War haunts the diaspora, see Grace M. Cho, *Haunting the Korean Diaspora: Shame, Secrecy, and the Forgotten War* (Minneapolis: University of Minnesota Press, 2008).
6 Ramsay Liem, "Silencing Historical Trauma: The Politics and Psychology of Memory and Voice," *Peace and Conflict: Journal of Peace Psychology* 13.2 (2007): 153-174.
7 As an example of how art creates the space for communal remembrance, Ramsay Liem points to the example of *Still Present Pasts: Korean Americans and the "Forgotten War"* (2005-2011), a multimedia art exhibit comprised of visual and media art, performance art,

and oral histories that explore the legacies of the war. See Liem, "Silencing Historical Trauma," 168-171.
8   "Interview with Playwright Lloyd Suh," *Bina's Six Apples* program, Children's Theatre Company, 13.
9   Ibid.
10 Clara Han, *Seeing Like A Child: Inheriting the Korean War* (New York: Fordham University Press, 2021), 5.
11 "Interview with Playwright Lloyd Suh," *Bina's Six Apples* program, Children's Theatre Company, 13.
12 "Interview with Director Eric Ting," *Bina's Six Apples* program, Children's Theatre Company, 12.
13 "Interview with Playwright Lloyd Suh," *Bina's Six Apples* program, Children's Theatre Company, 13.
14 Sally Henry Fuller, "Behind the Story with Playwright Lloyd Suh," *Bina's Six Apples* program, Alliance Theater, 7.
15 A co-production between Children's Theatre Company and Alliance Theater, *Bina's Six Apples* had its world premiere on January 9, 2022, at Children's Theatre Company in Minneapolis, before moving to Atlanta's Alliance Theater from March 11-27, 2022.

References

Cumings, Bruce. *Korea's Place in the Sun: A Modern History.* New York and London: W. W. Norton & Company, 1997, 2005.

Cho, Grace M. "Performing an Ethics of Entanglement in *Still Present Pasts*: Korean Americans and the 'Forgotten War,'" *Women & Performance: a journal of feminist theory* 16, no. 2 (July 2006): 303-317.

Cho, Grace M. *Haunting the Korean Diaspora: Shame, Secrecy, and the Forgotten War.* Minneapolis: University of Minnesota Press, 2008.

Frahm, Jill. *So Power Can Be Brought into Play: SIGINT and the Pusan Perimeter,* Series V, Volume 4. Fort George G. Meade, Maryland, National Security Agency, 2000.

Fuller, Sally Henry. "Behind the Story with Playwright Lloyd Suh," *Bina's Six Apples* program, Alliance Theater, 4-7.

Han, Clara. *Seeing Like A Child: Inheriting the Korean War*. New York: Fordham University Press, 2021.

"Interview with Playwright Lloyd Suh," *Bina's Six Apples* program, Children's Theatre Company, 13.

"Interview with Director Eric Ting," *Bina's Six Apples* program, Children's Theatre Company, 12.

Liem, Ramsay. "Silencing Historical Trauma: The Politics and Psychology of Memory and Voice," *Peace and Conflict: Journal of Peace Psychology* 13, no. 2 (2007): 153-174.

Stack, Liam. "Korean War, a 'Forgotten' Conflict That Shaped the Modern World," *The New York Times,* January 1, 2018.

Bina's Six Apples premiered as a co-production between The Children's Theatre Company (Peter C. Brosius, Artistic Director) and Alliance Theater (Susan V. Booth, Artistic Director).

The Children's Theatre Company production opened in Minneapolis, Minnesota, on January 11, 2022. The cast was as follows:

Bina	Olivia Lampert
Father/Boatperson	Albert Park
Jinsoo/Soldier	Joseph Pendergrast
Youngsoo/Another Mother	Shelli Delgado
Mother/Merchant	Sun Mee Chomet
Hamee	Elizabeth Pan
Boy	Jayden Ham
Director	Eric Ting
Scenic and Lighting Designer	Jiyoun Chang
Costume Designer	Junghyun Georgia Lee
Music and Sound Design	Fabian Obispo
Movement Director	Marcela Lorca
Production Stage Manager	Chris Schweiger
Assistant Stage Manager	Kenji Shoemaker
State Management Fellow	Cortney Gilliam

Understudies were Malia Berg, Michelle de Joya, Meghan Kreidler, Zakarin Ratsabout, Eric Sharp, and Clay Man Soo.

The Alliance Theater production opened in Atlanta, Georgia, on March 11, 2022. The cast was as follows:

Bina	Olivia Lampert
Father/Boatperson	Albert Park
Jinsoo/Soldier	Joseph Pendergrast
Youngsoo/Another Mother	Shelli Delgado
Mother/Merchant	Sun Mee Chomet
Hamee	Elizabeth Pan
Boy	Alexander Chen
Director	Eric Ting
Scenic and Lighting Designer	Jiyoun Chang
Costume Designer	Junghyun Georgia Lee
Music and Sound Design	Fabian Obispo
Movement Director	Marcela Lorca
Assistant Director	Raiyon Hunter
Production Stage Manager	Liz Campbell
Assistant Stage Manager	Skylar Burks

Understudies were Chloe Gia Bremer, Caroline Donica, and Clay Man Soo.

Bina's Six Apples was originally commissioned and produced by The Children's Theatre Company.

Characters

Bina, female, 10.
Father, male, 30s.
Mother, female, 30s.
Hamee, female, 60s, Bina's grandmother.
Jinsoo, male, teens. Bina's brother.
Youngsoo, female, teens. Bina's sister.

Another Mother, female, 20s or 30s.
Soldier, male, late teens.
Boatperson, any age, any gender.
Merchant, female, any age.
Boy, male, about 6.

Doubling is encouraged, except for **Bina** and **Boy**.

Setting

Between Geochang and Busan, South Korea.
Fall 1950.

1.

> *A clearing in Moon's Family Farm & Apple Orchard. One tree is prominent. Apples on it, and on the ground surrounding.*
>
> **Father** *stands holding a worn cloth knapsack.*
>
> **Bina**, *10, is beside the tree.*

Bina   Wait, what's happening?

Father   We have to leave.

Bina   When?

Father   Right now.

Bina   Right now?

Father   Right now. We can hear the fighting getting closer by the hour, by nightfall it might just be right on top of us. As soon as we gather what we need we're headed out.

Bina   Where are we going?

Father   Busan.

Bina   Where's that?

Father   The furthest edge of the country, touching the big blue ocean on the southeast point of Korea.

Bina   How far is it?

Father   About 70 miles.

Bina   How long's it gonna take to get there?

Father   I figure it'll take around 30 hours of walking total, mixed with meals and sleep and shorter stops to rest, not to mention adjustments for the terrain, with luck we'll make it in a few days, but we should be prepared for more.

Bina   What's it like there?

Father   Safer than here I hope.

Bina   I don't wanna go.

Father   We don't have a choice now, Bina.

Bina   I hate the ocean.

Father   You love the ocean.

Bina   I hate Busan.

Father   You've never even seen it.

Bina I hate war.

Father Mm. Mm-hm. Yeah, well . . . I do too, Bina. But sometimes that's how the world is, it's full of hateful things as much as it is full of things to love. Best we can do is try being one of the lovely things.

Bina What about my treehouse?

Father Maybe we'll come back when the war's over, maybe it'll still be here.

Bina You think we'll come back?

Father Honestly, Bina, I really don't know. But I promise if we can't get back or if it's gone when we do, we can build a new one and a whole new home besides.

Bina Can I bring Ji Hyun?

Father Who's Ji Hyun?

Bina My corn husk doll with the burlap dress.

Father Corn husk whatnow? You haven't played with that doll in years, what do you need Ji Hyun for?

Bina I just feel like maybe I'll need her.

Father Well if you think you can carry her in addition to the rest, that's your decision to make. What's happening now, Bina, means I gotta trust you to make good decisions on your own.

Bina What else am I supposed to carry?

Father *drops the knapsack.*

Father Apples.

Bina Apples?

Father We can't carry much but we each gotta carry our share. Only what we need. What we need the most is food.

Bina What are you gonna carry?

Father As much rice as I can.

Bina What's Mama gonna carry?

Father Bag of jars full of kimchee and vegetables.

Bina What about Jinsoo and Youngsoo?

Father Your brother and sister carry pots for the cooking and canteens of water, hopefully we'll get the chance to refill them time and again on the journey.

Bina What about Hamee?

Father Your grandma, she carries wisdom. And that's the heaviest, most important thing we've got.

Silence.

Bina   I can carry lotsa apples.

Father   See how many you can fit in there.

She starts picking apples and putting them in the knapsack.

Father   Make sure to pick the best of the best, they need to last.

Bina   I can only fit five.

Father   Five is pretty good.

Bina   Five apples is nothing, I can take more.

Father   Remember, these apples are the best in Korea. Denser, juicier, fuller than your average apple.

Bina   But I can carry more.

Father   Five Korean apples from Moon's Family Farm & Orchard are better than a dozen apples from any other spot in the world.

Bina   It's not even heavy. We just need a bigger bag.

Father   That's the only bag we got. Besides, what about your corn husk doll?

Bina   Corn husk dolls are for babies, this is war time Dad, we all gotta make sacrifices.

Father   That's a good kid.

Bina *picks up armfuls and holds them.*

Bina   I can hold way more, I can lift more than a dozen.

Father   Don't matter how much you can lift, it matters how much you can carry. There's a big difference between lifting and carrying, Bina. Picture treking through mountains and crags and traversing rivers, and consider how many apples you can hang on to when you're doing all that.

She drops a bunch.

Bina   I'll carry six.

Father   Bag only holds five you said.

Bina   There's six of us Moons, I wanna carry one apple for the each of us. I can carry one in my hand.

Father   You're gonna need your hands on the journey, won't be easy. Mountains crags and rivers, remember.

Bina   I'll carry it here.

She puts it in a pocket.

So it's always right beside me.

Father Good. One for each of us, that one's yours then.

Bina No daddy, that one's yours.

He conceals how much he loves this.

She hugs him abruptly. He holds her tight.

Father That's a good kid.

Bina Tell me we're gonna be okay.

Father We're gonna be okay.

Bina What's this war about, anyway?

Father Well I guess it's about the same thing all wars are, which is who gets to be in charge of things.

Bina Who's in charge of things now?

Father Around here, no one is. Past five years or so, which I guess is most of your life, there hasn't been anyone in charge. So right now there's two types of folks who want to do something about that.

Bina Whose side are we on?

Father I don't even know anymore. Sometimes you're in a spot when it seems like no one's looking out for you the way they should, so in situations like that, well. You gotta be on everyone's side. We've gotta look out for each other now, and that starts right here with you and me, see. I'm on your side. Always will be. No matter who's in charge of the country, no matter if we're here on the orchard or way down south in Busan, one thing I can promise is that we'll always be in charge of ourselves, and always in charge of each other. You understand what I mean when I say that?

Bina No, I don't think I do, Daddy, but it's good enough for now.

Father Alright then, strap on your bag and tell everyone it's time to go.

He walks off as she straps on her bag and turns to face offstage to shout:

Bina HEY EVERYONE IT'S TIME TO GO!

Father *returns carrying a jige on his back, filled to capacity.*

He has to hunch over to support it.

One at a time, the rest of the family lines up:

Mother*, carrying heavy bundles attached to a stick over her shoulders;*

Jinsoo *and* **Youngsoo***, each with two big, heavy bags;*

and finally **Hamee***, who walks slow, supporting herself with a wooden cane.*

They stand together, and then they walk.

Transition to:

2.

> *Walking.*
>
> *Somehow there should be a sense of distance:*
>
> **Father** *is at the very back of the line, with* **Hamee**. *Just in front of them is* **Mother**.
>
> *At the front are* **Jinsoo** *and* **Youngsoo**, *who walk with* **Bina**.

Bina   What's in that one?

Youngsoo   Don't worry about it.

Bina   Is it heavy?

Jinsoo and Youngsoo   Yes.

Bina   Gimme some of yours, I can carry more.

Jinsoo   It's fine, I got it.

Youngsoo   Trail's gonna get tougher up ahead, you just worry about your own bag.

Bina   No way, I can carry more.

Jinsoo   If you keep talking you'll wear yourself out.

Youngsoo   And stop bouncing around, you gotta pace yourself.

Bina   I'm feeling good though, lemme take an extra bag.

Jinsoo   These bags are heavy.

Bina   I'm strong though.

Youngsoo   These are big kid bags, Bina, just mind your apples.

Bina   I *am* a big kid.

Jinsoo   Alright fine, you wanna take a bag?

Youngsoo   Don't give her a bag, Jinsoo.

Jinsoo   Mind your business, Youngsoo. Here, Bina, take a bag.

Youngsoo   Don't take the bag, Bina.

Bina   I'm takin it!

Jinsoo   This is the lightest one I got.

He gives her a bag.

Youngsoo   She can't carry all that.

Bina   I can so.

Jinsoo   She wants a bag, she can take a bag.

She struggles with the bag.

They walk a little longer. After only a few seconds:

Bina   What's in this bag?

Youngsoo   Told you she couldn't handle it.

Bina   I can handle it! I'm just asking.

Jinsoo   She says she can handle it.

Bina   I just wanna know what I'm carrying. You know, so I can carry it appropriately.

Jinsoo   It's the smallest bag of the smallest jugs of water we got.

Youngsoo   You can give it back if it's too heavy.

Bina   It's not too heavy.

It's too heavy.

Youngsoo   Take the bag back, Jinsoo.

Bina   I wanna carry it.

Jinsoo   She wants to carry it, Youngsoo.

Bina   I can carry it.

She can't carry it.

Youngsoo   Alright, that's enough. Bina, stop. Stop, here. Gimme the bag.

They stop.

Jinsoo   I'll take the bag.

Youngsoo   Get off, I got it.

Bina   It's maybe just a little bit too heavy.

Youngsoo   Told you she couldn't handle it.

Jinsoo *sees how this bothers* **Bina**.

Jinsoo   Hey Bina, thanks for carrying it a little ways. It was really helpful. I can take it from here though.

Bina   After we drink some of that water in it, I bet I could carry it longer. Even just a little bit lighter and I bet I can handle it.

Jinsoo   I know you can, Bina.

He takes the bag back.

Thanks for helping me out. I really appreciate it.

They start walking again.

Bina   You're welcome.

Youngsoo   What are you smiling about?

Bina   I'm not smiling.

She's smiling.

Jinsoo   Let her smile if she wants.

Youngsoo   This isn't supposed to be fun.

Jinsoo   Just cause it's not *supposed* to be fun don't mean it can't be.

Youngsoo   That doesn't make sense.

Jinsoo   *You* don't make sense.

Youngsoo   Yes I do.

Jinsoo   No you don't.

Youngsoo   *That* doesn't make sense.

Jinsoo   What doesn't?

Youngsoo   What?

Jinsoo   Shut up.

Youngsoo   No you shut up.

Jinsoo   No you shut up.

Youngsoo   No you.

Jinsoo *and* **Youngsoo** *walk ahead.*

Mother *catches up to* **Bina**. *She's carrying big bags that hang off a stick she holds against the back of her neck and shoulders, with her arms wrapped around it. She's hunched a bit as she does this.*

Mother   Bina! Is your bag heavy?

Bina   It's not heavy.

Mother   We'll stop for lunch in an hour or so.

Bina   Okay.

Mother   Can you make it?

Bina   I can make it. Do you need help with your bags?

Mother   Oh no, this?! No, this isn't heavy.

It's heavy.

I'm fine.

She's not.

Bina   It looks really heavy, Mom.

Mother   It's easy! Because of the stick. See? I can carry so much more like this, I can put all the weight on my back instead of just my arms.

Bina   It looks really super heavy, Mom.

Mother   Oh no! No no no. Very easy. I've done this before, you know. And I didn't have such an excellent stick then. So this, ha! This is great. When your grandfather died, we had to move from our home in Seoul to live with my uncle in Geochang. We walked for weeks! Of course it was different then. We didn't have to bring as much food because you could buy things along the way. Sure, we didn't have money to buy things but we could stop in the villages, spend time, find work, wash clothes, sew, cook, clean, trade our clothes for lesser clothes, spend the difference on rice. It was fun! Kind of. Of course, sometimes there were soldiers, which was maybe a little bit frightening. But not all the time. We also sang songs while we walked.

Bina   Songs?

Mother   Sure. Singing helps to take your mind off of the walking, the soldiers, the bombs and the guns in the distance . . . growing closer and closer every day. But still, it could be worse! Right? Because what I remember most about those years long ago wasn't the fighting, or the walking. It was that we endured. We lived. We built a farm. A home. Had a family. An apple orchard. The best apple orchard in Geochang! Even though it's all gone now. Even though they fight again. . . . But anyway! This time, I am not worried. Because we have endured it all before. And we will endure it all again. And also, because I have this excellent stick!

Silence. They walk.

So. We'll stop for lunch in about an hour. I'll fix you something nice, okay?

Bina   Okay mom.

Mother   That's a good girl.

Mother *walks ahead.*

Hamee *catches up to* **Bina**.

Bina   Hamee.

Hamee   Mm.

Bina   Do you need help? Are you hot? Are you hungry? Do you need water? Do you need help to walk? Let me help you.

Hamee   Mrmph.

She waves her off.

Bina   Jinsoo and Youngsoo have water, I can bring some to you.

Hamee   Don't fuss. Worry your own worry.

Bina It's no trouble, I'll run ahead and come back again. It's hot, you should have some water.

Hamee Carry your own bag, child. Don't think of me, I carry nothing.

Bina Daddy says you carry wisdom.

Hamee Hrmpf.

Bina And he says that's the heaviest most important thing we got.

Hamee Well then we are in great trouble, child.

Bina I'm strong, you know.

Hamee Hrmpf.

Bina I'm carrying six apples even though the bag holds five. I can carry more! I may be small but I have grit and determination, if you're carrying any wisdom that's too heavy for you to bear, let me take some of it. I'll give it back when you need it, Hamee, but I'm happy to carry it for you awhile.

Hamee If I had wisdom to share, my child, I'd gladly put it in your knapsack. But all I'm carrying right now is Bitterness. Fatigue. Anger and Aches and Bewilderment that we still must walk this terrible walk. I thought I had walked enough in this life. You don't want to carry what I'm carrying, Bina. When it's your turn to run the world you make sure sure to fix it so you don't have to walk any more, okay? Or else you end up like me, now, carrying unnecessary heartbreak over mountains, a long long time in the hot summer sun.

Now go away, child. Leave me to my grumbles and my disdain.

Silence.

Bina Hey let's sing a song!

Hamee Heh?

Bina Mama says singing makes the walking better, do you want to sing a song with me?

Hamee No.

Silence.

Bina Okay.

Silence for a moment.

Until eventually, **Hamee** *sees* **Bina**'s *disappointment, and begins to sing.*

Bina *joins her.*

They sing together.

Bina's **Father** *catches up behind her.*

He joins in the singing.

They walk and sing a moment.

Until a whistle can be heard.

Father *looks up.*

Father   Wait.

Bina   What's wrong?

The whistle is a little louder.

Father   Oh no.

Bina   Wait what's that sound?

Father   RUN!

Out of nowhere, an explosion.

Blackout.

3.

> *A clearing.* **Bina** *is alone. She has been running. Her face and her clothes have traces of dust and ash on them.*

Bina Wait
Where

She looks around, in every direction.

Where did you go?
I'm here!
Mama! Daddy!
I'm here!
Jinsoo, Youngsoo, Hamee!
Bina! Bina is here! Where are you?
Where are you!? Where am I?!

She searches the stage as best she can.

She checks her bag. Counts the apples. They're all there. Momentary relief.

Until she checks her pocket. The sixth apple is gone. She panics.

Oh no. Oh no oh no no no no no...

On her hands and knees, running her hands through the rocks and dirt.

She finds it.

I found it! I found it oh thank you thank you thank you...

A woman enters, running slow, she's exhausted. She has a bag with her, it's tattered and torn. And empty.

This is **Another Mother**.

Bina Mama!

Another Mother Ji Hyun!

She runs to hug Bina but stops as she sees her.

Bina Oh! No.

Another Mother No. You're not
I'm sorry, I thought

Bina Are you lost?

Another Mother Lost. Yes.

Bina So am I.

Silence.

Another Mother Oh no

Bina What happened

Another Mother I don't know

Bina It was loud

Another Mother It was a bomb

Bina It was so close

Another Mother Out of nowhere

Bina I ran

Another Mother So loud

Bina I shouldn't have run,
I should have stayed close
But I was so scared
My family

Another Mother I don't know which way is north

Bina I don't know which way is south

Another Mother Where are you coming from?

Bina Geochang.

Another Mother How long have you been walking?

Bina Not long, only a few hours.

Another Mother A few hours from Geochang?, that's good, that's...

Bina But Geochang is north.

Another Mother Yes, I have to go north.

Bina But the bombs are north, the soldiers are north, at least I think that's yes, that's what he said

Another Mother I have to go north

Bina We're headed south, it's dangerous north, he said we have to go south

Another Mother *My daughter is north I have to go north.* I lost her. I lost my daughter. Ji Hyun. I've been trying to find her, it was north. I've been turned around. Do you have any food?

Bina I
No

Another Mother Please. I've been walking for days. I need to find my daughter. My daughter is missing. I'm missing. I have nothing left. I have this bag, it's empty but I carry it anyway. I have a canteen of no water. I have a bag of no rice. I have a jar of no food. I have a purse of no money. Please.

Bina I'm sorry I can't help you

Another Mother What's that

Bina What

Another Mother In your hand

Bina This isn't mine

Another Mother Is that an apple

Bina No
Yes

Another Mother Where did you get it

Bina I'm sorry I can't help you, I have to find my family

Another Mother You've been walking for only a few hours, you must have things. Still have things, to share. Please.

Bina I can't
It's my job I have to carry six apples
For my family

Another Mother Six apples?!
You have six apples?
That's
Please
I haven't eaten in
So long
Please

Bina I'm sorry
I can't give them to you
They're for my family

Another Mother Where is your family?

Bina I don't know

Another Mother They're not here, are they?

Bina I

Another Mother They've left without you, they don't need your apples, they're gone

Bina No, NO they're just
We got separated
I ran when I should have stayed
I ran too fast, too far

Another Mother They wanted one less mouth to feed

Bina   NO

Another Mother   You think it's better in the south?
It's not better in the south
You think you'll find your family before those apples rot?
You won't
I've been walking for days, first to the south and then to the north
You think that bomb was bad?
I've heard dozens of bombs
You'll never get those apples to your family
But hey
Look
We can help each other, you and me
Come with me
Come north

Bina   No I have to go south

Another Mother   Help me find my daughter

Bina   I have to find my family

Another Mother   Let me have an apple

Bina   I can't

Another Mother   You'll never make it alone

Bina   I will

Another Mother   You'll never make it alone

Bina   Stop saying that

Another Mother   I should know, I've been alone
I've been alone and *I'm not going to make it*

Bina   I'm sorry

Another Mother   No you're not

Give me an apple
Please
I'm not going to make it

Bina   I can't

Another Mother   I'm not going to make it
And neither are you

Bina *runs away.*

Linger on **Another Mother**, *before*

Lights.

4.

> **Bina** *walks. She approaches a large pile of rocks. Steps up onto a large boulder and looks up over it. She tries to climb the boulders, but struggles.*
>
> *As she does, we see below her—hiding in the rubble – is a* **Soldier***. He has a rifle. He is startled.*
>
> *He sees her, she doesn't see him. As she starts to descend the boulder, he jumps out and points his rifle towards her.*

Soldier Arms in the air!

Bina AAAAAAHHH!

She puts her arms in the air. He sees her and puts the gun down.

Soldier Oh man. What is that? What are you, are you a child?

Bina *is scared silent. Arms still in the air.*

You scared me! What's wrong with you?

Bina I'm I'm um um

Soldier This is a war zone, you know. What are you doing out here? Who's with you?

Bina I'm looking for my um my um

Bina *suddenly starts crying.*

Soldier Oh man. Come on. Oh man. Don't do that. Hey. Hey please? Don't cry?

She cries.

Soldier Okay look, I'm putting the gun away, see?
No don't put the gun away!
Yes I'm putting the gun away, she's just a kid.
You *are* a kid, right?
Of course you're a kid.
But I mean, you're like a real kid, right?, not some decoy sent here to distract and surprise me and force me out of the rock I'm hiding under in the middle of a craggy crossing so your evil collaborators can descend upon me in a surprise military maneuver, right?
Because I mean, that kind of thing
You know, it probably happens.
Please stop crying, I'm very confused!
Are you alone?
You're not alone, you can't be.
That doesn't make sense, a kid alone in the
Who are you with?

What's in your hand?
Arms in the air!
Is that a
That's not a grenade, right?
Please stop crying.
Okay I'm putting the gun away.
I mean it's not even loaded.
I forgot to bring any
No, never mind
I shouldn't have told you that.
Forget what I just said, it's totally loaded.

Even though he's probably put the gun away and then back up several times throughout this, he now puts it away definitively.

Alright fine it's not loaded.
Please stop crying, you're gonna make me start crying too.
There there.
Um.
Say.
Hey.
Where um where are your parents?

She cries louder.

Soldier   Alright alright let's um
Okay hey so . . . my name is Private Nam Moojin, 3rd Armored Brigade, Army of the Republic of Korea. What's your name?

Silence.

Bina   What?

Soldier   What's your name?

Bina   Bina.

Soldier   Hi Bina.

Bina   Who are you?

Soldier   Like I said. Private Nam Moojin, 3rd Armored Brigade, Army of the Republic of Korea. I'm a soldier.

Bina   Are there more of you?

Soldier   Right. Good question. That's a good question. Thing is, though, yes. There are more of me, the entire 3rd Armored Brigade, but as you can see for the moment I am alone. Why? Well, funny story. I'm kinda lost.

Bina   So am I.

Soldier   Where are you trying to go?

Bina   I don't know if I should tell you.

Soldier Why not?

Bina What side are you on?

Soldier I'm with the good guys.

Bina What does that mean.

Soldier Okay, fair enough. I guess if you asked someone on the other side they'd say they're with the good guys too. No one thinks they're on the bad guys' side, right? Wait. You're not on the bad guys' side, right?

Bina I don't think I'm on any side.

Soldier Oh good. I think that means we're on the same side? One side is coming down from up north—

Bina Is that the good side or the bad side?

Soldier Well like I said that depends on your perspective.
What's in your hand?

Bina What?

Soldier Whoa is that an apple?

Bina No.
Yes.

Soldier Shut up no it's not. Where'd you get it?

Bina From a tree.

Bina *starts to cry again.*

Soldier Whoa what the
Why are you crying again
What did I do

Bina I'm supposed to save it and carry it and I have to keep it safe

Soldier You gotta stop crying I can't understand what you're saying

Bina I have to carry it, for my family, it's an apple from Moon's Family Farm & Orchard and I'm carrying it to Busan because each of us Moons has to carry what we can and I can only carry six apples I wanted to carry more but I can't and now I'm lost and I don't know how to get to Busan and I'm hungry but I can't eat the apples I'm supposed to take them to Busan but I don't know where Busan is and I just want to go home I want my mom I want my dad I want my Hamee and maybe even my brother and sister but I'm scared and you're scary and I just want to go home!

She's really crying a lot now.

Soldier Okay man, alright that's enough, jeez.
Try to breathe or something. Try to—Okay. Yeah that's not good.
You're gonna hyperventilate. Yeah but see, it's kinda getting worse now. So. Don't.

He goes to his bag, she is startled, freezes in a panic.

Soldier No no no no no. It's okay. I'm just gonna show you something. Okay?

He takes a corn husk doll in a burlap dress out of his knapsack.

See this?

She nods, tentatively.

It's a corn husk doll. Now I'm gonna need this back cause it isn't mine, but if you want I can let you see it a sec. Do you want to?

She nods again.

He gives her the doll. She kinda likes it even though hers is better.

Soldier Guess who made it?

Bina . . . You did?

Soldier Ha no, I don't have that talent. My little sister made it. Her name is Soojin, she's eight. When I went off to the war, she gave it to me to keep me safe. I told her she should keep it. I said she needed help being safe too, but she said no, you're the one going off to war, and like an idiot I let her convince me to take it along with me. But now, they're headed down south. They're headed as far south as they can go, and Soonjin's right in the path so as soon as we got the order to meet the northern army up the pass, to try to fight em back, I knew I should just listen, I knew I shoulda just gone with em and taken it like a man and a soldier and a good guy, I know it's important to fight for my country and stuff, but none of that is more important than my little sister. Right? So I left the army. Ran away. Middle of the night, I packed up Soojin's doll and started running, I even forgot to bring any food, what a dope. But I'm headed back home. I'm a deserter. That's what they call soldiers who run away. I'm not lost, I ran away. Home. To Soojin.

Bina Where is your home?

Soldier Hadong. Have you heard of it? No? Probably not, it's not famous or anything but it's pretty good and I like it. Anyway, I gotta get there before the northern armies do. And so I'm real scared, you know? I'm scared of the bad guys, but I guess I'm scared of the good guys too, cause I'm supposed to be with em but I'm not.

She gives him back the doll.

Bina It's nice.

Soldier Yeah. It is, isn't it.

Bina Which way is Hadong?

Soldier Southwest.

Bina Do you know which way that is?

Soldier I think so. The army taught us a trick, to find out which way's north. Problem is you gotta wait til the stars come out. Once the sun goes down, I can show you.

Bina   So I gotta wait til the sun goes down to know where's Busan?

Soldier   Yeah but that'll be pretty soon, probably an hour or so from the look of it. And then, once the stars come out it's easy. As long as it's not too cloudy you can use the stars to face north, and from there just turn and go southeast.

Bina   Southeast?

Soldier   Busan is southeast. Hadong is southwest. Before you showed up, I was waiting for the sun to go down. Sleeping down here. In the shadow. It's less hot down here. Walking's so much better at night, you can check the stars to make sure you're headed the right way.

Bina   But you can't see nothing.

Soldier   Yeah but nothing can see you either.

Silence.

Anyway, if you wanna stick around til the stars come out, I can teach you how to read em.

She nods.

Good.

Thing is though. Um.

See, I haven't eaten in about a day and a half. Last thing I ate was about six grains of dried rice someone left on a spoon I found in a burned out jeep some miles back. I'll teach you the stars either way, but if you're able to share part of an apple, I'd be-

Bina   No.

She hurriedly clutches the apple bag to her, tight.

I'm sorry, I can't, I made a promise.

Soldier   No worries. I understand.
I understand, I really do.
Just. Figured it doesn't hurt to ask.

Silence.

I'm gonna go back inside my hole now to rest. We both got long walks ahead of us come nightfall.

Silence. He starts to head towards the hiding place, but stops.

If you want . . . you know what, you can use this one. It's pretty good. I'll move over there.

The soldier gathers his things and gestures for her to move to the crevice.

Bina   . . . Really?

Soldier   I mean you walked right by me before, and didn't even see me, right? So yeah it's a pretty good hole.

She makes her way into the crevice as the **Soldier** *moves to the other side.*

I'll be just out here. If you need anything, lemme know. And if there's any trouble I'll tell you about it.

Bina   Okay.

Soldier   I'm sure you're tired. Get some rest.
When the stars come out, I'll let you know.

They silently rest.

Bina   Thank you.

Soldier   . . . Do you want to hold onto the doll for a bit?

Silence.

Bina   Yes please.

The **Soldier** *walks over and hands the doll to her.*

Soldier   Yeah she's a pretty good doll.

Bina   Thank you.

Soldier   You're welcome.

They rest.

The sun goes down.

5.

> *Night, as before. The* **Soldier** *walks over to the crevice where* **Bina** *sleeps.*
>
> *He very carefully, very cautiously, very silently takes an apple from her knapsack. She stirs a little, and he stops sudden. She settles again. He places the apple in his own bag.*
>
> *He doesn't feel good about this, but he does it anyway.*
>
> *He starts to sneak away.*
>
> *In fact, he might even get completely off stage before returning.*
>
> *Because he's realized he totally forgot to show her about the stars.*
>
> *He thinks about this for a moment.*
>
> *Maybe he starts to go again and comes back.*
>
> *He makes a decision.*
>
> *Clears his throat.*

Soldier   Bina.

Bina.

Bina.

Bina *wakes.*

Bina   Mmm?

Soldier   It's night.

She emerges more fully from the crevice.

Soldier   Did you sleep okay?
I know it's not the most comfortable spot, but.

Bina   How long did I sleep?

Soldier   A few hours. It's been dark for awhile, but you looked really tired and I thought you could use the rest. But I gotta get going now, and first I have to show you:

He points to the stars.

Look. Up there. See those stars in a pattern, they look kinda like a soup ladle?

Bina   What?

Soldier   Like a handle there, and a spoon there. See it?

Bina   Yeah.

Soldier Well you look where the end of the spoon is pointing, just go straight up from there and there's another super big star just above it, do you see that one?

Bina Mm-hmm.

Soldier That's the North Star. No matter where you are, it's always there and it's always north, so if you want to get to Busan just turn about this much

He turns, holding his arm out.

Rotates from north to southeast.

That's southeast, exactly the right amount to get you to Busan.

Bina Wait

Soldier Just keep in that direction, but here's the thing. Are you listening?

Bina Yeah but

Soldier Two things I need to tell you. First, remember that direction. Always keep an eye on where I'm pointing. If you get turned around, just wait til nightfall and check the stars again to find your way. Got it?

Bina . . . Can you come with me?

Soldier Aw, jeez Bina. You know I can't.

Silence.

She holds out the doll for him.

He doesn't take it.

Look, why don't you keep the doll.

Bina No, you need it. Soojin needs it.

Soldier I'll learn how to make another one

Bina Just take it and go.

He reluctantly takes the doll.

Soldier Alright, but wait, there's one more thing I gotta tell you first. As you head southeast, you're gonna find a river. You're gonna hafta follow it. Find a way to go downriver, maybe if you're lucky you can find a boat or something. But here's the important part: at the end of that river, you'll be at a place called Yongsan. When you get there, it'll probably seem easiest to just go through it, but you need to take the extra time, and go around it.

Bina Why?

Soldier I've heard things. Bad things, about what's happened there.

Bina What things?

Soldier Just don't go there, promise me.

The sound of an explosion in the distance.

Bina   What if I don't make it?

Soldier   Oh Bina.

Bina   I don't know how to do this.

Soldier   Yes you do.

Bina   Please come with me.

Soldier   I can't, Bina, I have to get back to my family, I have to.
But hey. If. I mean, if you wanted. You could, uh. You could come with me?

Bina   What?

Soldier   To Hadong. You could meet Soojin, we could go there together.

Bina   But

Soldier   And we could look for your family after, when the fighting stops.

Bina   No. I can't.

Soldier   Yeah.

Bina   Thank you, but. No, I have to find them. They're waiting for me. I know they are.

Soldier   I know they are too.

Silence.

Another explosion in the distance, a little bit closer.

Soldier   Good luck, Bina.
Now . . .
I gotta go.

Silence. She doesn't know what to say.

Neither does he, so they stand in silence.

He leaves.

Linger.

She picks up her bag.

Checks it. Four apples.

Checks her pocket, the fifth.

Searches. Searches. Searches.

Thinks.

No. He didn't.

Searches some more.

Understands.

Looks out at the direction he left in.

Then sits.

Puts the pocket apple into the bag with the others.

Bina Don't worry, that one was mine. I still have five, the other five, one for each of you.

And she walks.

6.

> *A river.*
>
> **Bina** *stands looking out over it.*
>
> *A long while.*
>
> *She sits.*
>
> *She's so tired.*
>
> *She's so hungry.*
>
> *It's midday.*

Bina Hello, river.

How long are you, river?

How long has it been?
Since we left
Since I started walking
Since I've been away from my family
Since I've eaten

How long
Until this is all over?

How long would it take to get to the other side?

She opens her bag. Takes out an apple.

Hello, apple.

If I ate one of you.
How much further could I go?

If I wait here for someone
to come and get me
would they be good or bad?

Which side would they be on?

If they were good
How long would it take
for things to get better?

If they were bad
How long would it take
for things to get worse?

What's worse
The uncertainty
or the hunger?

If I ate one
How much longer would I last?
How much longer would this go on
and on and on this river
are you bad or good, river?

I said ARE YOU BAD OR GOOD RIVER?

Answer me, river.

You're a bad river.

This isn't fair, river!
It isn't fair.

Tell me what to do, river.

Not fair that you're such a long river
Not fair it's been such a long time

Where is my family, river?
Do you know?
Can you see them?
Have they been here?

Are they waiting for me?
Are they looking for me?
Are they ahead of me
or behind me
Are they safe
Are they hungry
Are they talking hopelessly to a river?

I hate you, river.
I hate this war
I hate this walking

The sound of a distant explosion.

I hate these noises
I hate the silence
I hate you, apples

She picks up an apple and shouts at it.

Stupid apples
I hate you!

No
no, I'm sorry apple
I didn't mean it
I don't
I don't hate you

I just
I don't know what to do

If I eat one
Will I need to eat another
and another

If I don't eat one
Will these apples rot
(if they haven't already)

If these apples rot
Will I still carry them?

If I rot.
Then
River
Will you carry me?

She gets on her knees. Bows a deep, honorific bow.

Please, river.
Help me.
River, please.
Help me.

There's something on the river.

Wait what.

. . .

The thing on the river approaches.

What the
What the heck.
Is that a
No way.

The thing is a boat.

Is that a boat?

The boat docks right beside her.

Bina   HEY THAT'S A BOAT!

Inside the boat, a **Boatperson**.

Boatperson   I know.

Bina   I've been staring at this river for hours and I didn't see a boat. Now I see a boat. Where did you come from?

Boatperson   I came from down the river. And then I came back up the river. On my boat.

Bina Oh.

Boatperson Do you want to go down the river?

Bina YES oh my, very much so, yes. How did you know that?

Boatperson Because everyone wants to go down the river.

Bina They do? I mean, of course they do.

Boatperson Just now I was carrying a family of five with their pig and two chickens down the river. Before that I carried a mother and her infant son down the river. Before that I carried an old man down the river with a very old goat, and this has been my pattern for many, many days. I carry people, and carry people, and carry people.

Bina There's no one in your boat now.

Boatperson They only go in one direction these days.

Bina So you just . . . I don't understand, this can't be real, you have no idea what I've been through—

Boatperson I do though.

Bina —it's like magic that you're here, you just seem so . . . *good*.

Boatperson Oh I don't do it from goodness.

Silence.

Bina What?

Boatperson Everybody wants to go down the river. Everybody *needs* to go down the river. And I have a boat. No one else has a boat. Don't I deserve something in return?

Bina I don't have any money.

Boatperson That's okay, money is worthless these days anyway. What do you have?

Bina I don't have anything.

Boatperson Is there anybody with you who has something to offer?

Bina No, they're . . . we got separated, I was

Boatperson Do you have any food?

Bina I . . . no

Boatperson What's that in your hand?

Bina Oh this?

She realizes she's still holding the apple.

It's an apple.

Silence.

Boatperson   That'll do.

Silence.

She holds the apple behind her back.

Bina   No, I—no, I can't.

Boatperson   Why not?

Bina   I just . . . I can't, I've already lost one, and it's my job to carry them.

Boatperson   Them? You have more than one?

Bina   Yes. No. Maybe.

Boatperson   Where are you supposed to take them?

Bina   To Busan.

Boatperson   Ah. Downriver.

Bina   Yes. So I can't give it to you, I have to keep it, and carry it, it's my job.

Boatperson   I carry things also.

Bina   Right.

Boatperson   That's *my* job.

Bina   I respect that.

Boatperson   I appreciate having a job. Yes? It makes me useful, which in turn gives my life meaning. Even in the face of calamity and warfare. Perhaps *especially* in the face of calamity and warfare. Because we are part of an ecosystem. A community! Those who fight, I hope this is what they are fighting for. The satisfaction and personal value of contributing to this ecosystem, this community. I do my job. You do yours. I have a boat. You have an apple. In fact you have more apples, yes? So in order to do your job, you need a boat. In order to do my job, I need to eat. Else the boat will lay abandoned. Captainless. Adrift. Else society will cease to function. Else your apples lay forever on the wrong side of this unmovable river. Do you understand what I'm saying?

Bina   Yes. No.

Boatperson   It seems to me there is a way we can help each other do our jobs.

Silence.

Bina   You know this river well?

Boatperson   I know everything about this river.

Bina   If I were to . . . walk? Instead of taking a boat. If I needed to keep this apple, or if I had no apple to give, no apple at all, then...

Boatperson Then you would walk forever. You would walk and walk and walk, and you would never walk on the other side of this river.

Silence.

Bina *stares at the apple in her hand.*

Bina Hello, apple.
I'm sorry I said the things I said to you.

Boatperson What are you doing.

Bina Just a moment please, I need to discuss this with the apple.

Boatperson Okay.

She pats the apple, tenderly.

Bina I was upset, but I didn't mean it.
I appreciate you, apple. And I'm grateful to you. For coming with me this far. For doing your job, here, now, so that I can do mine. Our very important jobs.

She might give the apple a little hug.

Thank you, apple.

She holds the apple out to the **Boatperson**.

Boatperson Great.

The **Boatperson** *helps her onto the boat, and then takes a bite of the apple.*

Boatperson Wow. Good apple!

They float away on the boat.

7.

> *Downriver.*
> *The boat is docked.*
> *It's dusk.*

Boatperson   Bina. Wake up.

BINA WAKE UP!

She wakes up.

Bina   WHAT WHO WHAT?

Boatperson   You're here.

Bina   Did I fall asleep?

Boatperson   You did. You talked in your sleep a little too.

Bina   What did I say?

Boatperson   You said a great many things that were so confusing I ceased paying attention. Anyway, you have arrived.

Bina   Arrived where?

Boatperson   As far south as the river will allow.

Bina   But I can see more river.

Boatperson   Yeah the rest of the river leads to the village of Yongsan. But you'd have to be crazy to go there.

Bina   Wait, Yongsan is where? Over there?

Boatperson   Please exit the boat now, I must go to back up the river.

Bina   But where am I?

Boatperson   I only know the river. Maybe you can ask the Merchant.

Bina   Who?

Boatperson   The Merchant.

*The **Boatperson** points to someone sitting on the side of the river with cart. This is the **Merchant**.*

Merchant   Goods for sale.

Bina   Oh!

Boatperson   Farewell, Bina.

Bina   Good job on the boat ride.

Boatperson   Good job on the apple. It was magnificent!

Bina   Best in Korea. Denser, juicier, fuller than your average apple.

*As **Bina** steps off the boat, she checks her bag.*

She still has her remaining apples.

The boat departs.

Bina *and the* **Boatperson** *wave to each other.*

Boatperson   Good luck, Bina!

Bina *approaches the* **Merchant**.

Merchant   Goods for sale.

Bina   Hi.

Merchant   Hello.

Silence.

Bina   Do you know the way to Busan?

Merchant   I can sell you a map.

Silence.

Bina   I'm trying to make my way to Busan. To meet my family.

Merchant   I'm trying to make my way in the world. Through the sale of goods.

Bina   I understand. But all I need is to know the best way to Busan?

Merchant   And all I need is to sell the goods I have on offer, which lucky for you I can sell you a map.

Bina   I don't have any money.

Merchant   Do you have any apples?

Bina   Wait what?

Merchant   I heard the Boatperson say something about apples. There is value in apples.

Bina   Can I just look at the map very quickly without buying it?

Merchant   Can I just eat an apple very quickly without buying it?

Bina   Good point.

Merchant   But I can see you have no apples. For I can see you haven't eaten in days, have you? In that case, I have rice. I have cabbage. I have an egg. And a potato. Make me an offer, I will give you a fair trade.

Bina   I have nothing to trade.

Merchant Ah too bad. It is a very fine potato!

Silence.

Bina Wait—do you stay here all day, by the river?

Merchant I stay for the crossing passengers. I sell goods. It is a prime location for the sale of goods.

Bina You've seen all the people who have crossed?

Merchant If I haven't seen them all, I have seen most.

Bina Have you seen a family?, five people. My family, we got separated, I—

Merchant Don't tell me the story, I've heard plenty of stories already. It's the one thing I do not need more of, for they are all the same.

Bina Have you seen them?

Merchant If they did not trade with me, I would not remember.

Bina Five people. A brother and sister. They fight though they agree, they speak in the same rhythm even though they're as different as north and south. A father, patient and kind. A mother, strong and willful inside but gentle of gesture.

Merchant I can't possibly remember such things, child. The faces I've seen, so many.

Bina A halmoni who carries wisdom so heavy it grumbles.

Merchant I cannot see wisdom. I cannot see patience or kindness, I cannot see gentle gestures. In the faces of those I've seen, all I see is the same thing I see in yours.

Bina What is that?

Merchant Hunger. Sadness. Fatigue.

Bina Oh.

Merchant But in some, I see determination as well, ambition and gumption. In those faces, I can see they have enough of value in their possession to reach their destination.

Bina Can you help me?

Merchant I can sell you a potato. I can sell you a map.

Silence.

Bina *softly cries.*

Merchant Do not insult me with tears! I cannot be swayed by the fragile emotion of a child. Not when my own children are gone, when my own family is gone. There is only one way forward: I can sell you a potato. I can sell you a map. I cannot barter with guilt. I cannot accept cries for payment, and you should not offer me sadness in exchange for the hard-earned value of these goods. I have toiled for them. I have worked for them. They are mine, and if you want them to be yours you must pay me what they have cost me. For there is always a cost, you see? The strangers struggle too. The strangers are desperate too. So I can sell you a potato. I can sell you a map. If you are strong enough to pay for such things, I believe you will reach your destination. But if you are so weak that all you have to offer are tears, then you will not make it any further.

Bina *takes her time. She wipes her eyes.*

Bina   What kind of a map is it?

The **Merchant** *studies her.*

Merchant   Ah! You wish to know the map's value.

Bina   I do. Yes, that.

Merchant   It is a beautiful, detailed map in excellent condition, and it shows all of Korea.

Bina   Will it show me how to get to Busan?

Merchant   Yes it will. Actually hold on.

The **Merchant** *double checks the map to be sure.*

Yes it will. It will show you how to get to Busan.

Bina *thinks.*

Bina   Does it show a village called Yongsan?

Merchant   What do you know of Yongsan?

Bina   I was told this village of Yongsan was on the path to Busan, and I should avoid it.

Merchant   This is good advice.

Bina   You know this village?

Merchant   I used to.

Bina   What do you mean?

Merchant   Yongsan is no more. One cannot sell any goods there, for it is replaced by destruction. It . . . it appears on this map, yes, but it doesn't matter, for it isn't there anymore anyway.

Silence.

Bina   Okay. I'll give you an apple for the map and the potato.

Merchant   For one apple?

Bina   Apples from Moon's Family Farm & Orchard are the best in all of Korea.

Bina *shows her the apple.*

Merchant   Wow. That is a very fine apple.

Bina   Denser, juicier, fuller than your average apple.

The **Merchant** *considers.*

Merchant   For one apple you can choose. The potato. Or the map.

Silence.

Bina   Three is still good. We can each have half an apple.

Merchant   What?

She opens her bag. Takes out an apple.

Bina   I'm sorry, apple. Thank you for everything.
Thank you for your value.
I'll miss you, and I hope you'll be safe and happy here.

To the **Merchant***:*

Map please.

She gives the apple to the **Merchant***.*

The **Merchant** *gives* **Bina** *the map.*

Bina *unfolds it, and studies the map intently.*

She looks around, trying to understand where she is.

She turns the map upside down.

Looks around again, and then turns it right side up again.

She does this a few times.

The **Merchant** *notices her confusion.*

Merchant   I can sell you a compass.

Bina *looks at her.*

Then she looks at the sky.

The stars are faint, but visible.

Bina   No. No need.

As **Bina** *scans the skies, she sees what she's looking for, and she tracks the soup ladle upwards to the North Star. She holds her hand out and points, tracing the journey of the stars upward.*

She turns, just like the Soldier taught her. From north to southeast.

She holds her hand like that for a while. Southeast to Busan.

She aligns the terrain with what she sees on the map.

And begins to walk.

Merchant   Good luck.

8.

> *Later, as dusk gives way to growing darkness.*
>
> **Bina** *walks. Stops. Puts her knapsack on the ground.*
>
> *Looks ahead. At the map. And then ahead again.*

Bina Okay that's a mountain.

She takes her time.

That's another mountain.

She looks behind her.

That's the river.

She looks at the map again, and then ahead again.

And that's Yongsan.

She sits.

Takes out the apples from her knapsack.

Lines them up in a row.

Bina Okay.

Here's the deal, apples.

I know we said we'd take the extra time to avoid Yongsan. That we'd go around it. Right?

But look.

She shows the map to the apples.

I don't see a way around it.

Do you?

She stands up again, looks toward Yongsan.

Maybe it's not so bad. Maybe whatever happened has already happened, and now it's full of happy healthy people, happy that the worst has passed, happy to see someone like me, happy to help me get to where I'm going. Maybe they'll have food, maybe they'll have apples! And their apples won't be as good as Moon's Family Farm & Orchard apples of course but maybe I can get a few more, so I'll have six again, six to carry in my knapsack on my way to Busan, maybe they'll have rice and vegetables too and I'll be belly full and happy on the rest of the road southeast. Maybe. Maybe it's not so bad as they say.

But maybe it is.
Maybe it's worse.

She sits again. Talks to the apples.

Alright, apples.
How about this.

If we have to go through Yongsan after all, we need to be ready. I know you're tired and you're weak and you haven't eaten in days. I know you're lonely and hungry and smelly and terrified too, so if we're going to do this, I'll tell you what. I'm going to hafta eat one of you. Okay?

But I'll make you a deal. If any of you has a better idea, I will consider it.

So.

What do you say?

The apples do not respond.

Okay then.

She considers which apple to pick. She takes one and places the rest in her knapsack, stands up.

Please apple, give me all the strength and energy you can, and I promise I will do my best to be worthy of what I'm about to do.

She takes a bite.

It's so amazing.

Oh wow . . .
Wowee zowee.

Mmmmmmm.

She takes another bite.

That's right, apple.

Oh yeah.

I can do this.

She eats as she walks towards the village of Yongsan.

9.

The streets of **Yongsan**.

This is awful.

Hollowed out buildings, broken wood and strewn straw from what once were huts. A gray dust. Random patches of smoke and fire.

Bina *walks on.*

It gets worse.

As she walks, she sees a dead animal, like a raccoon or a possum. She looks away and keeps walking.

A smear of blood on a wall. A blackened fence charred from some sort of explosion.

Something in the distance, maybe a human body.

She looks away, walks quickly, but stops and steals a glance back at it before moving on again.

Worse now.

Everywhere.

Now, a gray dust covers everything.

Dust from rocks, dust from gunpowder, dust from burning.

We see less and less as the air grows dustier.

Bina *coughs and covers her face, but walks on.*

Until she sees a **Boy**.

He's sitting on a step that once led to a hut. The hut is gone.

He is covered in this dust. He is dirty, hair unkempt, eyes blank.

He is about six years old.

Bina Hello?

He stares, blankly.

Boy There's nothing left.

Bina What?

Boy She's coming back.

Bina Who's coming back?

Boy My mother. She's coming back. She told me to wait here.

Bina Where did she go?

Boy I'm not supposed to tell.

Bina How long have you been waiting?

Boy I don't know.

Bina Are you all alone?

He looks away.

Bina You can't stay here.

Boy I don't have anything left, please go away.

Bina I can't just—you can't just stay like this.

Boy You can take anything you want but there's nothing to take. There's no food, I've looked. There's no water, I've looked. Whatever you find, just take it and leave.

Bina I'm not here to take anything.

Boy Then why are you here?

Bina I have to go to Busan. I have to pass through.

Silence.

It's not safe here.

Boy She's coming back.

Bina What happened here?

Boy Everyone left. The men and the boys they went to the war. They took things. Most things. For the war. They needed the things. Then other men and other boys came. Different men, different boys. I couldn't understand the things they said, they used different words, but they took things too. For the war, they said. They needed more things. And there was a fight. They had guns. We said they couldn't have the things because they were the only things we had left and so they fought and then they took the things anyway.

And they took people too. They took my mother. She didn't want to go with them but they took her and she said I should wait here. Everyone else left.

I am waiting for my mother.

Sometimes people come. People like you. They say they are going to Busan. They look for things to take. Some try to take me. But they can't take me.

I am waiting for my mother.

Silence.

Bina What's your name?

Boy My name is Hyunsoo.

Bina *takes an apple out of her bag and holds it out to him.*

Bina I want you to have this apple, Hyunsoo.

Boy I don't have any money.

Bina I don't want any money.

Boy I have nothing to trade.

Bina Not to trade. I'm giving it to you.

He doesn't take it.

But she gently places it into his hands.

This is a very special apple, Hyunsoo. It comes from the greatest apple orchard in all of Korea, and I have carried it a long way across mountains and rivers and kept it safe. I want you to eat this apple and stay strong and wait for your mother.

He takes the apple. It's the most beautiful thing he's ever seen.

Silence.

Here is a map.

She takes out the map, opens it and shows him.

With this you can see where you are. Here. If you go this way, you will find a river. When you are thirsty you can drink. It isn't far. You can go there quickly, drink water, come back and wait. If your mother comes while you are gone, she will wait for you.

I'm sorry I can't stay to wait with you. I have to find my family.

When you learn the way to the river and back, you can sell the map. There is a merchant who stays by the river and sells rice. She trades with the people who pass. Sell her the map. She knows its value.

She thinks for a moment.

She takes the final apple out of her bag.

She puts the apple in her pocket.

She gives the **Boy** *her bag.*

Take this bag. You can use it to carry these things, or if you don't need it you can sell it as well.

He takes the bag, but says nothing.

I have to go to Busan, to find my family, but when I do and when this war is over I will come back this way, to check on you. I will come back, on my way home.

She wants to give him something more but she has nothing more to give.

He wants to say something to thank her but he doesn't know how.

She walks away.

He sits and looks at the apple.

Lights.

10.

Sunset.

Bina *walks. The village of Yongsan is in the distance behind her.*

She has nothing but the apple in her pocket.

She walks and walks but suddenly stops.

Bina I have one left.
One apple.
I'm so close.
To what?
What if you're not in Busan
What if you went north, to try to find me
What if you went back home, to wait for me
What if I show up in Busan
with only an apple
and you're not even there?

She collapses onto the ground.

What if you are there?
What if I arrive in Busan,
and there you are?
All of you, healthy and safe,
worried sick about me?
You knew I would make it,
you knew I would find my way to Busan
because you know I am strong,
you knew I could do it even on my own.
And so I arrive.
And there you are, washed, clean,
you've eaten all the rice you took,
you've eaten all the vegetables,
drunk all the water,
you have nothing left,
and when you see me
we hold each other and we cry.
We cry the other kind of tears
the kind that come from happiness
and I show you the apple
and I say I saved it
I carried it all this way
the other five are gone
Stolen
Bartered

Traded
Eaten
Given
But this one made it
This one perfect apple
I wanted to bring six
one for each of us
but this is better

it is better that there is only one
because this way
we can share.

We are together and we can share.

And Father will take his knife
and he will cut the apple into six perfect pieces
and we'll eat it together
and smile
and enjoy

And then we can sleep.

She curls up in a fetal position, clutching the apple.

We can sleep for a long time
Until the war is over
And then,
We'll make our way home again.

She falls asleep.

The sun sets.

Darkness over everything.

Nothing but the sounds of the countryside.

Until the sun rises. Slowly.

We hear singing.

When the sun rises, first we see:

It's **Hamee**. **Bina***'s head is in her lap.*

Hamee *gently strokes Bina's hair as she sings.*

Bina *wakes.*

Bina   Hamee?

Hamee   Yes my child, oh yes my child.

Bina   It's you! It's you!

Hamee   Yes Bina, yes my child.

Bina   It's you is this where am I what

Hamee   Shhhh shhhh

Bina   Is this real?

Hamee   Shhhh the others are sleeping

Bina   Are you real are you really here?

Hamee   I'm really here my child, I'm really here and so are you. We walked. We passed the village of Yongsan, we came to this clearing and found you sleeping, we almost walked right by, it was so dark we almost didn't see you but I saw you, I saw you.

Bina   Where is everyone else?

Hamee   We're all here. All of us.

And now we can see the others are there too, surrounding them, asleep at first.

They wake. **Father**, **Mother**, **Jinsoo** *and* **Youngsoo**, *and they all rush to her, and hold each other.*

Bina   How are you here?

Mother   We looked and looked, we looked a long time

Father   But the army came

Youngsoo   It wasn't safe to stay there, wasn't safe to keep looking

Jinsoo   And we knew you would keep on going

Hamee   We knew you would keep on going to Busan.

Father   Everywhere we went, we asked about you

Jinsoo   We knew you were close

Mother   We knew you were still walking

Youngsoo   The boatperson told us you had been there just one day before us

Jinsoo   And the merchant on the other side remembered you

Mother   She said she didn't remember faces,

Youngsoo   Could not even remember a child

Father   But she remembered the apple.

Silence.

Hamee   And the little boy in Yongsan

Mother   He remembered the apple too.

Jinsoo   And his mother, who arrived at the village the very same time we did

Youngsoo   We took the same boat!

Father   She heard him talk of the apple you gave him

Hamee   And we were so proud of how good a thing you did.

Bina   I have only one left.

Bina *removes the apple from her pocket.*

She holds it out with both hands.

Stunned silence.

They all touch the apple.

They hold it together, everyone's hands, hers at the bottom.

Jinsoo   We saved nothing.

Youngsoo   You saved the apple, but we couldn't save anything

Father   The rice, stolen

Mother   The vegetables, rotten

Jinsoo   The water we drank, and the jugs were broken

Hamee   But we are together

Father   We are safe now

Mother   And we have an apple.

They stare at the apple.

Bina   Father, do you still have your knife?

Father   No knife. Nothing.

Hands still on the apple.

Bina   Then we will bite. One at a time.

Mother   Yes.

Bina   Hamee first.

They push the apple back and forth towards each other, but no one takes it.

Hamee   No Bina, you carried it, you eat first.

Bina   I carried it for you, you eat first.

Jinsoo   I'll eat first.

Youngsoo   No Jinsoo!

Jinsoo   Shut up Youngsoo!

Father   We'll eat together.

They all smile.

Hamee   But not yet. Let's just look at it a little longer first.

Mother   Yes.

Hamee   And appreciate that it is here.

Father   Yes.

They look at it a moment.

Bina   It's such a beautiful apple.

They smile as they look at the apple.

The sun rises to fullest height.

End of play.

Postscript

Revisiting the Korean War through a Young Korean Girl with Hope

Jiyoun Chang

When I was growing up in South Korea from the 1970s through the mid 1990s, 6.25 was only ever discussed politically, and we rarely learned in depth about what really happened. '6.25' (Six Two Five) signifies the start of the Korean War on June 25, 1950. Every 6.25 anniversary during my childhood, we had a speech contest to express our patriotism for South Korea and our hatred against North Korea, and an art contest to pick the best poster image depicting this. Oftentimes, North Koreans were illustrated as wolves in those posters. One of the most popular songs about 6.25 defines North Korea as the enemy who torn our country apart. The song assured us not to forget the war and our enemy. This was how we were taught to see the war.

In 1983, *Finding Dispersed Families* was aired by KBS, and it created many long days of looking for families separated by the war. Pictures of families and relatives were pasted on hundreds of temporary walls in the biggest public park in Seoul. The special broadcast aired live for four and half months, but the effort to find separated family members continued afterwards. The live program motivated political officials to help the families to meet with families living in North Korea. I believe this event helped us as a nation to rethink the war and see North Koreans altogether in a different angle.

Our family moved from North Korea to South Korea during the war. My grandmother was separated from her husband and took the responsibility to bring the rest of the family down to the South safely, including her in-laws' families. She rarely talked about it, so I learned little of her experience then, but I believe she was the center of the family with the strength to survive the following years to come with her two little children. She didn't get to find her husband through the TV program although a little hope sparked in her eyes for a short while.

In *Bina's Six Apples*, there is no definite enemy, there is no never-changing good people or bad people. There are only people trying to survive the war, trying to keep their family together, and trying to keep a family's legacy safe and last, generation after generation. Most of all, what is special and unique about this play is that it tells a story of hope through a 10-year-old girl. She is the one who proves that our family bond is strong and sacred, that our children will continue that beautiful culture no matter how challenging this world might be. I had never understood 6.25 in this way, and I felt an urge to tell the story to as many people in Korea as I could.

In 2022, I was invited to be a part of the creative team of the play as a scenic and lighting designer at Children's Theatre Company, which was a co-production between CTC and Alliance Theatre Company. As a Korean Immigrant with an American Family, with a young babygirl about Bina's age, I immediately connected with Bina. I admired her courage and determination. My initial approach was very personal for many reasons. I tried to comb through my personal feelings about 6.25 as a Korean all very carefully to make sure that it's inviting no matter what cultural background you have. I believe anyone who went through some manner of war could relate to the play and the creative team under the leadership of the director, Eric Ting, made a collective effort to make the production inclusive and inviting to those families with similar histories.

Lloyd Suh wanted to make sure *Bina* was a three-generational play, not just a children's play, and Eric Ting honored that throughout the whole process. The visual images were family friendly, but very minimal overall and very neutral with just a hint of the Korean Landscape, which was inevitable but not overpowering. Three walls were textured like old Korean paper. The walls were white, which is Korea's favorite color, which we see a lot in common people's clothing in the old times. Empty space in old Korean paintings was considered beauty that we valued and Bina's world reflected that aesthetic, with simple lines and empty space, minimal essential props, and colors you would find in flowers like 진달래꽃 or azaleas, and apples. While the props and costumes followed the timeline and culture during the war, the simplistic wall created a timeless universal world.

Our director, Eric Ting, focused on the storytelling through Bina's eyes and understanding war through a child's scale, which escalated throughout her journey. Eric wanted to make sure her physical environment conveyed that feeling so we began the play in a small space, then it expanded slowly. The world started like a two-dimensional painting: the wall was set flat meeting the proscenium portal in the preset, and that foreground wall moved further away from the spectators as Bina was separated from her family and started her journey by herself to Busan, the biggest southern harbor at that time of the war. As the wall moved, her world got bigger while she got smaller physically in the space. As night fell and stars sparkled in the sky, she became even smaller. Her physical world was a mirror to how fast she had to grow, but also how strongly she was, with her six apples from her family apple orchard. She didn't have family with her to keep her safe, but she did have her family's legacy, and that was enough to keep her going. At the end of the show, we found her alone in a big room, and when she woke up from a long sleep, she was united with her family. Bina ended up with one apple after using the rest so very carefully. As a family, they shared the last apple together after gazing at it for a long while.

The lighting design of the play was also quite minimalist. There were moments in the play where we needed to see time passing, but mostly the lighting was more abstract, an emotional reflection of the world: painfully sunny if not gloomy and feeling lost in danger. My abstract approach in lighting supported the stylized movements that slipped into the naturalistic exchanges between characters. While some characters were bigger than life, they always stayed real. The overall design of the production created the same idea.

Lloyd Suh's plays often start somewhere real, a piece of history. For me, what is amazing about his intention with history is that we are learning about real events and real peoples. When I worked on *The Chinese Lady* at Long Wharf Theatre in 2021, an audience member asked during a talk back, "Why did you write the play?" I will never forget Lloyd's answer. He said very simply, "I wanted to make sure people remember her." Whenever I work on his plays, I think about this answer. There is an extreme compassion in his attempt to make the historic into a play, and I find that it is not easy to complete this mission without tears and heartache because so much resonates with me. As much as it was a hard process, I became more empathetic and compassionate, and most of all, I was so proud of the young girl, the Bina that my grandmother might have been like. The Bina that my baby girl will be.

Charles Francis Chan Jr.'s Exotic Oriental Murder Mystery

Preface

Origin Stories

Christine Mok

Monkey ... You will forego the pacifist hippie mentality and start your own community! You will light a fuse that will set off a new political and artistic movement that will change the course of history!

Frank An oriental movement?

Monkey Not oriental, you reject that word!

Frank I reject that word!

Monkey You have your own word!

Frank Asian American!

Monkey Asian A– really? You think that's gonna catch on?

Frank ASIAN AMERICAN!

Monkey Okay! Let's go with that! (223)

In 1968, Emma Gee and Yuji Ichioka, two graduate students at University of California, Berkeley, coined the term "Asian American" when they created the political organization Asian American Political Association (AAPA) to unite civil rights and antiwar activists of Asian descent. To build their coalition, the couple called everyone with an Asian surname on the roster of the Peace and Freedom Party (PFP) and invited them to their apartment.[1] One evening in May, Floyd Huen, Richard Aoki, Victor Ichioka, and Vicci Wong joined Gee and Ichioka at 2005 Hearst Avenue. This meeting marked a vital moment in the Asian American movement, an origin story.

In *Charles Francis Chan Jr.'s Exotic Oriental Murder Mystery,* Lloyd Suh imagines an earlier origin story for Asian America. It is 1967, still the Bay Area, and Charles Francis Chan Jr. (Frank) has flunked out of UC Berkeley, "as an act of protest against the ethnocentric content of the campus curriculum" (214), two years before the start of the Third World Liberation strike. He now faces a military draft that would send him overseas to fight in the Vietnam War. His girlfriend Suzy has dumped him to film a Hollywood movie, *Charlie Chan and the Insidious Vietcong,* in the Philippines. In frustration, he hurls a book (perhaps *Journey to the West* or another text from the Chinese heroic tradition) from his nightstand and Monkey appears. What is an angry young man to do but take Monkey to a Chinatown bar and coin the term "Asian American"?

Lloyd Suh's *Charles Francis Chan Jr.'s Exotic Oriental Murder Mystery* is a metatheatrical genre mashup that charts the triumphs and trials of Asian American invention in the face (and yellowface) of racist representation. The play was Suh's first foray into exploring Asian American history. Originally commissioned and produced by the National Asian American Theater Company (NAATCO) by Mia Katigbak, co-founder and actor-manager, it started as an adaptation of Agatha Christie's *The Mysterious Affair at Styles,* which introduced the detective, Hercule Poirot. In November 2015, *Charles Frances Chan Jr.'s* premiered at Walkerspace. Notable productions include Theater Mu's production, directed by Randy Reyes, at The Playwrights Center (2016) and at the Guthrie Theater (2017), and the 2022 virtual reading directed by Ralph B. Peña in the second season of Paula Vogel's Bard at the Gate, in partnership with the McCarter Theatre Center.

The play, at its heart, explores inheritance, what has been and what might be passed between generations. It is both an homage and exorcism of real and fake figures from writer and provocateur Frank Chin, activist and performance artist Kathy Change, Earl Derr Biggers' fictional detective Charlie Chan, to Warner Oland/Sidney Toller/Roland Winters and countless others who played Charlie Chan[2] in the movies. The play looks back at the late 1960s to contest the durability of racist representations like Charlie Chan, first introduced to readers in 1925, and to remember both the revolutionary and retrograde impulses that have shaped the Asian American movement. Suh stages a battle between the ideologies instantiated in stereotypes and racist performance practices, and the hero and villain origin stories of Asian American theatre, in the era of political possibility that birthed the Asian American movement, alongside the feminist movements and civil rights movements. The play works its way through several genres, announced in the title, from the play-within-a-play to the detective story to the murder mystery, while also showing how deadly and deathly the "exotic" and "oriental" are as generic traps. These ugly racist representations, too, are part of our inheritance as Asian Americans.

Charlie Chan is Dead

With the 1993 publication of *Charlie Chan is Dead: An Anthology of Contemporary Asian American Fiction*, playwright, novelist, and editor Jessica Hagedorn, announced the demise of the infamous "Oriental detective." In her preface to the volume, Elaine Kim offers the following eulogy: "Charlie Chan is indeed dead, never to be revived. Gone for good his yellowface asexual bulk, his fortune-cookie English, his stereotypically Orientalist version of 'the [Confucian] Chinese family.'"[3] Yet, his spectre haunts Asian American representation.

Charlie Chan was a highly popular fictional Chinese American detective, featured in six mystery novels and a long-running film series played by white actors in yellowface, a racist performance practice of racial masquerade. Though culturally "dead," Charlie Chan as a figuration of accommodation persists as the pop cultural flipside to Fu Manchu's yellow peril. Chinaman-incarnate, Chan was a rotund figure of the model minority, an immigrant who dropped aphorisms in his broken English, was emasculated yet with a preponderance of sons and daughters, and filial to the law.

After learning about the real Honolulu Police Department detective Chang Apana (1871–1933), writer Earl Derr Biggers (1884–1933) created a fictional detective who appeared in his novel *The House Without a Key* (1925), a murder mystery set in Waikiki, Hawai'i. Charlie Chan is introduced like this: "He was very fat indeed, yet he walked with the dainty step of a woman. His cheeks were as chubby as a baby's, his skin ivory tinted, his black hair close-cropped, his amber eyes slanting."[4] Initially conceived as a minor character, Charlie Chan's chubby cheeks, slanting eyes, and mincing step captured the imagination of readers. After *The House Without a Key,* Chan appeared as the protagonist of five other popular novels,[5] each serialized in the *Saturday Evening Post* prior to full-length publication.

Chan always began as a type. Biggers created Chan as a "good" stereotype to Fu Manchu's "bad" stereotype, offering readers a Chinese American protagonist who solved crimes for his white superiors rather than plotted global domination. With Chan on one side and Fu Manchu on the other, Frank Chin and Jeffrey Paul Chan, in their 1972 essay "Racist Love," offer a reading of Charlie Chan as the model minority as an object of "racist love," because "each racial stereotype comes in two models, the acceptable model and the unacceptable model."[6] These models, acceptable and unacceptable, are co-constitutive binaries of "racist hate" and "racist love."

As popular as he was in fiction, Chan became a pop culture icon through film. 47 Charlie Chan movies were released between 1925 and 1949. In most of those films, Chan was played by a white actor in yellowface. Beginning with 1931's *Charlie Chan Carries On,* Swedish actor Warner Oland (1879-1938) played the detective in 16 films. After Oland's death in 1938, the mantle of Chan passed to another white actor, Sidney Toler (1874-1947) for 11 more films. With the outbreak of World War II, Chan moved from Hollywood to Poverty Row with Toler purchasing the rights to the character from Eleanor Ladd, Biggers's widow, and bringing it to budget studio Monogram, where he starred in 11 more Chan movies before his death in 1947 (Roland Winters, still white, replaced him in 6 more films, up until 1949).

Chan's legacy as yellowface performance cemented his place as a racist icon. Yellowface is the popular entertainment form and performance practice in which actors applied makeup (like the burnt cork of blackface minstrelsy) to darken or make their skin shiny, prosthetics and tape were used to make their eyes look slanted to create "yellowface" masks.[7] In addition to makeup and prosthetics, costume, setting, gesture, and voice reinforced the foreignness necessary to the fantasy of the "Oriental."

Chan's yellowface built on the long tradition[8] of nineteenth and twentieth century yellowface performance and Oriental stereotypes in plays and vaudeville, which featured the "Chinaman" character type. As Harvey Young notes, the "Chinaman" and his yellowface portrayal "appeared with increasing frequency in performances about the American "West" in recognition of the significant Asian, specifically Chinese, immigrant population whose presence made westward expansion possible."[9] Yellowface performance thus indexes both appearance and disappearance. The "Chinaman" first enters the vaudeville stage alongside Chinese migration to the United States when laborers built the transcontinental railroad and sought their fortune in the gold rush.

Yellowface performance then dominates during their disappearance enacted by the Chinese Exclusion Act of 1882, passed with bipartisan support and on the heels of anti-Chinese violence, ushering in an era of exclusion and restrictive immigration policies. As a result of these laws, as James Moy notes, "the notion of Chineseness under the sign of exotic became familiar to the American spectator long before sightings of the actual Chinese."[10] Biggers' character comes to prominence from 1925 to 1949 during a period of exclusion and discriminatory national-origins quotas, introduced in 1921 and only changed in 1965.

Chan in yellowface is America's racist habit. Readers and audiences are habituated to the convention, which overwrote any modicum of representational intervention Biggers may have thought he was giving the world through Chan. Indeed, Chan is the binary to Fu Manchu, suturing the emasculated, yet paternalistic, immigrant model minority to Fu Manchu's queer third world yellow peril. The fungibility of yellow peril is even contained within Chan's family unit. In the films, Chan's eleven children are simultaneously referred to not by name but by number ("Number One Son") while being performed by Asian American actors, not in yellowface.

Rather than sparking dissonance, the erasure of Asian American names and overwriting of Asian American bodies further entrenches Chan's yellowface performance. This reentrenchment of yellowface through the (dis)appearance of actual Asian bodies speaks to its durability through its iterability. Racist repetition transmutes the subjects of racial representation. To unpick the iterative of racial subjects and objects, Josephine Lee turns to Eddie Glaude, Pierre Bourdieu, and Helen Ngo to examine the "persistent reincarnation of racial stereotypes" and "repetitive and ingrained nature of racial habits"[11]: "Stereotypes exist not only as the strange relics of a racist past but as a set of constantly reanimated enactments. Nineteenth and early twentieth-century American theater served as both the point of origination for many of these character types and as one of the most important cultural practices that helped ingrain racial fantasy into conventional perspective."[12] Biggers creates Chan as an Orientalist character type, with his chubby cheeks, slanting eyes, mincing steps, which the filmic Chan in yellowface further ingrains into "racial habit": one that feels like a forced routine and a burdensome inheritance for Asian Americans, who are relegated to being nameless, numbered descendants.

The Asian American Movement

When Gee in *The Far Country* reminds Yuen that "[n]ames, names, names are important" (122), he offers a pronouncement that is plural and shared. Like Gee (perhaps a spiritual descendant) and Ichioka, Frank in *Charles Frances Chan Jr.'s* embraces the name "Asian American" not as an individual identity, but as a collective recognition. Ju Yon Kim underscores this same scene at the bar as "a moment of critical insight" when Frank "does not call *himself* Asian American, but names the movement that he hopes will be a medium of social transformation."[13] Asian American, as conceived by Gee, Ichioka, and Frank, marks a direct line to social and political change that was deeply influenced by and connected the Black Power Movement, the Vietnam War and antiwar movement, with anti-imperialism, decolonization, and revolutions throughout the Third World.

The Asian American Movement encompassed a range of radical sociopolitical activities sparked by Asian American students, in the late 1960s and early 1970s, who sought to gain political power for their ethnic communities. Building on past social activism and work in Asian American communities and ongoing efforts to increase political enfranchisement, the movement emphasized coalitional politics across national and ethnic backgrounds and borders, political activism (grassroots and electoral), the establishment of ethnic studies programs and reforming curriculum, and combatting racism, poverty, and police brutality in their communities. The movement combined a focus on the local community conditions to better social services with global anti-imperialism, forging a pan-Asian identity in solidarity with Black, Latinx, and Indigenous Americans, at home and abroad.

Like many ethnic movements, the Asian American movement also called for aesthetic and cultural revolution, with particular attention to Asian American history and heritage. Or, as Daryl Joji Maeda notes, "to make visible the long history of Asian Americans, expose the struggles they faced in a racist and exploitive nation, celebrate the communities and cultures they built, and envision a more just and equitable society."[14] Indeed, the debate between writers Maxine Hong Kingston and Frank Chin, which lasted from the 1970s to the 1990s and straddled the fault lines of "real" and "fake," "un-Chinese" and "authentic," demonstrated the political stakes of representation to these histories.[15]

It is in this heady moment that Lloyd Suh dramatizes the spirited exchange in a San Francisco Chinatown bar between his fictional Frank Chan and Monkey. In doing so, Suh imagines and stages a prior moment of inception for Asian American as a political identity. Suh offers a speculative dramatic precursor that captures the spirit of the moment and the movement. Asian American, as Karen Ishizuka notes, is "more than a descriptor, the term subverted the Orientalist tradition of lumping all Asians together —this time as an oppositional political identity imbued with self-definition and empowerment, signaling a new way of thinking."[16]

For Frank, with a new name in hand, this "new way of thinking" requires a new tradition, a new civilization, and a new language: "I will build a vibrant and progressive community of Asian Americans to populate a new and empowered cultural tradition that takes our protest and our culture and our voices to the people!" (224). It is telling that protest, culture, and voice are given equal weight. For when Monkey asks Frank exactly how he will do all this, Frank exclaims, "I'm gonna I'm gonna I'm gonna I'm gonna write a play!" (224). In his moment of self-definition and empowerment, Frank declares that he will write a play titled *Charles Frances Chan Jr.'s Exotic Oriental Murder Mystery! And Sing-Song Minstrel Show.* Frank's play becomes the play-in-progress within *Charles Frances Chan Jr.'s.*

Suh doubles the origin stories of "Asian American" and the Asian American movement with an origin story about Asian American theatre. By making Frank's understanding of Asian American both a politics and an aesthetic, the play directly connects Asian American theatre with the Asian American movement. Suh forges that connection through two fabulized historical figures, Frank Chin (b. 1940) and Kathy Chang/Kathy Change (1950-1996), each were and are controversial figures. In the play, Kathy Chang/Change becomes Kathy Ching; Frank Chin becomes Frank Chan – by way of Charlie Chan. Because Charlie Chan is Asian America's coerced inheritance, Suh turns to the history of Asian American theatre and performance art to offer up alternative legacies in Chin and Change.

Frank Chin's Sons & Kathy Change's Daughters

Frank Chan's shout of "ASIAN AMERICAN!" disrupts the open-mic night at the bar causing Kathy Ching to stop singing mid-song, smash something, and stalk her way to the bar. Monkey stage-manages Frank, transforming his disruption and her outburst into a meet cute. When Frank is pushed by Monkey into a conversation with Kathy, he calls himself an Asian American playwright. For Kathy, "[t]hat's not a thing," to which Frank acknowledges, "Not yet it isn't. But it will be" (226). In this exchange, the play stages a prophecy, one that follows each of these characters. The first is of the Asian American playwright, pitting the exorcising of Charlie Chan in the crucible of the play-within-a-play with the invention of Asian American. The second prophecy is a life unknown for Kathy Ching, a future unwritten and spooling out when she exits the play.

Frank Chin (b. 1940) is a complicated figure in Asian American letters. With Jeffery Paul Chan, Lawson Fusao Inada, and Shawn Wong, he co-edited *Aiiieeeee! An Anthology of Asian American Writers*[17], an anthology of Asian American literature, published in 1974. As a critic, Chin is known for his literary feud with Maxine Hong Kingston, along with several incisive and polemical essays and manifestos, including his piece with Jeffrey Paul Chan on "racist love" and "racist hate." As a pioneering playwright, Chin is a father of Asian American theatre. *The Chickencoop Chinaman* was the first Asian American play to have a major New York production. Chin wrote the play to submit to the East West Players' Asian American playwriting contest, winning the contest in 1971. In 1973, he founded the Asian American Theater Workshop (later renamed the Asian American Theater Company) in San Francisco.

While Chin, the self-proclaimed "Chinatown cowboy," has an outsize presence in Asian American studies, Kathy Change (1950-1996) is the lesser known. For a period of five years from 1971 to 1976, Kathy Change was married to Frank Chin.[18] A performance artist, political activist, and writer, Change (formerly Kathleen Chang) frequently occupied the University of Pennsylvania campus, and put on performances, as Vivian Huang notes, "to critique the US government's neoliberal collusion with corporate interests and advocate for world transformation."[19] Change chose the Ivy League institution as a site to disrupt and induce the next generation to act.[20] On October 22, 1996, for her final act of protest, by the Peace Symbol sculpture, Kathy Change doused herself with gasoline and set herself on fire, all while dancing. She was 46.

Suh plays with the origin stories of Asian American theatre and the Asian American movement. There is a witty playfulness to Suh's treatment of historical figures, fake and real, from Earl Derr Biggers, Charlie Chan, and Frank Chin (who is a slob). Yet, a different register of play is at hand with his resurrection of Kathy Change. Change's profoundly political death refigures how she is remembered. Rather than write her character as one of inevitable death, Suh imagines a counterfactual history for Kathy, who we meet as a young woman with solid political convictions and less solid taste in men. A pregnant Kathy Ching leaves Frank to provide a different future for herself and her unborn daughter. She walks out on Frank and walks out of the play. As much as the play overtly structures inheritance between fathers and sons, Suh offers for spectators another alternative: a genealogy for Kathy and her daughter. *Charles Frances Chan Jr.'s Exotic Oriental Murder Mystery* is both a history play and a myth. As myth, *Chan* offers an elucidation of Asian American experience not as an identity but as a political and artistic movement. It is an origin story of the Asian American movement as the origin story of Asian American politics, theatre, and performance. It offers an alternative history to combat "racist love" with other acts of love, even speculative ones.

Notes

1. In an interview, Ichioka recalls: "We figured that if we rallied behind our own banner, behind an Asian American banner, we would have an effect on the larger public. We could extend the influence beyond ourselves to other Asian Americans." Yen Le Espiritu, *Asian American Panethnicity: Bridging Institutions and Identities* (Philadelphia: Temple University Press, 1992), 34.
2. Peter Ustinov (1921-2004) played both Charlie Chan and Hercule Poirot in film.
3. Jessica Hagedorn, *Charlie Chan is Dead: An Anthology of Contemporary Asian American Fiction* (Penguin, 1993), xiii.
4. Earl Biggers, *House Without a Key* (Bobbs-Merrill, 1925): 76.
5. *The Chinese Parrot* (1926), *Behind That Curtain* (1928), *The Black Camel* (1929), *Charlie Chan Carries On* (1930), and *The Keeper of the Keys* (1932).
6. Frank Chin and Jeffrey Paul Chan, "Racist Love," in *Seeing Through Shuck*, edited by Richard Kostelanetz (Ballantine, 1972): 65.
7. For more on yellowface performance, see Sean Metzger's article "Charles Parsloe's Chinese Fetish: An Example of Yellowface Performance in Nineteenth-Century American Melodrama," *Theatre Journal* 56.4 (December 2004): 627-651, and his chapter on "The Queue" in his monograph *Chinese Looks: Fashion Performance Race* (Indiana, 2014) and Esther Kim Lee's monograph *Made-Up Asians: Yellowface During the Exclusion Era* (Michigan, 2022).
8. For more see Krystyn Moon, *Yellowface: Creating the Chinese in American Popular Music and Performance, 1850s-1920s* (Rutgers, 2005); Jack Tchen, *New York Before Chinatown: Orientalism and the Shaping of American Culture, 1776-1882* (Johns Hopkins, 2001); Esther Kim Lee, *Made-Up Asians: Yellowface During the Exclusion Era* (Michigan, 2022).
9. Harvey Young, *Theatre & Race* (Bloomsbury, 2013), 52.
10. James Moy, *Marginal Sights: Staging the Chinese in America* (Michigan, 2008), 9.
11. Josephine Lee, *Oriental, Black, and White: The Formation of Racial Habits in American Theater* (University of North Carolina, 2022), 9.
12. Josephine Lee, *Oriental, Black, and White: The Formation of Racial Habits in American Theater* (University of North Carolina, 2022), 9.
13. Kim, Ju Yon, "Korean American Theater and Performing Arts: Networks of Practice and Bodies of Work." in *A Companion to Korean American Studies*, edited by Rachael Miyung Joo, and Shelley Sang-Hee Lee. (Brill, 2018), 151.
14. Daryl Joji Maeda, "Documenting the Third World Student Strike, the Antiwar Movement, and the Emergence of Second-Wave Feminism from Asian American Perspectives" in *The Cambridge History of Asian American Literature* (Cambridge, 2015), 219.
15. Julia Lee eloquently frames their dispute as an ideological battle over "antiracist Asian American identity." Chin, the cultural nationalist, "insist[ed] upon an authentic Chinese American sensibility derived from the Chinese heroic tradition," pitting himself against "Kingston's deconstructive approach that privileges the ambiguity and complexity." Julia H. Lee, "The Railroad as Message in Maxine Hong Kingston's *China Men* and Frank Chin's "Riding the Rails with Chickencoop Slim."" *Journal of Asian American Studies* 18.3 (October 2015), 265-287. For more, see King-Kok Cheung's essay "The Woman Warrior versus The Chinaman Pacific: Must a Chinese American Critic Choose between Feminism and Heroism?" *Conflicts in Feminism*. Ed. Marianne Hirsch and Evelyn Fox Keller (Routledge, 1990), 234-251. For a literary and graphic treatment, see Karen Tei Yamashita's *I Hotel* (Coffee House Press, 2014), Box 4, "1971: Aiiieeeee! Hotel," chapter 4, "War & Peace."

16 Karen L. Ishizuka, *Serve the People: Making Asian America in the Long Sixties* (Verso, 2016), 62.
17 *The Big Aiiieeeee: An Anthology of Asian American Writers*, a follow-up, was published in 1991.
18 In the 1978 production of Chin's *The Year of the Dragon* at Asian American Theater Workshop, Change played Sissy to Frank Chin's Fred Eng.
19 Vivian Huang, ""What Shall We Do?" Kathy Change, Soomi Kim, and Asian Feminist Performance on Campus," *TDR* 62. 3 (Fall 2018): 170.
20 Her performances and protests, which warned of the consequences of human-wrought ecological disaster, the violence of US militarism, and white supremacy, could be construed as extreme, yet, as Joseph Shahadi notes, "in retrospect many of her hyperbolic pronouncements proved to be alarmingly prescient." Joseph Shahadi. "Burn: The Radical Disappearance of Kathy Change." *TDR* 55.2 (Summer 2011): 52–72.

References

Biggers, Earl. *House Without a Key*. Indianapolis: Bobbs-Merrill, 1925
Chan, Jeffrey Paul, Frank Chin, Lawson Fusao Inada, Shawn Wong, eds. *The Big Aiiieeeee: An Anthology of Asian American Writers*. New York: New American Library-Meridian, 1991.
Cheung, King-Kok. "The Woman Warrior versus The Chinaman Pacific: Must a Chinese American Critic Choose between Feminism and Heroism?" In *Conflicts in Feminism*, edited by Marianne Hirsch and Evelyn Fox Keller, 234-251. NY: Routledge, 1990.
Chin, Frank. *The Chickencoop Chinaman; And, The Year of the Dragon: Two Plays*. Seattle: University of Washington, 1981.
Chin, Frank and Jeffrey Paul Chan. "Racist Love." In *Seeing Through Shuck*, edited by Richard Kostelanetz, 65–79. NY: Ballantine, 1972.
Chin, Frank. Jeffrey Paul Chan, Lawson Fusao Inada, Shawn Wong, eds. *Aiiieeeee: An Anthology of Asian American Writers*. Seattle: University of Washington Press, 1974.
Espiritu, Yen Le. *Asian American Panethnicity: Bridging Institutions and Identities*. Philadelphia: Temple University Press, 1992.
Hagedorn, Jessica. *Charlie Chan is Dead: An Anthology of Contemporary Asian American Fiction*. NY: Penguin, 1993.
Huang, Vivian. " 'What Shall We Do?' Kathy Change, Soomi Kim, and Asian Feminist Performance on Campus," *TDR* 62, no. 3 (Fall 2018): 168-174.
Ishizuka, Karen L. *Serve the People: Making Asian America in the Long Sixties*. New York: Verso, 2016.
Kim, Ju Yon. "Korean American Theater and Performing Arts: Networks of Practice and Bodies of Work." In *A Companion to Korean American Studies*, edited by Rachael Miyung Joo, and Shelley Sang-Hee Lee, 150–171. Boston: Brill, 2018
Lee, Esther Kim. *Made-Up Asians: Yellowface During the Exclusion Era*. Ann Arbor: Michigan, 2022.
Lee, Josephine. *Oriental, Black, and White: The Formation of Racial Habits in American Theater*. Chapel Hill: University of North Carolina, 2022.
Lee, Julia H. "The Railroad as Message in Maxine Hong Kingston's China Men and Frank Chin's 'Riding the Rails with Chickencoop Slim.'" *Journal of Asian American Studies* 18, no. 3 (October 2015): 265–87. https://doi.org/10.1353/jaas.2015.0023.
Maeda, Daryl Joji. "Documenting the Third World Student Strike, the Antiwar Movement, and the Emergence of Second-Wave Feminism from Asian American Perspectives." In *The*

Cambridge History of Asian American Literature, edited by Rajini Srikanth and Min Hyoung Song, 221-236. NY: Cambridge, 2015.

Metzger, Sean. "Charles Parsloe's Chinese Fetish: An Example of Yellowface Performance in Nineteenth-Century American Melodrama." *Theatre Journal* 56.4 (December 2004): 627–51

Metzger, Sean. *Chinese Looks: Fashion Performance Race*. Bloomington: Indiana University Press, 2014.

Moon, Krystyn. *Yellowface: Creating the Chinese in American Popular Music and Performance, 1850s-1920s.* New Brunswick: Rutgers, 2005.

Moy, James. *Marginal Sights: Staging the Chinese in America.* Ann Arbor: University of Michigan, 2008.

Shahadi, Joseph. "Burn: The Radical Disappearance of Kathy Change." *TDR* 55, no. 2 (Summer 2011):52–72.

Tchen, John Kuo Wei. *New York Before Chinatown: Orientalism and the Shaping of American Culture, 1776-1882*. Baltimore: Johns Hopkins, 2001.

Yamashita, Karen Tei. *I Hotel.* Minneapolis: Coffee House Press, 2014

Young, Harvey. *Theatre & Race*. NY: Bloomsbury, 2013.

Charles Francis Chan Jr.'s Exotic Oriental Murder Mystery had its world premiere at Walkerspace in New York City, produced by The National Asian American Theatre Company (NAATCO) (Mia Katigbak, Artistic Producing Director), in October 2015. The cast was as follows:

Frank/Hastings	Jeffrey Omura
Kathy/Linda	Jennifer Ikeda
Suzy/Eleanor	KK Moggie
Sergeant/Charlie	Jeff Biehl
Chuck/Cop/Bartender/Alfred	Peter Kim
Monkey	Orville Mendoza
Director	Ed Sylvanus Iskandar
Set Designer	Jason Sherwood
Costume Designer	Loren Shaw
Lighting Designer	Seth Reiser
Sound Designer	Jeremy S. Bloom
Projection Designer	Olivia Sebesky
Dramaturg	Kimber Lee
Production Stage Manager	Andrea Jess Berkey

Charles Francis Chan Jr.'s Exotic Oriental Murder Mystery had its regional premiere at the Guthrie Theater's Dowling Studio, produced by Mu Performing Arts (Randy Reyes, Artistic Director), in May 2017. The cast was as follows:

Frank/Hastings	Eric Sharp
Kathy/Linda	Hope Nordquist
Suzy/Eleanor	Stephanie Bertumen
Sergeant/Charlie	Luverne Seifert
Chuck/Cop/Bartender/Alfred	Song Kim
Monkey	Randy Reyes
Director	Randy Reyes
Set Designer	Sarah Brandner
Costume Designer	Samantha Fromm Haddow
Lighting Designer	Angelina Vyushkova
Sound Designer	Matthew Vichlach
Projection Designer	Kathy Maxwell
Properties Designer	Abbee Warmboe
Production Stage Manager	Lyndsey R. Harter

Charles Francis Chan Jr.'s Exotic Oriental Murder Mystery was originally commissioned and developed by The National Asian American Theatre Company (NAATCO).

Characters

Frank Chan, as **Hastings** – Asian American male, 23
Kathy Ching, as **Linda** – Asian American female, 20s
Suzy Takigayama, as **Eleanor** – Asian American female, 20s
Sergeant David Fitzwallace, as **Charlie** – white male, 30s or 40s
Chuck Chan, as **Cop**, **Bartender**, and **Alfred** – Asian American male, late 20s
Monkey, Asian American, any age, any gender

Setting

Berkeley, California, 1967.

Mandarin translations by Yilong Liu

Act 1, Scene 1.

> *A mansion in the Marina, San Francisco, California, 1967. It contains the largest television that a person might have in 1967, facing the audience. On screen, at low volume, is a news broadcast about military conscription. It plays as the audience enters.*
>
> *There is a telephone, prominently placed on a decorative telephone table. Beside it is a very expensive-looking armchair. The back of the armchair faces the audience. In it sits a man. We can see his arm. In his hand is a drink. There is ice in it.*
>
> *The phone begins to ring.*
>
> *It rings about three or four times before a voice from offstage can be heard.*

Eleanor   Earl, darling, telephone!
I said Earl!
Telephone!

There is no response from Earl.

My gracious, Earl, I'm taking a bath!
Can you please answer the telephone please?
EARL!

Still nothing from Earl.

Eleanor *enters in a bathrobe. We may not be able to tell, but she is a white woman in her 70s played by an Asian American woman in her 20s, with heavy makeup.*

And you left the TV on too, good heavens!

She turns off the TV.

The phone continues to ring.

Yes alright I can hear you, I'm coming I'm coming!

She answers.

Eleanor (*Cont'd*)   Hello! Biggers residence Eleanor speaking.
. . .
Who's calling please?
. . .
I beg your pardon!
. . .
Who is this?

WHO ARE YOU?

. . .

WHY I NEVER!!

Whatever she hears next causes her to gasp loudly and slam the phone down on the receiver and step away from it.

Earl, you won't believe what just . . .
Earl, wake up, I—

She goes to wake him and he slumps down off the armchair,

the drink falls,

his body lands on the ground with a thud.

He is dead.

AAAAAAAAAAAAAAHHHHH!

Blackout.

Act 1, Scene 2.

> **Frank** *is getting his physical with the local draft board.*

Frank   The purpose of stereotypes is to maintain order. The dominant culture assigns a system of behaviors to a group of people with the expectation that this model will become an actual pattern within the culture being stereotyped, and it works! We *assimilate* because this is our path of least resistance, we do the work of the white devil on behalf of the white devil by becoming what the white devil wants us to become. Does that answer your question?

Sergeant   No.

Frank   What was the question again?

Sergeant   What is your name?

Frank   My name is Charles Francis Chan, Jr., but referred to by the middle of my names, I'd appreciate you calling me Frank.

Sergeant   Your name is Charlie Chan?

Frank   My name is Frank.

Sergeant   Date of birth.

Frank   August 6, 1945.

Sergeant   August 6, 1945?, wait, isn't that the date that

Frank   Yes it is! At precisely 8:15am on August 6, 1945 Hiroshima time, the Enola Gay releases the Little Boy gravity bomb which takes 43.3 seconds to fall to its detonation height of 1,967 feet above the city. Meanwhile it is 3:15pm, August 5 in Oakland, California where my mother believes she is still several weeks away from delivery; however!, shockwaves from that nuclear blast traveled at a rate of 4.4 miles per second, tapering at a rate of .08 miles per mile, meaning those waves reached the shores of the San Francisco Bay at precisely 12:04am Pacific Standard on August 6, 1945, causing me with no contractions or labor pangs to just pop out of my mother golden yellow and naked.

Sergeant   Okay, so then birthplace is Oakland, California.

Frank   For the first of my births, yes, but I have been severally reborn!, once at the tender age of six, on a trip to visit my grandmother in Canton province (the Chinese Canton, mind you, not the one in Ohio), and of course you say, I assumed you meant the one in China!, but wouldn't you know that one is closer to home, and don't bother to guess which one!, it's the one you did not assume, but when my grandmother spoke in our blood's indigenous Cantonese mother tongue, it sounded to me like a litter of cartoon kittens; it was there I knew that even if by eyesight I am Chinese, by every other measure from geography to culture I am not simply Chinese but Chinaman! American born!

Sergeant   Got it. So—

Frank I was thirdly born in Berkeley, California. 1964! An undergraduate Golden Bear sitting outside Sproul Hall in a wave of civil rights activism; they tried to squash this political activity but hell no we would not go (except that we had to because one of the pigs grabbed me by the beard and flipped me into a paddy wagon), but as I was cast into a holding cell it was like falling out of a womb all over again, for if birth is emerging from the grip of a vag into some new world, then those piggy cops were the vag and my life will be a life of protest.

Sergeant Look man.

Frank What.

Sergeant You gotta stop doing that.

Frank Doing what.

Sergeant This is a monotonous job so that was fun for a second, but I got a line of punks like you out there to get through, so let's cut this off now. You wanna get out of here, don'tcha?

Frank Sure.

Sergeant Then just answer the questions.

Frank Okay.

Sergeant Are you a homosexual?

Frank Would that disqualify me?

Sergeant Only if I believe you.

Frank I'm totally a homosexual.

Sergeant I don't believe you.

Frank You have beautiful eyes.

Sergeant Shut up. Have you been diagnosed with any of the following conditions?

Frank Yes.

Sergeant I haven't listed them yet.

Frank Right.

Sergeant Heart disease.

Frank No, but I once dated a man who likened my inscrutable disregard for his affections as a disease of the heart-kind.

Sergeant Diabetes.

Frank Not yet.

Sergeant Asthma.

Frank Wait, asthma gets you out?

Sergeant   Yeah.

Frank   <gasp> yes.

Sergeant   Remove your pants please.

Frank   Gladly!

The **Sergeant** *puts on a rubber glove.*

Sergeant   Undergarments as well.

Frank   Usually I have to pay for this.

Frank *takes off his pants.*

Sergeant   Bend over and shut your face.

As the **Sergeant** *checks* **Frank***'s prostate:*

Frank   Oh but is this not an apt metaphor for the Chinese in America!!

Lights.

Act 1, Scene 3.

> *Back at the Marina. Chief Inspector* **Hastings** *of the San Francisco police is there with a* **Cop**. *The room is marked off as a crime scene with all the various crime scene indications.*

Cop Toxicology's back, Inspector Hastings. Poison. Strychnine, to be precise. Immediately after exposure comes a slow paralysis of neural pathways, seeping silently through the bloodstream, numbing everything, a whirl of confusion, a tingle at first, then complete incapacitation as everything slows to a deadly pace. Slowly. Slowly. Slowly. And then you die.

Hastings Okay, so who's the mug?

Cop Earl Derr Biggers. Author of some renown, wrote chintzy murder mysteries in the vein of Agatha Christie, some got made into Hollywood B-movies which explains the luxurious living quarters.

Hastings Good. I'd like to talk to the widow now.

Cop Me too, but you might want to wait on that.

Hastings What, why?

Cop Just got a call from the station, and apparently the Major's sending in an independent investigator.

Hastings Oh crap on a candlestick!

Cop I know, he'll be here soon and we're to provide support, but he's gonna be the lead on this case.

Hastings This is from the Major?

Cop Nope, this comes from even higher up.

Hastings Well dammit to hell, but alright, who's the ringer?

Cop Charlie Chan.

A thunderclap.

Hastings Oh wow. Charlie Chan, eh?

Cop Yep.

Hastings Hoo boy. Is this gonna be weird, Chad?

Cop How do you mean?

Hastings Well I'm not prejudiced or nothin, but his kind kinda does things funny, don't they?

Cop Oh I dunno. They seem harmless to me. Sure they eat strange things and talk like a whistle but the good ones enjoy being helpful to white folks. And Charlie Chan's got a rep for loving the white man.

Hastings   Well we'll see about that. When's he getting here?

A ring at the door.

Then a thunderclap.

Dramatic music and lights.

Act 1, Scene 4.

Frank's *apartment.*

Suzy   I have news.

Frank   So do I.

Suzy   Me first.

Frank   I had my physical for the draft board.

Suzy   WHAT?

Frank   Yeah, I quit school, so my deferrment was nullified.

Suzy   Are you insane?

Frank   Because fuck school! Fuck writing workshops, fuck art, man! It's just a bunch of white people stories for a bunch of other white people.

Suzy   So you'd rather get drafted?

Frank   I won't get drafted, I have asthma.

Suzy   No you don't.

Frank   Technically I don't but I know a guy who can say I do.

Suzy   What guy?

Frank   Okay so I don't know a guy but I have flat feet. So.

Suzy   You can't quit school Frank!

Frank   Too late!

Suzy   You didn't quit, you got kicked out, didn't you?

Frank   Okay yes technically I flunked out, but it was totally on purpose as an act of protest against the ethnocentric content of the campus curriculum.

Suzy   I'm going to the Philippines.

Frank   What?

Suzy   That's my news, I got cast in a major Hollywood motion picture and so I'm going to the Philippines.

Frank   What film?

Suzy   It's called *Charlie Chan Versus the Insidious Vietcong.*

Frank   Holy shit.

Suzy   I play a prostitute in an opium den.

Frank   So not cool, man.

Suzy   I have one line.

Frank   Holy shit.

Suzy   I think we should break up.

Frank   WHAT?

Suzy   This just isn't working for me anymore.

Frank   But Baby!

Suzy   I mean our whole situation Frank, it's just totally unmanageable, you're going nowhere fast and my life choices are clearly incompatible with your whole, like, ethos. Besides, I'm gonna be in the Philippines for three weeks starting Tuesday and

Frank   Three weeks?

Suzy   Yeah in the Philippines.

Frank   One line and it's three weeks?

Suzy   Most of what I do isn't talking.

Frank   I feel sad.

Suzy   Look, an actor has to go where the rodeo takes her.

Frank   Shut up, that's not acting!

Suzy   It's a major Hollywood motion picture!

Frank   Exactly!, fuck Hollywood and its malappropriation of our cultural identity! Suzy baby, don't let those imperious neo-colonialists exploit your exoticized orientalist otherness!

Suzy   Right, and do what instead?, live a disempowered nonparticipatory life, listening to you bitch about white people all day?

Frank   Ouch.

Suzy   And that's *if* you don't get drafted.

Frank   Let's get married.

Suzy   You are the dumbest person in the history of the world.

Frank   Come on baby, marry me!

Suzy   Frank, we just broke up!

Frank   When?

Suzy   We broke up like two minutes ago!

Frank   Let's get back together!

Suzy   You know what your problem is?

Frank   Yes.

Suzy You call yourself a writer but you've actually never written anything and I'd be surprised if you ever did. Because you're all talk.

Your mustache is stupid.

You think that just because you have a big penis it makes you desirable, but you're such a selfish, inattentive and lazy lover that no, it doesn't.

Your hygiene is despicable.

Your apartment is disgusting and if you don't clean your bathroom soon I won't be surprised if you get hepatitis.

Frank You raise some valid points.

Suzy You know what, Frank, maybe you *should* go to Vietnam.

Frank Say what now?

Suzy Yeah maybe that's exactly what you need!

Frank Are you – WHAT?

Suzy That's something you never see in the movies – an Oriental, fighting for the good guys!, dressed in US Army greens, an Oriental who *cares* about participating in the life and welfare of this country, willing to put his life on the line to prove it!

Frank Oh sure, you want me to Step 'n' Fetch it, too? Put on the white man's suit and fight and die for the colonialist policies of an Aryan-normative world view?

Suzy Yeah, maybe!

Frank What do you think I'd be in Vietnam? With my face and my eyes? What do you call a Chinaman in Vietnam?, you call him a gook, what do you call a Chinaman in US Army greens baby, you call him a chink. If I'm out there what side do you think they'll think I'm on?

Suzy What side *are* you on, Frank?

Frank From WWII to Korea to Vietnam, this country has been at war in Asia our entire lives, you ever think about that?

Suzy No baby, *you've* been at war with the whole goddamn world your entire life, you ever think about *that*?

Frank THAT'S ALL I EVER THINK ABOUT!

Suzy I'm gone, babe.

She heads for the door.

Frank I love you!

Suzy Don't call me.

Frank I hate you!

She exits.

Frank *screams, grabs a book from a nightstand and throws it against the wall.*

A **Monkey** *emerges from the book.*

Monkey Far out brother.

Frank What?

Monkey She crazy, dig?

Frank You're a monkey.

Monkey I know it.

Frank Did a monkey just emerge talking and wearing tie dye from the pages of that book?

Monkey That's power, brother. Words are power and power is words.

Frank Am I on drugs?

Monkey Well if you ain't then just say the word, I got some shit.

Frank Who are you?

Monkey Oh me? I'm just a monkey journeyed west from the olde thyme traditions of the heathen Chinee. Like a Confucian Mark Twain on a Timothy Leary deadhead trip and I'm diggin this Berkeley. I heard what you said about higher education, pumpkin, and I'm right there with ya. Fuck academia with its Campanile ivory towers! Chinese-town is where it's at, we're gonna do some great things, you wave me? Cause I wave you.

Frank Wave?

Monkey Exist on the same sociospiritual wavelength.

Frank Right on.

Monkey Let's get out of here. Buy my a drink, willya?

Frank I don't have any money.

Monkey We're gonna have to steal then.

Frank Where to?

Monkey Where else but Chinatown.

Lights.

Act 1, Scene 5.

> *Back at the Marina. Chief Inspector* **Hastings** *stands with* **Cop**, *facing* **Charlie Chan**.
>
> **Charlie Chan** *is played by a white actor (the* **Sergeant***) in yellow face.*

Hastings   Your reputation precedes you, Detective Chan. I'm Chief Inspector Arthur Hastings, SFPD. I'll be your right hand in this investigation.

Cop   And I'm Chad.

Silence.

Hastings   Long way from home for this, eh?

Charlie   Nature of home is elusive and transitory as sparrow.

Silence.

Hastings   What?

Charlie   Have been able to ascertain hour of victim's demise?

Hastings   Discovered around 12:04 last night, toxicology estimates time of death around 8:15.

Charlie   Have exchanged words of queried information with widow?

Hastings   Not yet, thought I'd wait for you so we could question her together.

Charlie   Have inspected all entries of egress to domicile?

Hastings   No sign of any forced entry.

Charlie   Most aggressive force is kind which leaves no sign.

Hastings   Right. Anywho, we've got a list of everyone who had access to the house – CHAD! Can you get that list?

Cop   Right on it, sir.

The **Cop** *goes.*

Hastings   Say, what brings you all the way out this neck anyway?

Charlie   Once was acquainted with gentleman departed. Have personal interest.

Hastings   Is that right? Buddy of yours?

Charlie   Buddy no. He was my father.

A thunderbolt from outside.

The sudden sound of torrential rain.

Hastings   Come again?

Charlie   I am not leaving.

Hastings   What?

Charlie   What?

Hastings   What?

Charlie   What?

Hastings   I'm confused.

Charlie   Inspector Hastings say come again, which is phrase often heard in laundry stores and fish markets upon departure of customer, but no need for self to come again for self does not depart.

Hastings   You said he's your father.

Charlie   Understand one's confusion.

Hastings   But

Charlie   Please, Inspector Hastings. A man is dead. Let us focus to one mystery at a time.

Another thunderclap.

The **Cop** *re-enters.*

Cop   Got that list for you, sir.

Hastings   Super. Bring the widow down, we'll be ready for her in a bit.

Cop   Yes ma'am. I mean sir. SIR! Sorry, I was thinking about something else.

The **Cop** *exits again.*

Hastings   Alrighty then. This list has the names of anyone who's been inside the house in the 24 hours prior to discovering the body.

Hastings *hands him the list,* **Charlie** *reads.*

Charlie   Sheaf of thinly pressed wood pulp reveals to me only four known suspects.

Hastings   That should make it easier, eh?

Charlie   Linda Wong.

Thunderclap.

Hastings   The widow's acupuncturist.

Charlie   Alfred Wong.

Thunderclap.

Hastings   Part-time manservant, Linda's husband.

Charlie   Eleanor Biggers.

Thunderclap.

Hastings   That's the widow, obviously she was here but we put her name there just to be thorough.

Charlie Arthur Hastings.

Thunderclap.

Hastings Jesus, how are those things so perfectly timed?!

Charlie Such name, Inspector, is same as name which belongs to you.

Hastings Right! I was called here this morning, Biggers complained of some threatening phone calls and so I popped by for a tea and some questions.

Charlie Ah so.

Hastings Appears someone's been calling periodically and breathing deeply into the phone like a deviant, talked creepily about the dead guy's children. We agreed it was likely a wrong number as the Biggers have no . . . or as far as we knew, they had no children.

Charlie Full content of presumptive fiberoptic conversation was?

Hastings Right, I have it here:

Hastings *checks his notes*
"I will murder you in your home for the sins of your son you sick white racist fuckface. Fuck you. Fuck your face. Die you disgusting fat fuckface."

Cop *sticks his head in.*

Cop Mrs. Biggers is here when you're ready.

Charlie Much gratitude for sensitive presentation of bereaving for conversatory diagnosis.

Silence.

Cop What?

Hastings Send her in.

Charlie Widow shall be first for inqury, then Wongs, and Hastings Inspector shall be interrogated further upon the final!

A thunderclap.

Lights.

Act 1, Scene 6.

> **Frank** *and* **Monkey** *at a Chinatown bar. A* **Bartender** *hovers.*
>
> *It's open mic night, so of course there is a young Chinese American woman with rainbow sunglases and flowers in her hair singing a 60s era protest folk song (possibly in Chinese), and playing either the harp or the guitar or at least a tambourine. Her name is* **Kathy**.

Monkey   I appear as a monkey, but am mammalian only by metaphor. I was born from a stone at the very same time as the origin of the universe, and have spent my entire existence fighting against ill-gotten authority and institutionalized power, on behalf of tricksters, warriors, malcontents, and all other types of underdog racounteurs.

Frank *to* **Bartender**   Another round?

Bartender   What another? You mean *two* more drink even though you all alone?

Frank   Yeah man, two of the same.

Bartender   Two dollar.

Frank   Put it on my tab?

Bartender   Hmmmmmmmm.

A moment where he studies him.

Yeah okay.

He pours two drinks and sets them down.

Monkey   But enough about me, let's talk about you.

Frank   What?

Monkey   Why have I been summoned here?

Frank   I wouldn't know.

Monkey   Oh but you would, my mustachioed friend. I do not appear to well-adjusted and self-actualized gentility, sir! So do not play coy with me. Tell the Monkey what's troubling you.

Frank   Oh Monkey, where to begin, where to begin.

Monkey   Let it out, sweetie.

Frank   My entire life is falling apart.

Monkey   True, true.

Frank   I got kicked out of school, I have no money, no job, no friends, no skills. My heart is broken.

Monkey Come on, no it's not.

Frank I miss her so much.

Monkey She's only been gone for like five minutes.

Frank Do you know how hard it is for an Asian guy in America to be seen as a sexual being?

Monkey No, I don't have that problem.

Frank Also, I think I'm about to get drafted.

Monkey Ah yes, the draft. Sending the youth off to kill our Vietnamese cousins. This is not the war for you. For there is another war you are already engaged in. Isn't there?

Frank There is?

Monkey A war between who you really are and who you are *perceived* to be by the world around you. And this war cannot be won by simply changing yourself, you can only rise victorious by changing the world around you, dig?

Frank That's heavy.

Monkey I know it is, boy. I know it is.

Frank But how? I can't go to Vietnam, I can't dodge, I don't think I'd last long in prison, I can't go on the run cause I don't have any money, maybe I could be a hippie and join a commune but I think that's just for white people, right? Oh shit Monkey I'm so fucked.

Monkey No you ain't, peanut, cause I'm here now. All you need is a little Monkey.

Frank Huh?

Monkey The warrior tradition is serious in our ancestral memory, but has yet to journey west. They brought us here to build the railroads, to replace the loss of slave labor in Reconstruction times through an indentured coolie trade. We looked for opportunity in America but died in giant waves of unremembered millions, mass graves beneath the mountains and gulches that carry the rails which bind this country together, and yet we have no heroes to speak of that history.

Frank Exactly! That's what I'm talking about! I grew up listening to the stupid radio, all these white racist so-called heroes fighting Japs in service of the flag; I turn on the TV now and there are no heroes that look like me!

Monkey Why do you look to TV for heroes?

Frank Huh?

Monkey Look at your history! look to your forefathers, look at the courage and the strength it takes to immigrate across oceans to a new world, I mean look at *me* motherfucker! And yet we were the last people in America to be allowed citizenship, and we are therefore perpetually seen as foreign. Someone must fight against this.

Frank   Totally.

Monkey   Frank! *You* can be that someone.

Silence.

Frank   Wait, me?

Monkey   Oh yeah baby. This is why I am here.
Charles Francis Chan, Jr.
Frank.
This is why you have summoned me.
We're gonna start a revolution, brother. I mean come on, it's 1967! The world is screaming for change, and you're gonna bring it!

Frank   I am?

Monkey   You will tell the draft board to kiss your golden ass, you will tell the police department to suck your golden cock! You will forego the pacifist hippie mentality and start your own commune instead, your own community! You will light a fuse that will set off a new policial and artistic movement that will change the course of history!

Frank   An oriental movement?

Monkey   Not oriental, you reject that word!

Frank   I reject that word!

Monkey   You have your own word!

Frank   Asian American!

Monkey   Asian A—really? You think that's gonna catch on?

Frank   ASIAN AMERICAN!

Monkey   Okay! Let's go with that!

Frank   I reject the present idiomatic parlance! I reject Jap Gook Chink Chop Suey!

Monkey   You reject it!

Frank   And in it's place I will build a new heroic tradition that screams across the continent like a mythical bullet train on the beautiful rails of our ancestral legacy!

Monkey   Speak!

Frank   I will start a new civilization!

Monkey   I'm with ya!

Frank   And a new language!

Monkey   Work!

Frank I will build a vibrant and progressive community of Asian Americans to populate a new and empowered cultural tradition that takes our protest and our culture and our voices to the people!

Monkey Tell the people how, preacher!

Frank I'm gonna I'm gonna I'm gonna I'm gonna write a play!

Silence.

Monkey A play?

Frank Yeah I'm gonna be a playwright.

Monkey You kinda lost me there, baby.

Frank Not just a play but a manifesto!

Monkey Okay?

Frank A manifesto of a movement! A history of grievances! A polemic on the disposession and invisibility of the Asian American identity! An indictment of counterrevolutionary assimilation into grateful inscrutable subservience!

Monkey Do you know anything about writing plays?

Frank Absolutely nothing, so it's perfect! I eschew traditionalist norms and embrace a new and individual set of cultural aesthetics!

Monkey Fine!

Frank The play will be called:

Monkey Lay it on me.

Frank *The Children of Charlie Chan!*

Monkey Meh.

Frank It will be called:

Monkey Take two:

Frank *Charles Francis Chan! And . . .*

Monkey Yeah?

Frank *Death of the . . .* no. *Murder! of the . . . Oriental Murder Mystery! Charles Francis Chan Jr.'s Exotic Oriental Murder Mystery! And Sing-Song Minstrel Show.*

Kathy *abruptly stops her song.*

Kathy Hey asshole you're interrupting my song!

Frank Oh! Sorry! I'm sorry.

Kathy I'm trying to do something here, nerd! I'm trying to *create!* And *express* myself in a cold and disinterested world! *Jesus*, with the yelling!

Frank   I wasn't – I didn't – I'm sorry.

Kathy   Whatever, this is stupid anyway.

She smashes something and goes to the bar, where the bartender wordlessly makes her a Singapore Sling and slides it across to her, she catches it and drinks.

Monkey   Oooooo boy go get it.

Frank   Huh?

Monkey   Go talk to that girl, I said!

Frank   What girl?

Monkey   The only girl in this bar, boy!

Monkey *pulls him off the barstool and slaps him across the face so hard that he ends up standing right next to* **Kathy**.

Frank   HI!

Kathy   Hi.

Frank   Hi.

Kathy   Hi.

Frank   I'm Frank.

Kathy   Kathy.

Frank   That's a nice name.

Kathy   Bullshit, it's boring and common.

Frank   I like your hat.

Kathy   It doesn't even fit.

Frank   Your song was really beautiful.

Kathy   No way it sucked, I did the last part all wrong but it doesn't matter, art is pointless and insufficient at making any lasting impact on the cultural conversation. Besides, we all die alone anyway.

Frank   Well it was nice to meet you.

Frank *starts to go but* **Monkey** *slaps him across the face and he goes right back to standing next to her.*

Frank   Have you ever done any acting?

Kathy   Seriously?

Frank   Yeah, I'm writing something that I think you might be right for.

Kathy   Shut up.

Frank No really, I'm a playwright.

She studies him a second.

Kathy I've never heard of an Oriental playwright.

Frank Asian American.

Kathy Say what?

Frank Not Oriental. Asian American.

Kathy That's not a thing.

Frank Not yet it isn't. But it will be.

Silence.

Kathy What kind of a play is it?

Frank A mystery.

Kathy Oh yeah?

Frank A *murder* mystery.

Kathy What's it about?

Frank Well you see, I can't tell you that. Because it's a mystery.

Silence.

Kathy Alright you can buy me a drink.

Lights.

Act 1, Scene 7.

> **Frank**'s *apartment. He and* **Kathy** *lie in bed, half undressed but very still.*

Frank Sorry about that.

Kathy Don't worry, it happens to lots of guys.

Silence.

Kathy I'm hungry.

Frank Me too.

Kathy Do you have any food?

Frank No.

Kathy Well maybe we can go get something somewhere later?

Frank Look, before you get any ideas, I should let you know that I'm kind of emotionally unavailable at the moment.

Kathy Oh.

Frank Yeah I just don't have time for frivolous things like love. See, I had to end my most recent relationship to focus my attention on some really serious artistic and political commitments.

Kathy You mean your play?

Frank Oh it's not just a play. It's a manifesto. Of a nascent revolutionary identity politic that establishes Asian America as a new but permanent social movement that will rise up in defiance of our gross misrepresentation in American culture, and our cruel subjugation in American society.

Kathy Cool.

Frank I know, right? And sure, that sounds easy, but it's sort of complicated because I'm also inventing my own language.

Kathy Language?

Frank Yes because American English is a colonialist system of cultural biases that cannot accurately contain the full force of what I have to say.

Kathy I know what you mean.

Frank Yes, you what wait, you do?

Kathy I speak Mandarin, Cantonese, and Japanese, with a fairly advanced understanding of Hawaii'an, Hawaii'an pidgin, and other Pacific Polynesian dialects, and I often find there are many concepts and semantic modalities of each that are nearly impossible to translate into American idiomatic English.

Silence.

Frank Exactly.

Kathy Will your language be an amalgam based on the root systems of other linguistic sets, or have a new and original phraseology?

Frank You know what, I haven't decided yet actually, it'll depend on some other, um stuff. That I'm still trying to figure out.

Kathy You're a Leo, aren't you?

Frank What I'm a yes I'm a Leo. How did you know that?

Kathy I'm deeply empathic. What year were you born?

Frank Guess.

Kathy 45.

Frank Wow.

Kathy The year of the cock.

Frank Wait what?

Kathy I'm more into the Eastern zodiac. 1945 was the year of the cock and in terms of elements it's the cycle of wood, so you're a Wood Cock.

Frank Wait what?

Kathy I'm a Fire Mouse myself. A Gemini Fire Mouse. Gemini, so there are two of me.

Frank What does that mean?

Kathy It means what it sounds like. It means everything.

Frank Right. Right, so . . . um. Hey. What's your . . . I mean, what's your deal?

Kathy What?

Frank Where are you from?

Kathy You mean where am I "really" from?

Frank No, just like: Who Are You?

Kathy Who am I?
Wow. Um let's see.

I was born in Canton, Ohio. My father is an engineering professor at Kent State, he doesn't understand me. He and my mother immigrated after the repeal of the Chinese Exclusion Act in 1943. I'm a junior at Berkeley, double major in Studio Art and Chemical Engineering. My hobbies are algebra and performance poetry. I'm a vegetarian, my favorite color is gold and my favorite animal is the capuchin monkey.

My mother killed herself when I was 14. Gunshot to the face. I discovered her body myself.

I worry that suicidal tendencies are hereditary. Especially when I wake up from dreams believing I'm the Messiah. That happens sometimes. But it doesn't answer your question, does it?

It's an impossible question to answer.

Frank   What do you want to be?

Kathy   Fuck you I want to be important! I want to feel like I'm contributing in some way to the good of humanity and the pursuit of universal world peace. I want to be an artist. Even though I can't draw and don't know music and can't dance and hate myself. I want to be loved by a family because I've never had that and probably won't until I have a child of my own. Which I do want, in fact, 12 of them, 12 like the star signs or disciples of Christ. One Black, one Chinese, one Native American, one Persian, one Chicano, one Romani Gypsy and the rest should all be mixed race, but I'll probably never have any children at all.

Frank   Why not?

Kathy   Look at my hand.

Frank   What?

Kathy   Here.

She holds her palm out so that he can examine it, he holds it.

Frank   What am I looking at?

Kathy   You'll see my love is strong. It's scattered and it wavers but it's always the deepest part of me. You'll see my life is quick. It's so so full but will not endure. You'll see I have two minds. They intersect in spots but mostly they run in opposition, out of convergence. I look at my hands daily. This is who I am.

He touches the lines on her hands gently.

Show me yours.

Frank   Nah.

Kathy   Show me.

Frank   I don't think so.

Kathy   Are you afraid?

Frank   Pshaw.

Kathy   Be brave, Frank. Show me.

He gives her his palm.

She looks and is shocked.

AAAAH!

Frank   What.

Kathy Oh you poor poor man.

Frank What?

Kathy Everything you are, and everything you will ever be is in conflict with itself. Your fate attacks itself. Your hands are violent. The lines at war with each other.

Frank That sounds about right.

Kathy Do you know what that means?

Frank I have an idea.

Kathy It means you're just like me.

They look at each other for a moment.

He puts his other hand on top of their ball of hands.

The **Monkey** *enters with a guitar and starts to play an elegant classical etude, haunting and balletic.*

Frank *and* **Kathy** *move their hands in a dance of limbs and desperation, they separate and touch, palms hovering over palms as they never stop looking at one another.*

When the song ends:

Kathy You're not like most Oriental guys.

Frank That's cause I'm not Oriental.

Kathy Oh right.

Frank I'm Asian American.

Kathy Asian American.

Frank And so are you.

Silence.

Frank Let's get married.

Kathy Shut up.

Frank No I'm serious.

Kathy Hot shit you are, aren't you?

He is.

Well then. Um? Okay.

They get on each other's bodies.

The **Monkey** *puts down his guitar and takes a martini out of his pocket.*

Monkey Oh yeah, babies. That's what I'm talking about.

Let's give them a little privacy while we set up for the next thing.

But just to stay thematically pertinent while they're doin what they're doin, let's talk about love.

What do I love about love?

I love bodies jumbled together but I love souls jumbled together even more, slippin and slidin like noodles in a big big plate of chicken chow mein. You don't know where one of em ends and one of em begins, because in that big ol plate, them noodles is all just noodles together, dig? Swimming in a big ol sea of chicken and Chinese vegetables.

In this way, it is just like being Chinese in America.

See, we are urged to believe that it is irreconcilable to be Chinese and American.

That in order to be truly American, one must assimilate and overcome the brutal barbarism of Chinese culture. One must not only lose the gross staccato accent but also eliminate from themselves all those vile indications of otherness.

You gotta be just like the white man.

And then you can go to a Chinese restaraunt and order in English.

And the Chinese storekeeper will look at you and say, "You Chinese?" and you will say "Nope". And she will think about it, hmm, "You Japanese?" and you say "Nope!", this time getting a little prouder of the "No", but now she's on a roll, "You not Korean!", and you both laugh at this absurdity, of course you are not Korean!, and to end the conversation and because your food is now ready (you ordered General Tso's), you tell her confidently:

"I'm American".

And the proud way you say it makes this Chinese storekeeper gleam with admiration.

Wow, she will think, maybe one day I can be like this enlightened American.

. . .

And that's what it looks like to hate yourself.

Wedding music begins to play.

Now here's what it looks like to love.

Dearly beloved.

We are gathered here today to witness the marriage of two beautiful young souls in humanist matrimony until their looming, inevitable divorce.

The rest of the cast assembles as wedding guests.

Frank *enters in a powder blue tuxedo with tails and a cowboy hat.*

Kathy *enters in a white dress with a spaceman helmet adorned with Christmas lights.*

Do you, Charles Francis Chan, Jr., take Kathleen Ching to be your life partner, to have and to hold, in full commitment to a new paradigm for Asian America?

Frank Hell yes.

Monkey And do you, Kathleen Ching, take Charles Francis Chan, Jr., to love and to cherish, with the same cosmic yin-yang entwinement as the spiritual wholes of Asia and America do so harmoniously dwell in thee?

Kathy You betcha.

Monkey I now pronounce you married.
You may kiss each other's faces please.

They kiss.

Triumphant science fiction music plays as the crowd applauds and fireworks go off.

Act 1, Scene 8.

*The **Sergeant** stands in front of a mirror, dressed in a white undershirt and white pants. Beside him is a small table with a makeup box. Very slowly he puts on a white dress shirt, white suit jacket, and black tie. He does this deliberately, looking at himself and taking in the look as he does.*

When he's placed the necktie just so, he takes a powder puff from the side table and applies makeup that gives his skin a yellowish hue. He then removes from the box, one at a time, a false moustache and a false goatee, applying spirit gum to each and placing them onto his face.

After he has placed the facial hair, he removes from the box some black eyeliner and very carefully draws an arch to his eyebrows, over his own, elevating them upwards. This takes some effort, and he has to try a few times to get the right look. When he's satisfied, he applies more of the makeup to the outer edges of his eyes to create an upward slant on either side.

He then begins to contort his face, squinting and pinching his nose and manipulating his cheeks in improvisatory ways, studying himself and the transformation in the mirror as he does.

He removes a tin of pomade from the box and slicks his hair back, experimenting with various awkward smiles as he does.

Sergeant   Herro.

He hunches his shoulders. Stoops. Walks around, looking in the mirror. Then he waddles a bit. Satisfied, he takes a white derby hat with a black trim from the table and places it on his head.

Sergeant   Herro! Herro. Ah! So. Herro.

in his own voice
How's that?

Frank *speaks from the audience.*

Frank   Can I see your teeth?

Sergeant   My teeth?

Frank Yeah, like in the bucktooth kamikaze cartoons of Japanese war criminals, you know the ones I mean?

Sergeant Of course.

He shows his teeth.

Frank Good, but more like a rabbit face, you know? Just scrunch your whole face up a little.

Sergeant Ah! So!

Frank Perfect.

Kathy *enters from the side.*

Kathy What is happening right now?

Frank Kathy! Perfect. Meet my friend Dave. He's playing Charlie Chan. Dave this is Kathy.

Sergeant Herro!

Kathy Who is this person?

Frank He's my friend Dave. He was my draft officer.

Sergeant Staff Sergeant David Fitzwallace, ma'am, but recreationally I've been in numerous community theater productions in and around the Bay Area, it's long been a passion of mine and—

Kathy Frank this guy is white.

Frank *unbearable anger way out of nowhere* CHARLIE CHAN IS WHITE!

Kathy What?

Frank The guy who created Charlie Chan is white, the people who make Charlie Chan films and the culture in which Charlie Chan exists in are entirely white!

Kathy Wait though.

Frank Charlie Chan is a white racist lie, so in order to represent that white racist lie he must be played by a real white racist in real white racist yellowface! To cast an Asian American as Charlie Chan would be to legitimize and endorse his white racist fakery!

Kathy Oh Jesus.

Frank What.

Kathy Oh Jesus Christ oh sweet Jesus Christ why does this keep happening to me?

Frank What do you mean?

Kathy This is Ohio all over again! It's just like that blues singer in Omaha and that weird beard guy Jerry and his stupid hippie jam band! Why do I keep attaching myself to strange disappointing men with unusual face hair?!

Frank Babe!

Kathy How did I not see this coming!? You roll up on me in some bar with this line about political and emotional community building and convince me to marry you oh my God Kathy you're better than this you stupid bitch!

Frank No that's not what I –

Kathy I have to get out of here!

Frank Wait, you don't understand!

Kathy You're right, I don't! I thought this play was about empowering Asian America in a positive and self-actualized way, but instead I walk in on this pasty disgusting white guy and the same Ching Chong Charlie Chan horseshit I get from everyone else, YOU'RE JUST LIKE EVERYONE ELSE!

Sergeant I can do it better.

Frank No, baby listen! We have to expose the white racist lie as a white racist lie in order to allow a non-white-racist representation of an empowered Asian American identity to emerge from the white racist fallacy!

Kathy No baby, you legitimize the white racist fallacy by engaging in it as a white racist threat, when the real white racist menace is real white racism, not just white racist stereotypes!

Frank Baby, white racist stereotypes are real!

Kathy Baby, stereotypes are *not* real!

Frank Oh baby no baby, stereotypes are *so* real, they are real white racist fictions that fuel a real white racist reality!

Kathy Baby what?

Frank You heard me, baby!

Silence.

Kathy Baby what?

Frank Okay – okay okay okay, let me show you.
Please? Baby?
Just watch. I'll show you.

Kathy *is skeptical but she sits.*

Frank *stands next to the* **Sergeant**.

Frank Is there any way that you could make yourself seem fat, but also somehow very small and insignificant at the same time?

Sergeant Absolutely.

He tries this.

Frank Hey that's not bad.

Sergeant   Thanks!

Frank   So lemme ask you something.

Sergeant   Great.

Frank   What's the difference between you and an Asian guy?

Sergeant   What do you mean.

Frank   Name some things. What do you think are the differences.

Sergeant   Um. Okay. Um. The eyes.

Frank   Sure, but you've got that covered nicely with the makeup. What else?

Sergeant   Um.

Frank   Don't be shy, this is important. We're getting to the heart of the character.

Sergeant   Okay.

Frank   Whatever you can think of.

Sergeant   Okay, um. Less body hair?

Frank   Good.

Sergeant   And um, I'd be . . .

Frank   Yes?

Sergeant   Bad at driving?

Frank   Okay.

Sergeant   Perhaps on account of the smaller eyes? Hee hee.

Frank   Good, keep going.

Sergeant   I should try to be shorter, too, maybe, right?

Frank   Sure.

Sergeant   And um . . . Penis?

Frank   Penis?

Sergeant   Penis.

Frank   Good. What about it.

Sergeant   Smaller?

Frank   Interesting.

Sergeant   And well, of course I would be . . . you know. Naturally inscrutable.

Frank   Naturally.

Sergeant   Which is to say, not terribly demonstrative or expressive. Timid? Or just emotionless.

Frank   Which one, timid or emotionless? They're not the same thing, right?

Sergeant I don't know.

Frank What do you think?

Sergeant Um. Both?

Frank That's the stronger choice, yes.

Sergeant Also I'm probably really hateful to women. Or not hateful, more like . . . I consider them inherently subservient. To me. And that their feet should be bound and they should be demure and obedient while simultaneously well-versed in all sorts of exotic and physically improbable sexual arts.

Frank Good, good, keep going.

Sergeant Um. Well, I . . .

No, never mind. That's all I can seem to think of.

Frank No you were about to say something else?

Sergeant No.

Frank Come on Dave.

Sergeant Yes. Well, there's another thing. I don't know if I can articulate it completely, but.

Frank Let's give it a shot.

Sergeant Okay. It's like . . . That Orientals, well. They kinda just don't value human life?

Frank Mm.

Sergeant At least not in the same way that regular people do. That Americans do. Because they're emotionless. Or at least their emotions aren't as important to them. They are a more cerebral people. Right? More intelligent than normal people, maybe, at least in terms of things like math and science, you know the book-smart stuff, but they lack gut. Instinct and intuition. They're more like robots than people. When they die it's no big deal because they're actually just small cogs in a big Oriental robot machine. Which explains things like kamikazes and hara-kiri ritual suicides and stuff. They just don't care about beauty or feeling or love. They're more like cockroaches. They breed and breed and breed and that's more important than like quality of life, right? Because they can totally live in squalor and like, huts or whatever, cramped overpopulated cities filled with smog and their backs are hunched over cause they're always carrying these heavy bags of rice and sticks on their backs until they're like 80 and then they die but that's no big deal because another one will come along and just do the same thing because they just don't . . . yeah, you know, they just don't value human life.

Silence.

Sergeant (*Cont'd*) In a way it's because . . . okay, it's probably because there are so many of them. You know what I mean? And you know, they also all kinda look the same. The men are all kinda weak and asexual and the women are all exotically hot until they reach a certain age at which point they become totally dumpy and wizened?

And not only do they look the same, they kind of all are . . . the same.

And I don't mean that in a bad way.

It's actually kind of admirable. Like maybe you're more evolved. Like originally we were all apes and then we were all African people and then at a certain point people migrated all over the rest of the earth and some of them became civilized and they became white people and they built cities and became normal and stuff. And other people, the Orientals, well they're actually even further away from apes than white people are, they're smaller and have the aforementioned less body hair, and they're less primal and instinctual– in general, I mean, I don't want to generalize – but they're smarter and emotionless so maybe it's part of the natural evolution of apes to become less and less animalistic and more and more robotic and cockroach like.

Silence.

So in a way, it's good that you're so much less emotional and that you don't care as much about human life.

Right?

Because it makes you more efficient. At things like overpopulating the earth. And building machines. And hoarding wealth. Because you don't care so much about actual human emotion.

Silence.

I mean I'm not making this up, you know what I'm saying, right?

Silence.

Frank   Whaddya think, baby?

Kathy   Yeah okay, I get it, baby.

Lights.

Act 1, Scene 9.

> *The Marina.* **Charlie Chan** *and* **Hastings** *talk to* **Eleanor**.

Eleanor   I believe in America. We have lived an American life. Have we been perfect? Who has? We do what we must, in pursuit of the great ideal of American exceptionalism, and yes we have thrived. Sure some were disgruntled, but in this country, there are winners and there are losers. Without losers there are no winners, and without winners there is no America.

Charlie   Ah so.

Eleanor   We are winners, Mr. Chan, and so yes we have left many losers in our wake.

Charlie   Any such loser in particular maybe you recall hear about recently?

Eleanor   Countless! For losers abound, sir, throw a cat outside and you'll hit one.

Charlie   No thank you. Upon inspection of departed gentleman's private notebooks, appearing that much of daily notations written in such inscrutable language.

Eleanor   He was paranoid.

Charlie   Such markings bearing any meaning to thee?

He shows her a notebook, she glances at it.

Eleanor   It looks like the scribbles of a capuchin monkey toddler.

Charlie   Ah so. Your husband ever he insinuate fearfulness of threatening upon life?

Eleanor   Naturally.

Charlie   And yet Madam knows not any who might have been so feared of such crime?

Eleanor   Goodness no, I was completely in the dark about all of his affairs.

Charlie   Include his affair with. . . . Linda Wong, your acupuncturist?

Thunderclap!

Eleanor   I beg your pardon!

Hastings   Hold on, Chan, do you really have to do it like this?

Charlie   Among notation papers find one in very such simple language.

Chan *holds up a piece of paper folded up in an origami flower.*

Hastings   Wow okay I guess so.

Chan *opens the paper.*

Charlie   Childlike missive upon revelation learn to be so:
"Meet me. Downstairs. After. Heart XOXO – L."

240   Once in the Countryside

Thunderclap!

Eleanor   Let me see that!

Charlie   Apologies for inability to share active evidence.

Eleanor   L?, what is that, that's not Linda, L could mean anyone! It could mean Larry, Luke, Lorelai!

Charlie   Please to elucidate re Larry Luke Lorelai.

Eleanor   There is no Larry Luke Lorelai, I'm just throwing out random words to demonstrate the commonality of names that start with the letter L, there's no way Earl was stepping out with Linda!

Charlie   And yet.

Eleanor   He couldn't even get it up at this point, an affair?! Please!

Charlie   Sometimes it gets up for some more easy than for others.

Hastings   Whoa, Chan!

Eleanor   Why I never!

Charlie   In light of discovered miscegenation Madam, perhaps can discuss possible confliction of Mrs. Linda with husband?

Eleanor   I can't even
What?
This is absurd, I can't believe that
It doesn't make sense, Linda wasn't that kind of
No
I'm sorry
I'm processing

Charlie   You likee nose towel?

He offers her handkerchief, she accepts and blows her nose into it.

Eleanor   How could she do this to me
How could she

blows nose
I built this life
I made that man

blows nose
My special universe of dreams
and it's all destroyed

blows nose, hands the handkerchief back to **Chan**, *who takes it and now uses it to blow his own nose*

Charlie   Special universe of dreams can rebuilded be with substantial payment of life insurances, yes?

Hastings Oh Chan.

Eleanor What did you say to me?

Charlie Policy evidence suggesting voluminous restitution amounting one million US dollar, this many monies can dreams new created buy?

Eleanor How dare you! I'm not talking about *money*, I have money! LOTS OF IT! I am talking about dignity! You you you silly Chinaman, it must be nice, to come in to this country and judge me?! Give me that handkerchief back, sir!

He does.

She blows her nose again.

Hastings Mrs. Biggers, if I may. I know this is a confusing, complicated time, so perhaps . . . if you might be able to provide any information about some of your employees, in particular Linda Wong, or her husband Alfred, it might help to—

Eleanor Alfred!

Thunderclap!

Hastings That's right, Alfred Wong, he—

Eleanor Yes! Of course! It must have been him! Alfred Wong! Her stupid shifty awful husband, he's the man who did this!

Thunderclap!

He must have discovered her infidelities just as I'm discovering them now, oh sir yes, I would stake my fortune upon it!

She blows her nose, simultaneous with another thunderclap!

Charlie Ah so.

Hastings Is there anything in particular about Alfred you could share that would help tie him to—

Eleanor Gladly! Earl hired him as a favor to Linda, part-time manservant but he ruined so many a dinner service it got unbearable. We had to fire him just a few days back and lordy! What a scene that was!

Hastings Aha! So Alfred must have been pretty upset about that, right?

Eleanor My goodness yes, he was crying and wailing like a little white girl!

she blows her nose

Weeping in the foyer and begging for a second chance, well fie upon you Alfred Wong, what second chances did you give my Earl?

She blows her nose emphatically and wads up the handkerchief, throwing it at **Hastings**.

Please tell me you will find that man, sirs! Find that Alfred Wong! He did it!

Hastings *takes the handkerchief and blows his nose into it.*

I will testify against him, I will go to court and tell the world how he resented our wealth, our position, our whiteness! I said give me back that handkerchief sir!

Hastings *gives her the handkerchief. She blows her nose again.*

Promise me. Promise me you'll make him pay!

Charlie   Promise to devote full being in direction of justice.

Hastings   I think we can let the lady rest now, Chan.

Charlie   Such condition acceptable for now, yes.

Hastings   I know it's been a difficult day, ma'am. Thanks so much for everything, you're free to go.

Charlie   However please to remain proximal such that further query may forthcoming be.

Eleanor   I wonder about your tone, sir. Don't forget, I'm the victim here!

Charlie   Victim clothing sometimes most suspicious disguise.

Eleanor   What?

Hastings   Apologies, Mrs. Biggers, you see...

Hastings *whispers something to* **Eleanor** *that the rest of us can't hear; they laugh and look at* **Chan**.

Eleanor   Yes. Well, good day to you Inspector.

She gives a slight nod, then blows her nose.

Missster Chan.

She gives him back the handkerchief, and exits.

Once she's gone:

Hastings   Look Chan. Lemme give you some advice.

Charlie   Ears happily open for prescriptive feedback.

Hastings   I know you're not from around here, but my God you really gotta work on your people skills.

Charlie   People skills?

Hastings   I mean this old lady's a widow not 12 hours, for sweet Jesus' sake. I know you gotta get these questions out but holy shit Chan you don't hafta be so . . . so.. inhuman.

Charlie   Ah so.

Hastings   Don't get me wrong, boy, I'm on your side here. But you should know the Chinese are expected to be, you know, appeasing and deferential foreigners just happy to be in the country. Do that and you'll put folks at ease, capice? Cause no one's gonna trust a Chinaman who don't act the way a Chinaman's supposed to.

Charlie Thousand of thanks for valuable advice.

Charlie *bows.*

Hastings Wahoo! See, there! That's more like it!

Hastings *smacks him on the back triumphantly!*

Now what say we take a break and get some donuts?

Charlie No.

Hastings Okay.

A thunderclap.

Lights.

Act 1, Scene 10.

> **Frank**'s *older brother* **Chuck** *is with* **Frank** *and* **Kathy**.

Kathy So let me get this straight. Your dad's name is Charles Chan.

Chuck and Frank Yes.

Kathy Your name is Charles Chan.

Frank and Chuck Yes.

Kathy And his name is Charles Chan.

Frank and Chuck Yes.

Kathy How did that happen?

Frank Dad was mysterious.

Chuck Dad went by Charles, I go by Chuck, and Frank goes by Frank.

Silence.

Kathy Got it.

Chuck So tell me more about this character.

Kathy His name is Alfred.

Chuck What is he, a tough guy? A bad guy? A tough mean old alpha male bad guy? I can do that.

Kathy He's more like a weak and impotent representation of emasculated Asian American victimhood.

Chuck What else you got.

Kathy That's the only open role available.

Chuck What about Inspector Hastings?

Frank You're not playing Hastings, I'm playing Hastings.

Chuck I just think I'm more of the Hastings type.

Frank I knew you were gonna be like this.

Chuck Like what?

Frank You always have to make everything a competition!

Chuck Well sure, I'm a competitive person, so are you.

Frank I know. I'm more competitive than you.

Chuck No you're not.

Frank I am!

Chuck   I've always been more competitive.

Frank   I'm *so* much more competitive, because you made me *hafta* be competitive, you think it was easy being your little brother?

Chuck   It was a hell of a lot easier than being your *older* brother, I can tell you that!

Frank   See you're being competitive again!

Chuck   So are you!

Kathy   You guys are idiots.

Chuck   Wait, who are you again?

Kathy   I'm Kathy.

Frank   This is Kathy.

Kathy   You don't have to do that, I already said I'm Kathy, you don't have to also tell him I'm Kathy.

Chuck   Yeah, Frank! Have some respect! Very nice to meet you by the way, Kathy.

Frank   She's my wife.

Chuck   No shit.

Kathy and Frank   No shit.

Chuck   In that case. *Hiya.* How ya doin'?

Frank   You're such a fuckface.

Chuck   You're a fuckface.

Frank   You're a bigger fuckface.

Chuck   Okay well if I am then that makes you a *little* fuckface, ya little fuckface.

Frank   That doesn't even make any sense.

Chuck   Sure it does, if I'm a big fuckface then you're a little fuckface, you said it yourself, how could you get married without inviting me you little fuckface, I woulda been your best man! THIS WOUNDS ME FRANK! WE'RE SUPPOSED TO BE FAMILY!

Kathy   PLEASE STOP IT.

Frank   Sorry.

Chuck   Really sorry, it's all his fault.

Frank   Shut your face.

Chuck   No YOU shut YOUR face.

Kathy   NO BOTH OF YOU SHUT YOUR OWN FACES.

Frank Sorry.

Chuck Once again, so sorry.

Kathy Are you gonna help us with this play or not?

Chuck Of course I am.

Kathy Oh praise Jesus.

Frank Thanks, man.

Chuck Absolutely, bro. I'm always here for you. To save the day. To bail you out when you're lost and in dire need of my transformative support.

Frank Hey, lemme be clear: we don't need saving.

Kathy We kind of do though.

Frank We're actually doing pretty great.

Kathy It's largely been a disaster.

Frank The show's in terrific shape, we just need a few extra hands is all.

Kathy It's mostly a random assortment of race jokes and diatribes that don't seem to be building to any coherent message or story.

Frank HEY LOOK. Yes it's messy but that's the whole point, we're dealing with the most difficult shit to unpack about our entire cultural identity politic, so if it gets complicated sometimes well that's just the price of revolution.

Chuck Got it. So then what kind of help do you need?

Kathy Well we've been collaboratively rehearsing for about three months now and the play is still only halfway written, we have no money, neither one of us has a job and I've been cutting class to come to rehearsal so I'm probably going to fail out of school which means we'll get kicked out of my dorm room which is the only place we have to work so it would be amazing if you could stake us for remaining rehearsal costs plus whatever production costs might happen should this play ever end up in front of an audience?

Chuck How much we talking?

Frank $50.

Kathy $60.

Frank $60 includes a contingency.

Chuck And you also need me to play this Alfred character?

Kathy You also have to double as a random policeman.

Frank And a Chinatown bartender.

Kathy Chinatown bartender? What scene is that?

Chuck Done.

Chuck *spits on his hand and holds it out to shake.*

Frank *is about to shake, but* **Chuck** *pulls his hand away.*

Chuck Wait though, one question first.

Frank What.

Chuck Tell me honest. This play is about Dad, right?

Frank No.

Chuck Come on. Charlie Chan?

Frank No! It's about the other Charlie Chan, the racist movie Charlie Chan.

Chuck Come on.

Frank It is.

Chuck Come on.

Kathy Wait why, what's the story with your Dad?

Chuck Wait, she's your wife and she doesn't know all this?

Kathy All what?

Chuck You want me to tell it?

Frank G'head.

Chuck Nah, you tell it.

Frank You.

Chuck Just tell it.

Frank I don't want to.

Chuck Fine, I'll tell it.

Frank Our dad was a vaudevillian. He was trained in Peking Opera back in the mother country but they changed his name at Angel Island to Charlie Chan, and with that on a handbill he managed to pull some serious crowds who were ultimately disappointed as they expected a harmless and non-threatening yellowface murder mystery, and instead got a confusing and grotesque metatheatrical Chinese-infused operatic American freak show.

Chuck So in order to have a career he converted his routine into an orientalist sing-song puppet minstrel act for white people.

Kathy Typical. Does he still perform?

Silence.

Frank He died.

Kathy Oh.

Frank He was murdered.

Chuck He wasn't murdered.

Frank He was murdered by white racists.

Chuck He was hit by a train.

Frank Under mysterious circumstances.

Chuck It wasn't mysterious, he was drunk and passed out on the railroad tracks.

Frank Mysteriously.

Chuck No, he was always drunk, no mystery about it.

Frank That's easy for you to say.

Chuck Why is that easy for me to say?

Frank Never mind.

Chuck You mean because you had unresolved issues with the man and he died before you could come to a sense of closure and understanding?

Frank Shut up.

Chuck And that I was always his favorite?

Kathy Why were you his favorite?

Chuck I joined the family business. That's why I'm such an amazing actor and feel so comfortable on stage, I did it all throughout my youth and some things just never go away.

Kathy You're a professional actor?

Frank Formerly.

Chuck I stopped after dad died.

Kathy What do you do now?

Chuck Guess.

Kathy You work in a Chinese restaraunt.

Chuck Nope.

Kathy Laundry.

Chuck Nope.

Kathy You're a student in some scientific or mathematical field.

Chuck Nope.

Kathy I have no other guesses.

Chuck   No you were right the first time I work in a Chinese restaraunt.

Silence.

Frank   Anyway, the play's not about Dad.

Chuck   Okay.

Frank   It's not.

Chuck   Okay.

Kathy   Then what's it about?

Silence.

Frank   He had this one bit that he did. The most popular part, he ended almost every night with it. A song, called The Heathen Chinee. It went like this.

They sing together.

Frank and Chuck   Hi! Hi! Hi! Ching! Ching! Ching!
Chow, chow, wellie good, me likie him.
Makie plenty sing song, savie by and bye.
China man a willie man, laugh hi! hi!

Silence.

Frank   That's the end.

Chuck   So then it is about Dad.

Frank   No!

Kathy   It really isn't, is it?
I get it, babe, cause it's about *you*. Isn't it?

Frank   Yeah. It's about me.

Kathy   And that's why it doesn't make sense, isn't it? Cause you don't make any sense at all.

Frank   I mean.

Kathy   None of us do, we're a lost generation, ain't we babies, we're the children of Chan and what do we do with that?

Frank   And that's why I have to play Hastings. Because the play is an investigation. Of myself and our entire cultural identity. And I'm the Inspector.

Chuck   Great. You play Hastings, I'll play Alfred.

Frank   Thanks man.

Chuck   No problem, I can play anything.

Silence.

Frank Hey so I've never told anybody this, but as long as we're sharing: I have an imaginary mythical capuchin monkey avatar who visits me sometimes. Like a voice in my head. He gives me guidance. It helps.

Kathy You have a monkey that talks to you?

Frank Yeah.

Kathy And you respond?

Frank Yeah.

Silence.

Kathy For me it's Jesus.

Frank What?

Kathy I know it's not really Jesus. He knows it too. Sometimes he takes off his face and he's my father, sometimes he's The Virgin Mary or Malcolm X, Fa Mulan, or Joan of Arc. But usually he's Jesus Christ and he speaks for Messiahs and Martyrs. He is very clear that I am not his disciple, but I am Him. I resent him unbearably and when he appears I am always afraid, but in the end I just want him to be proud of me.

Frank *and* **Kathy** *look at each other intensely, and then abruptly start making out.*

Chuck Goddammit seriously?

Frank What?

Chuck How come *I* don't get an imaginary psychosomatic avatar to give me guidance?

Kathy Maybe you don't need one.

Chuck But I do! I do need one! I know I look amazing and my life seems so awesome but it's not!
I'm so lonely! I'm so lonely!

Chuck *starts to cry,* **Frank** *and* **Kathy** *put their arms around him and they have a group hug.*

Kathy There there, Chuck.

Chuck You guys get me, don't you? Do you get me?

Frank Yeah man.

Kathy Yeah baby, we get you.

Silence, as they separate from the hug.

The **Monkey** *appears and looks at them.*

Monkey O for a muse of fire that would ascend
The brightest heaven of invention!
Pardon, gentles all, these flat unraised

Spirits that have dared on this unworthy
Scaffold to bring forth so great an object:
Can this cockpit hold that Golden Mountain?
Or may we cram within this wooden O
Those steps led to and fro Angel Island?
Let us, though ciphers to this great accompt,
On your imaginary forces work.
Think when we talk of monkeys, that you see them,
Flinging their foul poop in the fucking air;
When we speak of whiteness, bring to this please
Not the absence but the weight of a word;
And when we say Asian America,
Imagine if such a thing existed.
Imagine a movement so united,
So clear of purpose and so understood,
It could be recognized by all the world.
Admit me Chorus to this history,
And I will sing its hopeful, mournful tune.
O let us stay to see what once was done:
What battles in that war have yet been won.

Now. Before we take a quick break, let's play a little game.

Who here can answer me a question.

Simple question.

Who.

Who can name me:

In all of popular culture.
Movies, TV, books, all cultural media anywhere ever.
Who is the greatest Asian American character of all time?

Everyone waits.

They think about it.

This should take a very long time because the audience should also think about it.

If someone says something, then feel free to respond organically. Either by correcting factual errors, or by determining that their selection is, in fact, the greatest Asian American character of all time.

Feel free to feel how that feels.

If no one says anything, then at least thirty second should pass.

When Asian Americans are equitably represented in media, then everything Monkey just said after his iambic pentameter section should be deleted.

Let's take an intermission, I need a drink.

He picks up his guitar.

Let's all go to the lobby,
let's all go to the lobby,
let's all go to the lobby,
and have ourselves a snack!

End of Act 1.

Act 2, Scene 1.

> *The Marina.* **Charlie** *and* **Hastings**, *interrogating* **Alfred**.

Charlie   Ni hao, Alfred.

Alfred   What?

Charlie *very slowly*   NI HAO, ALFRED.

Alfred   I'm sorry I don't speak Chinese.

Charlie   Oh Alfred, you no speakee Chinese?

Alfred   Sorry no I was born in Stockton.

Charlie   Ah so, Alfred. You parents no teaching to you?

Alfred   Well no they tried, I guess I just wasn't very interested at the time. Sorry.

Charlie   How come why not?

Alfred   Oh I don't know. I guess I figured well, I'm in America, so I'm American I guess, I didn't really see the point to learn Chinese when I already spoke American. I mean English. I had my my my my American friends and they only spoke American, I mean English, so I figured why do I need to learn English? I mean American I mean Chinese I mean Mandarin.

Charlie   Such pity.

Alfred   Yeah in this way I dishonor my family.

Charlie   Please then to describe whereabouts of self during day of this one?

Alfred   You mean . . . today?

Charlie   Yes, day of this one.

Alfred   Oh, okay, um. I don't remember really, I was I guess I was . . . at home?

Charlie   At home what time?

Alfred   Um. The whole time?

Charlie   Whole day?

Alfred   I guess.

Charlie   Wake up stay home no go outside never nothing?

Alfred   That's right.

Charlie   Just stay home all day all time.

Alfred   Yeah.

Silence.

Charlie   This very sad, Alfred.

Alfred   I know. I know! I guess I've been pretty sad lately.

Charlie   How come why for?

Alfred   Oh I don't know. It's just, cause I got fired and my wife doesn't respect me and I don't feel very good about myself. Or my appearance. Or my life.

Charlie   Make you sad to lose job?

Alfred   Yes.

Alfred *begins to cry.*

Charlie   How sad it make you?

Alfred   Oh I don't know, pretty sad I guess.

Charlie   Forgive intimate nature of next query forthwith, Alfred, but must to asking. Was sir aware of wife's illicit affair with elderly gentleman employer?

Alfred   Yes.

Charlie   Make you sad to wife have such sexy time?

Alfred   Yes!

Charlie   How sad it make you?

Already   Oh I don't know, really really really really really really really really sad I guess.

Charlie   Ah so. Great sadness most number one best ingredient in recipe for great anger.

Alfred   What?

Charlie   Great anger most number one best ingredient in recipe for . . . revenge!

Thunderclap!

Alfred   Wait!, you don't think that I -
NO.
I could never –
Not Mr. Biggers, no, I'm not -
I'm not a sus-
A sus-
A sussssssspekk
I can't even say the word
Suppex
Sups-pex
Sup
Pupspect
What's wrong with my mouth
Upspect
Am I a supspups

Am I a supspescht?
Oh God this day just keeps getting worse,
I'm so sad
I'm so upspect
Upsect
What's wrong with me
I can't even say upspet
Uspettttttth
Uppppppp
Upsot
Upsooooo
I'm so upstect
I'm so suspect!

A thunderclap.

Hastings   Do you have a key to the house, Alfred?

Alfred   What?

Charlie   Ability for access to house anytime self desires?

Alfred   A key, um. Well yes, I have a key, I used to . . . I mean my wife, she

Hastings   So you can basically slip in and out whenever you want, right?

Alfred   Um I guess but

Charlie   Okay so also. You go to school for scientific, yes?

Alfred   What?

Charlie   You have study . . . what was subject?

Hastings   He has a Master's Degree in Chemical Engineering.

Charlie   Ah yes, the chemistration. Ah so. So when you studying the chemistry, they learning to you much of such things as . . . POISON?

Another thunderclap.

Alfred   What? No.

Hastings   Really? Chemical Engingeering, and you never learned anything about poison?

Alfred   I mean, no, I guess yes I know a lot about poison and its uses and the manufacture of deadly poisons thereof, but I mean NO I WOULD NEVER!

Charlie   Did Alfred Wong poison Earl Derr Biggers to die?

Alfred   NO!

Hastings   Tell us the truth now kid and we might go easy on you!

Alfred   I DIDN'T! I SWEAR I DIDN'T!

Charlie   You no poison him, provide poison, help wife to poison or poison Mr. Man by self?

Alfred   NOOOO!!!

Silence.

Charlie   Oh okay.

Silence.

Alfred   What?

Hastings   What?

Charlie   Chan say okay. Chan agrees.

Hastings   You . . .

Alfred   Really?

Charlie   Mystery is like earthworm. One piece missing then make no connect piece together, so if earthworm not have all pieces, then is not earthworm no more.

Hastings   Listen, Chan

Charlie   Humble self is humbly certain. Alfred is not murtherer.
Murther.
Murdurdur.
Morrrdur
Strange mouth cannot articulate
Martyr
Mother
Murtherererer

Hastings   I think you mean Murterter
OH!
That's odd,
Murded
Murdeder
Merrrrrr
I also cannot seem to

Charlie   Mur

Hastings   Murt

Charlie   Morter

Hastings   Mirederer
Okay see, now we're just thinking about it too much, it's
Murmurrrr

Charlie   Murmadder

Hastings   Murmurmurmurderder?

Charlie   Anyway! Mr. Alfred Wong please to claim freedom for which to depart.

Silence.

Alfred   Really?

Charlie   Like River Chi'ang, flow the way of northerness.

Alfred   Okay. Thank you? Goodbye!

Alfred *runs out of the room as fast as he can.*

Chan *closes the door behind him.*

Hastings   What the sam hell was that?

Charlie   Patience makes ketchup remove from bottle more satisfactory.

Hastings   But he did it! The man couldn't even say the word suspups
I mean supspets
Never mind! He's got motive, opportunity, and access to poison! We can't just let him walk! What if he runs, what if he covers up his tracks in the meantime?

Charlie   None of above will he do, for his tracks already white as snow falling on cedars.

Hastings   How do I know this isn't some kinda weird Chinese conspiracy?

Charlie   Pardon?

Hastings   I mean look at him and look at you! You could be related for all I know, or comrades in some foreign communist plot!

Charlie   Inspector misunderstands.

Hastings   Yes! I do! Cause nothing you're doing makes sense! You gotta level with me Chan, what do you know?, what are you doing?, lemme know what you know and what you're doing!

Charlie   Knowledge sometimes more vicious weapon than action.

Hastings   What?

Charlie   He who rides back of tiger shall have difficulty on dismount.

Hastings   Stop that.

Charlie   Even if cut off dragon's tail, still it is dragon.

Hastings   I said stop it!

Charlie   Okay.
So then please.
Inspector is ready for resume job of active murder mystery investigation?

Silence.

Hastings   Alright fine! But I'm warning you, Chan. I'm gonna need some real answers soon.

Charlie Meantime, thousand pardons, lunch was chop suey dim sum, so must now to toilet for next fifteen minutes go.

Hastings Um . . . okay.

Charlie Better to run with dog than sleep with bunny rabbit.

Hastings Oh come on!

Charlie *exits.*

Fuckin' *chink.*

A thunderclap.

Eeeek!

Lights.

Act 2, Scene 2

> **Suzy** *stands in front of a mirror. Beside her is a small table with a makeup box. Very slowly she puts on an elegant but matronly black dress. She does this deliberately, looking at herself and taking in the look as she does.*
>
> *She takes various makeup items and begins to draw wrinkles on her face, around her eyes and near her mouth. She then takes a powder puff from the side table and applies a dusty white makeup that gives her skin a paler hue.*
>
> *After this, she removes from the makeup bag some mascara, and applies it heavily. Lipstick too. When she's satisfied with the amount, she sprays herself with perfume and then adds elaborate jewerly – a brooch, a necklace, rings.*
>
> *She then takes a gray wig from the wigstand and places it on her head, careful to conceal any of her long black hair just beneath.*
>
> *She adjusts her posture. She hunches at first, but then stands more upright than before. Shoulders back. Nose in the air.*

Suzy Hello.
Hellow.
Hallo.

She adopts a rich person's voice.

Eleanor Biggers.
Ellie-uh-nor.
Ella-nor.
Charmed. Charmed, I'm sure.

She takes a pair of elegant dinner gloves from the table and puts them on.

Over there, Jeeves. Darling, could you help me?
WHY I NEVER!
How's that?

Kathy *speaks from the audience.*

Kathy What happened in the Philippines?

Suzy They decided to go in another direction.

Kathy They cast a white person, you mean?

Suzy ANOTHER DIRECTION! That's all I know, another direction.

Kathy I'm sorry to hear it.

Suzy Not me, darling NOT ME! I never dwell on things. The world is the way it is! What is *really* wrong with this country are people who expect things to be handed to them. My father started from nothing, his father started from less, his father's father's father started from an amoeba in a primordial soup that had to walk to and from school uphill in the snow and yet he pulled himself up by the bootstraps!

Kathy Good.

Suzy I am a 70 year old white woman.

Kathy Are you?

Suzy A *rich* 70 year old white woman.

Kathy Good. So . . . what is that like?

Suzy Well. I imagine I don't even know. For I probably never have to think about it. How would I? Think about whiteness? About wealth? I've always had these priviliges, and so I feel entitled to this life, I have people beneath me who can perform tasks on my behalf, and this has made me a confident person who takes for granted the service of others. But I don't even realize I take it for granted because I never have to think about anyone else but myself!

Kathy That's pretty good.

Suzy EXCUSE ME I WAS TALKING!

Kathy Nice.

Suzy I was always excellent in school. Wheaton then Harvard, I studied Western Literature and Creative Writing but my poems were unremarkable; I only ever wrote about beautiful fields of flowers. For what else could I write about!? I couldn't write of struggle, of community, or culture, for I never thought of such things, they simply didn't exist!

Kathy It's funny you say that, because—

Suzy I said stop interrupting me! Because as I think about it, my dear, what I really love, what I *really* love more than anything?

Is whiteness itself. Oh yes.

How to describe.

Occassionally, I wish I was black. When I hear black men speak and march and call for change, I wish I had that kind of passion, that kind of *purpose*. And I think this makes me a good person, to have empathy for blacks, but I don't actually have to think about it beyond the few minutes I pretend; I envy it for a moment only, and then I can go right back to being white again.

Kathy What about Asian Americans?

Suzy Asian Americans. What does that mean, Asian Americans as in Orientals?

Kathy Sure.

Suzy Huh. To be honest, I've never given the matter any thought.

Kathy That sounds about right.

Suzy HOLY SHIT THIS IS AMAZING!

Kathy What do you—

Suzy HOLY SHIT I LOVE THIS!

Kathy Oh!

Suzy LOOK WHAT I HAVE BUILT! Look upon my castle of dreams! These stairways, these arches! These doric columns and marble bannisters, the cristal chandelier that hangs so dewlike in the foyer!

She pronounces foyer pretentiously.

This is my Xanadu! It protects me from those less fortunate, my goodness I'm able to go days months years without ever seeing a black, or a poor, or a Chinese except for when they're tending to me! Where was I?

Kathy The foyer.

Suzy Yes yes, the FOYER! My monument to whiteness! To sit atop this great country and look back on a history marked by victory and dominance, with no degradation or subservience in my family tree, to enjoy the myriad benefits of a society founded entirely around *my* history, *my* personhood, *my* standards of physical beauty and cultural values, *and not even have to admit those benefits even exist!* To blame others for their own subjugation and still enjoy the incredible comfort of this ABSOLUTELY FRICKIN GORGEOUS FOYER!

Kathy Alright, that's . . . really good, maybe a little *broad,* but

Suzy I MEAN LOOK AT THIS DECORATIVE VASE! THIS DECORATIVE VASE COSTS MORE THAN MY RENT FOR A YEAR AND I HAVE FIVE OF THEM!

Kathy You're mashing your pronouns a little, try to stay in character.

Suzy Oh you don't have to tell me twice, baby, I never want to leave this character ever like ever ever ever EVER EVER! I mean fuckin' a, if this is what it feels like to be white than please oh Christ Almighty let me start my life again!

Kathy Okay you're doing great, but remember this play isn't about *you,* so

Suzy How DARE you speak to me like that, don't you know who I am!?

Silence.

Kathy Apologies, Madam, it will never happen again.

Suzy Thank you my dear sweet Linda. You make me feel good don't you?

Kathy   I hope it is so, Madam.

Kathy *begins to prepare an acupuncture table.*

Suzy *begins to remove her evening gown to lie on the table.*

Suzy   I know not the mysteries of your dark art, but it certainly makes me feel at peace.

Kathy *stops with the table for a second.*

Kathy   Do you really think that?

Suzy   What?

Kathy   Do you really wish you were white?

Suzy *stops changing her clothes.*

Suzy   I mean. Sometimes, yeah. Totally.
Don't you?

Kathy   No.

Suzy   Bullshit. Never?

Kathy *starts to respond but doesn't.*

Instead, she starts again with setting up the acupuncture table.

Suzy *watches her a moment before she continues changing.*

Eventually she lies down on the table, and **Kathy** *begins to perform acupuncture on her back.*

Kathy   Sometimes.

Suzy   What?

Kathy   Sometimes.

Suzy   What are you talking about, are you being Linda right now, or Kathy?

Kathy   I don't know.

Suzy   Okay well I just need to know if I'm still Suzy or if I can be Eleanor.

Kathy   I wish it most when I think about children, you know?

Suzy   See, the best part of being white is the privilege of knowing you're normal.

Kathy   If I had a child, think of how different it would be.

Suzy   In fact it's not even about knowing . . .

Kathy   To never have to worry about how she'll fit in,

Suzy   I don't even have to think about it.

Kathy   how this country might pereceive her.

Suzy I just *am*.

Kathy What it might expect from her.

Suzy Normal.

Kathy All the extra ways this society might objectify her,

Suzy When a not-white enters a room, the first thing you notice is their not-white nature.

Kathy Suppress her,

Suzy With me, the first thing you notice is up to me.

Kathy Make assumptions based on the color of her hair

Suzy If I feel like fashioning my hair a certain way, then the first thing you notice is my hair.

Kathy Her eyes

Suzy If I want you to notice my clothing, I can select the apparel necessary to make that my leading characteristic.

Kathy What kind of a world would I be bringing her into?

Suzy But these are things I've not even aware of.

Kathy What kind of life would I be asking her to live?

Suzy Things I don't have to think about.

Kathy A life like mine?

Suzy Ahhhhhhhhh ohmigod yes that feels good, darling.

Kathy *takes one needle and dips it in a vial of strange liquid.*

Kathy *hesitates with the acupuncture needle hovering over* **Suzy***'s back.*

Throughout the following, **Kathy** *starts to put it in, then stops.*

Suzy Did you kill him?

Kathy I beg your pardon?

Suzy My husband. Did you kill him?

Kathy I'm stunned by your question, ma'am.

Suzy I can understand if you did, dear. He was an awful man, and deserved to die.

Silence.

Kathy Honestly?
. . .
I wish I had.

Kathy *places the needle into Suzy's back.*

If I had, I would have made him suffer.

Suzy Oh you are naughty.

Kathy Not enough poison to kill him in his sleep, no. That would be too nice. I would have given him tiny doses, just a prick here and a prick there, so that he would slowly lose power, a little bit at a time.

Kathy *begins putting needle after needle into the vial and then into* **Suzy**'s *back, throughout the following:*

Suzy Ha! He would have hated that.

Kathy At first he would have very slowly started to feel numb in his extremeties. His hands. His feet.

Suzy Oooooooh.

Kathy The slightest tingle.

Suzy Whatever you're doing right now, darling, it feels *soooooo* nice.

Kathy It might even feel nice at first, before becoming an itch he desired to scratch. But as he moves to scratch it, he realizes he cannot move his arms.
He tries to get up, but suddenly his legs too are unresponsive.

Suzy That's strange, I seem to be feeling a little...

Kathy And then his neck.

Suzy Woozy.

Kathy At this point he realizes he is in trouble.

Suzy Ho ah whaaaaa happaaaaaa neeeee

Kathy He thinks about the nature of power. How it feels for all of that power to slowly, limb by limb, fall away.

Suzy Ah grrr goo haaa rrrr ee.

Kathy He tries to scream. But his lips don't move either.

Suzy's *mouth seems to be paralyzed but she is completely lucid.*

Kathy And yet his mind continues to think. And it tells him he is dying.

And before his mind falls numb also, at the same time as the slow slow fade of his cold cold heart, his eyes do continue to reflect back what he sees. What does he see?

Kathy *takes the vial of poison and moves to face* **Suzy**.

He sees me.

She shows her the vial.

And staring deep into his eyes, I will say:
Do you see me now?

Look at me. Now I will be seen.

Eleanor *dies.*

Kathy *checks* **Suzy**'s *pulse.*

Satisfied with what she finds, she goes looking around the room for a place to hide the body.

She opens a closet door. Inside is the **Monkey**, *dressed like Jesus Christ.*

Monkey   Mark me.

Kathy   Oh Jesus not right now please!

Monkey   You're doing great, mama, there's a pile of detritus here, hide the old lady underneath.

Kathy   I don't know if I can do this.

Monkey   Thou shalt not be a whiny bitch!

Kathy   I'm not a violent person!

Monkey   We didn't land on Plymouth Rock, Plymouth Rock landed on us!

Kathy   Totally, I know, but—

Monkey   There is no light without the darkness.

Kathy   Yeah I got it, but there's something I have to tell you.

Monkey   Shhh mama.

Kathy   Something important.

Monkey   I have already heard the good news, mami.

Kathy   You really think it's good news?

Monkey   Oh mumsy it's the best news. But you should hurry. They're coming.

Kathy   Right! Yes, I'll . . .

Kathy *hides Suzy's body.*

Kathy   This is just so not me!

Monkey   Wrong, mi madre, you've never been the real you until now.

Silence as **Kathy** *thinks about this.*

I'm proud of you, Kathy.

She is somehow very touched by this. They share a tender smile before the door to the closet suddenly slams shut, along with:

Thunderclap!

and **Hastings** *appears.*

Hastings   Mrs. Wong.

Kathy   Inspector! I didn't hear you come in.

Hastings   Detective Chan should be joining us shortly.

Silence.

Hastings   I'll see what's taking him so long.

He starts to go.

Kathy   There's something we need to talk about.

He stops.

When you get the chance.

Hastings   Okay. You mean about . . . What?

Kathy   We can talk about it later. After we're done with . . . never mind.

Hastings   Everything okay?

Kathy   Yes. No. Maybe, I don't know. I'm just confused. And nauseous. And like really, really just super hungry.

Hastings   Okay. You mean because of this? Or...

Kathy   We'll talk about it later.

Hastings   Okay.

Kathy   Let's just do this.

Hastings   Okay.

Thunderclap!

Chan *appears.*

Charlie   Request excusing for arrival delay. Bathroom experience more productive than anticipated.

Hastings   Gross, Chan.

Charlie   Please Madam will forgive disruption and interrogation into matter of involvement, but in order to release pigeon from hand must first confirm incongruity of hand to bird prior.

Kathy   ...Okay?

Charlie   Excuse poor communication ability.

Kathy   (Perhaps the Honorable Detective would feel more comfortable speaking in Mandarin?)
Huo xu zhen tan xian sheng geng xi guan jiang zhong wen?
或许侦探先生更习惯讲中文？

Parenthetical text is supertitled in English.

Bolded text is the Pinyin romanization of what is spoken in Mandarin.

Charlie   Ah! You wish to converse in Mandarin!

Kathy   (It would be my pleasure.) **Fei chang le yi.**
非常乐意。

Charlie   In that case. Ching-chong-ching-chong sing-song she-shaw-shur?

Kathy   (Yes, I was here that morning attending to Mrs. Eleanor.)
Mei cuo, na tian zao shang, shi wo zai zhe li zhao gu Eleanor tai tai.
没错，那天早上，是我在这里照顾Eleanor太太。

Charlie   Lama lama ding dong?

Kathy   (Such details escape my memory.)
Wo ji bu tai qing le.
我记不太清了。

Hastings   Hey what's she saying?

Charlie   Mung mung tsing tao te ching wong tong fa chin chow hoo cho hee zip bong how who moo shoo wing yao sher ee hong ching tsai chang nar wo ni wong ai shu mai guy?

Kathy   (Yes.) **Shi de.**
是的。

Charlie   Ja ja myun?

Kathy   (I'm surprised you know that, but yes. It began one evening while Eleanor was sleeping. He asked if I would help him open a jar of raspberry preserves. I did, but in the process, I spilled some of the preserves on his pants. I began to wipe the preserves only to realize he had developed an extraordinary erection. I began to wipe much more slowly. He responded. I continued until the matter was concluded. We didn't speak of it. Until a day came when he asked me again whether I would help him open a jar of preserves.)
Mei cuo, ni jing ran zhi dao. You yi tian wan shang, Eleanor yi jing shui xia le, ta lai wen wo neng bu neng bang ta da kai yi guan shu mei jiang. Wo da kai shi, sa le yi xie zai ta ku zi shang. Bang ta ca gan jing de shi hou, cai fa xian ta ying de hen li hai. Wo kai shi gu yi man man de ca, ta de fan ying ye yue lai yue qiang, zhi dao ta de xu yao bei jie jue le. Zhi hou wo men zai mei you ti qi guo zhe jian shi, zhi dao ling yi ge wan shang, ta you gei wo yi guan shu mei jiang, jiao wo bang ta da kai.
没错，你竟然知道。有一天晚上，Eleanor已经睡下了，他来问我能不能帮他打开一罐树莓酱。我打开时，洒了一些在他裤子上。帮他擦干净的时候，才发现他硬得很厉害。我开始故意慢慢地擦，他的反应也越来越强，直到他的需要被解决了。之后我们再没有提起过这件事，直到另一个晚上，他又给我一罐树莓酱，叫我帮他打开。

Hastings   Come on, really?

Charlie Beef lo mein.

Kathy (For months, it remained in this fashion, an illicit handjob on irregular evenings. We no longer needed the pretext of jars. I found it empowering. I found him so needful. Despite all his power, all his wealth. He was so helpless. My husband is also helpless, but in a way that disgusts me.)
Zhe zhong qing kuang chi xu le hao ji ge yue, ou er wan shang wo hui bang ta shou yin. Wo men ye bu zai xu yao shu mei jiang zuo jie kou le. Zhe rang wo gan dao chong man le li liang, jiu suan ta you na me duo de quan li he cai fu, zai xu yao mian qian, hai shi na me wu zhu. Wo zhang fu ye shi zhe yang, dan ta de na zhong wu zhu que rang wo gan dao e xin.
这种情况持续了好几个月，偶尔晚上我会帮他手淫。我们也不再需要树莓酱做借口了。这让我感到充满了力量，就算他有那么多的权利和财富，在需要面前，还是那么无助。我丈夫也是这样，但他的那种无助却让我感到恶心。

Charlie Sing Sing Sing a Song?

Kathy (No. I never desired Mr. Biggers, not truly, not like that. What I desired was . . . was a baby.)
Bu, wo xiang yao de cong lai dou bu shi Biggers xian sheng, wo xiang yao de shi yi ge hai zi.
不，我想要的从来都不是Biggers先生，我想要的是一个孩子。

Charlie Goochie goo!

Kathy (Yes. But my husband is incapable. And as I looked at the ejaculate which coated my fingers, the viscous juice of a powerful rich white man, it enraptured me. So I rubbed it up against myself while he watched, and I saw this excited him.)
Shi de, dan wo zhang fu bu zhong yong. Dang wo kan dao yi ge you quan you shi de bai ren, kan dao ta de jing ye zhan man le wo de shuang shou, wo jiu xiang zhao le mi yi yang. Yu shi wo ba ta men mo dao wo shen shang, wo zhi dao guang shi kan zhe wo, jiu jiao ta xing fen.
是的，但我丈夫不中用。当我看到一个有权有势的白人，看到他的精液沾满了我的双手，我就像着了谜一样。于是我把它们抹到我身上，我知道光是看着我，就叫他兴奋。

Charlie Yin-yang buck buck bagaw!

Hastings Seriously, Chan, what are you guys saying? Please?

Kathy I didn't kill him. I took from him what I needed, and it was enough. I am grateful for what he gave me, but I didn't care enough about him to kill him. My life is no different with him dead than it was when he was alive. Perhaps you should ask Inspector Hastings if this is also true of his situation. I know that other people have secrets too.

Hastings What the hell is that supposed to mean?

Charlie   Glorious sunlight upon your beautiful field of ancient flowers, and one hundred years of thanks. Lady may now cordially dissipate as lotus flower in morning dew.

Hastings   Hold on a second!

Kathy *bows a deep bow to* **Charlie***, who returns it.*

She exits.

Hastings   Dammit Chan, that's it. I'm done with this soy sauce rice-pickin' freakshow once and for all! This whole slope eyed investigation of yours is totally out of control!

Charlie   Perhaps Inspector can comment upon Mrs. Linda remark?

Hastings   Say what?

Charlie   Allude to existence of secrets.

Hastings   Oh come on, I couldn't understand a goddamn thing that dragon lady nip bitch said!

Charlie   Secrets she is know about, hm? Secrets she seeming to know you know she know about, cannot help but wonder what such secret might be.

Hastings   Get outta here, ya Jap Dink Gook! You're the one who's put this investigation in jeopardy with your mongoloid mushu crap, so don't fuck with me, Hop Foo, I will end you.

Charlie   Such murderous words. Words of killing kind.

A blood-curdling scream from outside the door!

Cop *from behind the door*   Detective Chan! Inspector Hastings!

Chad *runs into the room.*

Inspector Hastings! Detective Chan!

Hastings   What is it, Chad?

Cop   Come quick, come quick!

Cop *slides the screen, revealing:*

the dead corpse of **Eleanor** *Biggers!*

Hastings   AAAAH!

Cop   AAAAH!

Hastings & Cop   AAAAAAAAAAAAAH!

Charlie   Most interesting.

Hastings   That's . . . that's Eleanor Biggers!

Cop   Why is this happening?

Hastings   I hope you're happy now, Chan! This blood is on your hands, you yin yang mustard zipperhead! Well I'm taking over now goddammit. Step aside, flat face!, I'm gonna find out who the killer is once and for all!

Cop   Are you allowed to do that?

Hastings   Of course I am! I'm a white man! Now get forensics in here right away!

Cop   Yes, sir!

Cop *exits.* **Hastings** *steps to* **Charlie***.*

Hastings   I hereby place you under arrest for impeding a criminal investigation! You're comin with me, Chino. I'm gonna get to the bottom of all your coolie secrets at last!

Charlie   Ah, but Hastings, secret bottom already has been revealed.

Hastings   Say what?

Charlie   Two persons now dead. Maybe killer of one same as killer of other, but maybe no. Maybe killer try to kill again. How many killing killer want to kill? All done killing or do killer want kill another someone soon?

Hastings   If you're trying to creep me out ya little rateater, it ain't gonna work.

Charlie   Dangerous world we live in, Hastings. Share room with killer, should feel some fear feeling no?

Hastings   I said stop that shit, you seaweed suckin' eggroll.

Charlie   Unless you person is the killer, then you person not need to fear killer because you know no killer gonna kill you because you the killer.

Hastings   I'm not the killer!

Charlie   I know.

Thunderclap!

I am the killer.

Three thunderclaps!!!

Hastings   YOU!? That's – Why would you kill a sweet old woman?

Charlie   Eleanor?, no I not kill her.

Hastings   Wait what?

Charlie   I didn't kill to her.

Hastings   But you just said.

Charlie   Oh, no! WOW! Okay, yes perhaps was confusing. No, I no to kill to Elcanor, somebody somewhere else kill to her.

Hastings   Oh, okay! WOW INDEED! I got confused there for a second because you said

Charlie   But Mr. Earl Derr Biggers yes, Chan did kill him!

Thunderclap!

Hastings   I KNEW IT!

Charlie   Really?

Hastings   Okay so technically I didn't, but I knew something weird was going on with you!

Charlie   Something weird indeed...

Rumbling thunder now!

For I am Charlie Chan . . . UNLEASHED!

LOUDEST THUNDER EVER!

Earl Derr Biggers create Chan, but now creation overtake creator!

Hastings   That's right! You said . . . you said he's your father!

Charlie   Yes! Created in one his image but I have been severally reborn!

Hastings *tries to tackle* **Chan** *to the ground and cuff him or something, but* **Chan** *knows kung-fu so throws him to the ground with ease and pins him down.*

Born to submission.
Born to assimilation.
Born to appeasement,
But not this time!

Chan *draws an ancient Chinese symbol on the palm of his hand.*

Hastings   What the hell are you doing?

Charlie   This time will I be born real.

He lightly blows the metaphor onto **Hasting***'s face.*

Hastings *dies from a fake Chinese curse!*

Hastings   AIIIIEEEEE!

Lights.

Act 2, Scene 3.

> **Frank** *in a chair as* **Kathy** *does his makeup. It is not evident right away, but eventually we should realize that she is making him look exactly like* **Monkey**.
>
> *He starts without any makeup at all.*
>
> *Mostly they speak to each other through a mirror.*

Kathy What's the worst thing you can imagine?

Frank What do you mean?

Kathy I've been putting together a list. Of the worst things ever. Slavery. Genocide. Torture.

Frank Yeah man, those are pretty bad.

Kathy Radiation sickness from nuclear fallout.

Frank Look babe, this is some really heavy shit for so early in the morning.

Kathy Because as terrible as these things are, they have all actually existed. Haven't they? I can't seem to imagine anything worse that doesn't already exist. These things still happen, every day.

Frank Look man, you're being kind of a drag.

Kathy But even though they happen all the time, all over the world, I still have moments when I'm happy. Morning coffee. Sex and music and sunsets and food, it all lets me turn my mind off and not think about it for a second, and if I found a way to do that all the time do you think I could actually be happy?

Frank Where is this coming from?

Kathy I saw your draft notice.

Frank Oh.

Kathy You put it in the garbage. Half burned, but you only burned the edges, not the part that says you have to report next Tuesday.

Frank Yeah, I guess I felt conflicted.

Kathy So then what are you going to do?

Frank I haven't decided yet, can we just finish this first please?

Silence.

Kathy I want a divorce.

Frank Whoa!

Kathy How can you not have a plan? This affects me too, we're supposed to be married, we're supposed to be building a future, and you don't even have a plan for next Tuesday!

Frank   Come on! I'm twenty-three years old, man, you're not supposed to think about that crap til you're like older!

Kathy   How old?

Frank   I don't know, like 25?

Kathy   Before you know it Frank, you're gonna be 25. And you don't even know whether you'll be in jail or in Vietnam when it happens.

Frank   Alright fine, you want a plan, here's the plan. Cause government bureaucray has gotta be pretty slow, right? So I probably have at least a few months before they find me, and even then I can miss my court date, jump bail, finish this play and by the time they catch up to me I'll have already firmly established Asian America as an irrefutable and conscientious objectionist political cause.

Kathy   And then what?

Frank   What do you mean and then what, then we can be happy! That's what it takes, babe! Cause there is something that's worse, you know, worse than slavery, or genocide, or torture.

Kathy   What.

Frank   It's worse if you're somehow *responsible* for such things. Not simply that they exist, but that they might be my fault. Someone else's subjugation. Their slavery. Their genocide. Their torture. If horror exists and I do nothing about it, then I'm tacitly endorsing its existence and therefore responsible.

Kathy   Babe.

Frank   There are people who save people. There are heroes in the world. There are people like Martin Luther King and Jesus Christ who have looked at the evil of the world and dedicated their lives to making it go away, and that's what this play is about.

Kathy   No it's not!

Frank   Well then what is it about?

Kathy   I don't know! I don't know what any of it's about, it's not even a play, is it? A play is supposed to have an audience, a theater, and we don't even have that, we've been rehearsing for nine months and I don't even know where the play starts and I begin!

She makes a mistake with the makeup.

Frank   Yo, you're messing it up.

Kathy   I'm agitated.

Frank   I look stupid.

Kathy   That's just how you look.

Frank   Gimme the thing, I'll do it.

She does. He starts to do his own makeup.

Kathy Look. Frank. Let's just leave.

Frank What are you talking about?

Kathy Let's get outta here. Hit the road. Forget the play, forget the movement, forget Asia and forget America, let's just pack up our shit and get a van and drive down south to Mexico and buy guitars and grow beards and wear hats and start a mariachi band and live in the world. If we need money we'll play Mexicali Blues on street corners enough for beer and nachos and we'll get a dog and a hacienda and learn Spanish and invent a hybrid fusion linguistic mash of Mandarin Cantonese Mexican Spanish English rebel poetry and when we get drunk we'll howl at the moon and when we sing we'll make up the words as we go and sing full throat from our gut cause that's how completely we'll be living.

Frank I just—

Kathy Don't that sound not half bad, babe?

Frank But

Kathy Don't that sound like a pretty decent life for a coupla Chinese westerners lost in the wilderness?

Frank No. It doesn't, babe. I'm sorry but it doesn't, not right now.
This is too important, this play, it's too important.

Kathy But it doesn't have to be. We can live a different way.

Frank I can't though!

Kathy Why not?

Frank Because I am Jesus Christ, babe!
I am Jesus Christ, or at least I gotta try to be!
I gotta smash the fucking evil of the world or else I'll never be free!
I gotta finish the scene, I gotta finish the play,
this is all I have, I gotta work on the play like the play is me,
and I am so close, babe, I am so so close,
I gotta play this scene, babe, can you just let me play the scene?

Kathy What difference will it make?

Frank I said I don't know, that's why I have to do it, so I can figure it out!

Kathy Well I'm getting tired of the figuring out, and all your pathetic Charlie Chan daddy issues, alright? I gotta do something, babe, right now. You don't even know what you're going to do next Tuesday, but right now I gotta know all of it. I gotta know where I'm gonna be in ten years, or twenty, I gotta know what the world is gonna be and it's all I can think about. What will the world look like in fifty years?

Frank Do we really have to have this conversation right now?

Kathy Yes.

Frank Why?

Kathy I'm pregnant.

Silence.

They stare at each other in the mirror for a long moment.

Act 2, Scene 4.

                           Kathy *as* **Linda** *with* **Chuck** *as* **Alfred** *at home.*

Linda   Are you gonna look for a job today?

Alfred   Me? Yeah, sure, I suppose so.

Linda   We can't just live off my salary, you gotta pull your weight around here.

Alfred   I know.

Linda   You're gonna be a father, okay? It's time to step up.

Alfred   I know.

Linda   Call that place, they're supposed to have some work.

Alfred   What should I say?

Linda   Whaddya mean? You say that you're looking for work.

Alfred   Oh right, sorry.

Linda   And try to be a little confident, okay?

Alfred   Sure, okay, confident. Yes, except I don't, um.

Linda   What?

Alfred   How?

Linda   Oh my Jesus, Alfred, this is why you keep getting fired from places.

Alfred   I know, it's just

Linda   I can't do everything for you.

Alfred   Sorry.

Linda   Alright, fine, here. Let's practice. Ring ring.

Alfred   What's that?

Linda   We're practicing, dipshit! Ring ring!

Alfred   Ring ring.

Linda   Hello.

Alfred   Oh hello, yes, um. Okay. Let's see. Um. I'm calling you because, um, my wife, um . . .

Linda   Who is this?

Alfred   Oh! Right, sorry. This is Alfred Wong?

Linda   Is that a question?

Alfred   Sorry. No. Alfred Wong. I'm married to . . .

Linda   Don't mention me.

Alfred   I'm married to my wife.

Linda   Oh okay, Alfred, what can I help you with?

Alfred   Um, well yes, sorry to bother you, but I'm . . . well, you see, I'm looking for work and um?

Linda   Alfred, that sucks.

Alfred   Sorry.

Linda   Stop saying sorry. It's irresolute.

Alfred   Sorry.

Linda   Let's try again.

Alfred   Ring ring.

Linda   Hello.

Alfred   Hello, my name is Alfred Wong. I'm looking for work?

Linda   Don't ask as a question, make it a statement.

Alfred   Sorry I'm looking for work.

Linda   Stop saying sorry.

Alfred   I'm looking for work.

Linda   What kind of work are you looking for?

Alfred   Oh, you know, um.

Linda   What skills do you have?

Alfred   Who me? Oh, I don't know. I can um, I have a master's degree in chemical engineering, but

Linda   Well that's useful!

Alfred   Oh well it's nothing really.

Linda   NO!

Alfred   What?

Linda   ALFRED WILL YOU BE A MAN!? FOR THE LOVE OF GOD, BE A MAN! WHAT IS WRONG WITH YOU?

Alfred   Sorry.

Linda   I can't deal with this okay, I have to do my tai chi.

Alfred   Okay.

Linda   Call the place! NOW!

She exits.

He picks up the phone, looks up a number, dials.

Alfred   Yes, hello, I um.

He hangs up.

And then starts to cry.

The **Monkey** *appears with a flourish.*

This **Monkey** *isn't played by the* **Monkey***, but by* **Frank** *in Monkey costume.*

Alfred   Who are you?

Frank   I'm a friend, Alfred.

Alfred   Oh.

Frank   You seem like you could use one of those, eh?

The Monkey holds out his palm and a flame shoots out of it or something.

Alfred   What the

Frank   Let me show you something, Alfred.

Alfred   Show me what?

Frank   Let me show you where you come from.

Frank *as* **Monkey** *takes* **Alfred** *on a tour of the troubled history of the Chinese in America, which appears in projected images of historical documents and stereotypical caricatures. The real* **Monkey** *appears, and plays accompanying music.*

Alfred *and* **Frank** *watch as they navigate these images, which should include:*

- 1885 broadside stating "The Chinese Must Go!"
- 1882 "Hip! Hurrah! Chinese Excluded" broadsheet
- Front cover sketch of the 1878 novel "Almond Eyed – The Great Agitator" by Atwell Whitney
- 1899 editorial cartoon captioned "Yellow Terror in All His Glory"
- Early 20th century Rough on Rats advertisement card
- 1907 postcard "He's a Yellow Peril Chink . . ." by Fred C. Lounsbury
- 1877 photograph of Hong Di, lynched by the citizens of Colusa.
- film still of Christopher Lee as Fu Manchu
- film still of Warner Oland as Charlie Chan

Alfred   Why are you doing this to me?

Frank   This is what you're up against, Alfred. This is your legacy. This is who you are.

Alfred   Okay, but

Frank   You gotta get mad. I mean nobody gives a fuck, do they?

Alfred   They don't?

Frank   No. You know who gives a fuck?

Alfred   Nobody?

Frank   Nobody gives a fuck. White people don't give a fuck. But do you know who gives even less a fuck?

Alfred   Who

Frank   You.

Alfred   Me?

Frank   Did your mother give a fuck?
No.
Did your father give a fuck?
No.
Did your sister give a fuck?

Alfred   I don't have a sister

Frank   What kind of father are you gonna be, Alfred?

Alfred   What?

Frank   A father like your father, so you can have a son like you? Are you gonna be the kind of father who tells his son to just do his homework, don't cause trouble, be a chemical engineer and listen to what the man says?

Alfred   Probably.

Frank   How's that worked out for you, Alfred?

Alfred   Oh God.

Alfred *weeps.*

Frank   Let it out, baby.

Alfred   Why does life have to be so hard?

Frank   Oh but it doesn't, baby. Look in your blood. We invented gunpowder, Alfred, we invented paper!, and the printing press!, and fermented alcohol!, and the noodle. You think Italians invented the noodle? No way, that was us, kid. Marco Polo stole that shit, he took it from us and just put tomatoes on it. He also took the Triads and turned it into the Mafia cause when he came to the Yangtze he could see that's how you get shit *done*. When European kings were still painting themselves green and humping rocks or whatever, we Chinese had already developed the most complicated and beautiful written language in history, we had silk weavers and porcelain artisans, we had fireworks!, and we had dignity.

Alfred   No way, dignity? Really?

Frank   Get that dignity back, Alfred Wong.

Alfred   How?

Frank   What skills do you have?

Alfred   Um.

Frank   Ring ring.

Alfred   What?

Frank   WILL YOU BE A MAN!?

Alfred   Why are you being so mean?

Frank   You're gonna be a father, okay? It's time to step up.

Alfred   Oh God.

Frank   Phone's ringing, Alfred.

Alfred   But

Frank   Pick up the phone.

Alfred   I don't know what to do.

Frank   I just told you what to do, boy. Pick up the phone!

Alfred   But the phone's not ringing.

Frank *as* **Monkey** *disappers in a cloud of smoke or something.*

Alfred   Is it?

. . .

Wait, where did you go?

. . .

Are you still here?

. . .

Is anyone here?

The phone starts to ring.
AHH!

Thunderclap!
AHH!

Linda *runs back into the room.*

Linda   DON'T ANSWER! I GOT IT!

Alfred   AHH!

She picks up the phone.

Linda   Hello.

. . .
. . .
. . .
Okay.
. . .
. . .
. . .

She hangs up.

Alfred   Who was it?

Linda   Where are the passports?

Alfred   What?

Linda   We have to get out of here.

Alfred   Who was on the phone?

Linda   Listen, babe, here's the thing: I kinda killed that old white lady Eleanor Biggers this afternoon so I think I'm in a lot of trouble, we're gonna have to run away to China.

Alfred   Um.

Linda   WHERE ARE THE PASSPORTS?

Alfred   WHO WAS ON THE PHONE, LINDA?

A thunderclap! Causing momentary darkness,

and when the light comes back on,

Charlie Chan *is standing there watching them.*

Charlie   It was me.

Alfred & Linda   AIIIIEEEEE!!!!

Charlie   Ni hao.

They back away from **Chan**.

Linda   Okay look, Chan, I know why you're here, but I swear what I did was self-defense! Let's be reasonable!

During this, **Linda** *makes hand gestures to* **Alfred** *in an attempt to get him to do something, but* **Alfred** *doesn't understand what she's trying to indicate.*

Alfred   What?

Linda   I had to do it! They were trying to ruin me! I know what Eleanor wanted, how she thinks, all the lies she was prepared to tell to pin her husband's murder on me!

Charlie   This is not why I am here.

Linda   I mean you should understand better than anyone, Chan! You know how these people are, they'd never believe me, over a rich old white woman?, the courts, the cops, the *system, man,* I had to do it! For the baby! For the baby!

Alfred *finally figures out that Linda wants him to distract Chan.*

Alfred   Hey! What's that over there!?

Charlie   What?

As **Charlie** *turns,* **Linda** *grabs something (the telephone?) and tries to attack him with it.*

But Chan blocks. Does a swift kung-fu thing.

Linda *counters.*

She knows kung-fu too.

They fight.

Charlie *is winning.*

Alfred *just stands there, crying and stuff.*

Linda *is on the verge of defeat.*

Kathy   Alfred, go get the swords!

Alfred   What swords?

Kathy   There are swords in the kitchen, second drawer on the left.

Alfred   Since when?

Kathy   JUST GET THEM NOW!

Charlie *is about to take* **Linda** *down completely when* **Alfred** *runs back in with two ancient Chinese swords.*

Alfred *attacks Chan, weakly.*

Chan dodges easily and takes his own sword out of his pocket.

This frees **Linda**, *who crawls to retrieve the other sword.*

Alfred   Why are you doing this? I didn't kill anyone, I'm just a weak and emasculated representation of Asian American victimhood!

Charlie   Exactly this is why you must die.

Charlie *kills him.*

Linda *stands with the sword in her hands.*

Charlie *turns to her.*

Linda   *I'm* not weak, Chan.

Charlie I know.

They fight, slow at first.

Linda I am strong like an ox.

Clink.

I am cold and dark as winter midnight.

Swing.

I am dangerous and beautiful like a jagged shard of ancient jade.

Slash.

And I strike like a dragon!

She makes a grand attack! but is easily defended.

Charlie And exactly this is why you must die.

Clink swing slash.

And then a stab wound to the gut. **Charlie** *with a killer move, right into* **Linda***'s stomach.*

Silence.

Linda *with a stunned look.*

Linda The baby.

Charlie Bye-bye baby.

Charlie *digs the sword in deeper. This can be super gruesome.*

He twists the sword, digs at the stomach, and enjoys it. It's almost perverted.

Linda *dies.*

He studies the carnage. He drops the sword.

He adjusts his suit and his hat so that it all looks great again.

Frank *emerges from behind* **Charlie***, still dressed as a Monkey.*

Charlie Hello my son.

Frank Hello Father. You know what I'm here for?

Charlie What you are *think* you here for yes this I am know very well.

Frank I have journeyed west for hundreds of years, in order to reclaim my true identity, my ancestral birthright, one rooted in a heroic tradition that will supplant your white racist fakery.

Charlie Ah so.

Frank I'm here to destroy the distorted image of the yellow man which you have perpetuated throughout this country, so that I can finally LIVE! As myself! As a new western Monkey King with the power and dignity of my ancient forebears! And that's why you must die.

Frank *takes a sword out of his pocket.*

Charlie Such different you are now than when was a boy.

Frank I know.

Charlie As a boy you cared not for such things, for such things you loved, America and Fred Astaire, GI Joe and bubble gum. As a boy were you wish to be such same like me, adored by white man, harmless but safe in America.

Frank At what cost?

Charlie Cost? Ha! Am I not most very best number one example of what you can becoming in America?

Frank No.

Charlie No? Let's see: I'm rich. I'm famous. White people all the time they love me, think I'm cute, think I'm funny. I am providing an acceptable alternative to the insidious and vile image of Fu Manchu as invader.

Frank Oh but you are far more insidious, fat man! The proverbial good Yellow alternative to that Fu Manchu devil; created out of the white desire to make us harmless.

Charlie True.

Frank You're the Uncle Tom of the Yellows. You're the Tonto alternative to Geronimo, Stepin Fetchit to Mandingo. The acceptable model of the savage foreigner, the one who does what the white man says, you're the one they can laugh at. Well I'm sick of being laughed at.

Charlie Ha ha ha ha!

Frank Stop it.

Charlie HA HA HA HA!

Frank STOP IT!

Charlie You think you kill to me and then no one gonna laugh no more? HA HA HA!

Frank I SAID STOP LAUGHING AT ME!

Frank *strikes at* **Charlie***, but* **Charlie** *dodges.*

Charlie You going to have baby, yes?

Frank How did you know that?

Charlie I remember when your mother she tell me she become pregnant with you.

Frank Shut up.

Charlie   She say "ai ya Charlie Chan, we have one another son to come." But at this time so poor we are, very worry, all the time for thing like money, for thing like clothings and food.

Frank   I don't believe anything you say.

Charlie   And this is why I am become policeman. Solve criminal crimes and try rid of this world violence, work with white man to make more safe the world. This is why I act like so harmless, all the time harmless, so my child can live safe in this America.

Frank   You think I feel safe? You think I feel always American?

Charlie   Think about one your new baby, son, this is change something no?

Frank   No! It doesn't change anyth- It-

Charlie   How you gonna raise your baby?

Frank   That's none of your business.

Charlie   Many my business, boy, I am grandpappy!

Frank   It doesn't matter.

Charlie   NOTHING ELSE MATTERS. WHAT KINDA BABY YOUR BABY BE, BOY?

Frank   A BABY JUST LIKE ME!

Frank *strikes at* **Charlie** *again,* **Charlie** *dodges.*

Charlie   Ah so.

Frank   He'll be a baby without a father.

Just like me.

A baby who has to find his own way, just like me, for he will have an unrighteous father incapable of giving him that much in advance. He will be a boy who deals with the very same lies I've had to deal with, the same invisibility and mockery, the same degredation and shame.

For he's the son of Chan. Like me.

And maybe I can build a different kind of world.
Maybe *he* can build a different kind of world.
But either way, I won't even know.
I won't even know because I won't be there.
I won't be there, Pop.

I won't be there.

Charlie   How come why not?

Frank   Cause I have to report.

Charlie Ah.

Silence.

Frank I don't know what to do. I don't wanna go to Vietnam, I don't wanna go to Mexico or Canada, I don't wanna spend my life running. I don't wanna be a bad father, I don't wanna be like you.

Silence.

Charlie Will tell to you one story.

Long ago time, when still very young persons you were, I stop to do police work in favor of traveling Chinese minstrel show puppet carnival, yes? Safer this way. Peddling harmless and humorous stories of the Chinese for American palate. This give me great shame, my son.

Frank I know.

Charlie One long ago night I take one walk.
Upon railroad tracks.
Strange land, this is.
The Sierras.
Look down see tracks.
Know these were tracks build by ancestor Chans.
My father, his father come to America build railroad.
Never did I really know my grandpappy.
Two times only I meet him.
First time I am so small, he seem to me so large.
Hands so calloused with markings of labor,
the callouses covered everything,
like his hands were their very own planet.
Their very own mountain attached to this mountain of a man.
His back was strong.
Strong from carry so many iron across American west,
Strong from build foundation of country.
But then, second time I meet him, he no seem strong no more.
Back no strong no more.
Look for callous on hands but he no more have hands.
Lose hands in accident.
Don't know how. Never tell story.
So sad to realize,
No one ever gonna know his story.
No one every gonna know him.
I think of this when I walk railroad tracks.
Tracks I walk, no one even use no more.
Now all cars. All roads.
No one care.
So many story no one talk about.
Many peoples probably buried there,

on rails that no one Chinaman ever never get to ride.
So upon this railroad track, son, I laid down.
I laid down to become somehow one part of it,
part of whole history of tracks and all what came before.
I think about you as I lay upon tracks.
I know I have no understand of how to tell you of my shame,
how to teach you some something different,
only I have to tell you how I hope.
Hope for you find better way.
But I can no help you.
And so I stay there, on tracks.
Long time.
Sunset on the Sierras.
A cold and lonely night in the American West.
And this is when I heard the train.
And this is how I died.

Frank   I know.

Charlie   I am so sorry, my son. Sorry for cause you shame.

Frank   Dad, I—

Charlie   But please must understand why I was this way.
What else could I do?
I know I look funny,
I know I talk funny,
but this is how I talk, okay?
Cannot change my face.
Cannot change my talk
any more than I can change whole world around me.
Any more than I can change my fate.

Frank   Oh, Dad.

Charlie   But maybe I can change yours.

Frank   You already have, Dad, you already have.
Maybe I can change yours too.

Charlie   No, my fate was long ago already written.

Frank   Maybe it can end different this time.

Charlie   No, I have long ago already died.

Frank   Let me write you a better death, dad. I can do that, but not the way I thought I would, not to destroy you and the shame you carry, but to honor it. To accept it, to understand where it comes from and take it up as my own.

Charlie   Yes.

Frank And then you can be . . .

Charlie Yes, my son.

Frank Asian American.

Frank *stabs him in the heart.*

Charlie *falls,* **Frank** *cradles him in his arms.*

Frank I got you, Pop. I got you. Because this time. This death. You will die in my arms. And I'll never let go, Dad, I'll carry you everywhere, your shame and your heartbreak, your hopes and your failures. And then, Pop. And then. I will avenge you.

Charlie *struggles to speak.*

Frank I love you, Charlie Chan.

Charlie I love you, my son.

Charlie *dies.*

Frank *reverently folds his father's arms over his chest and gently closes his eyes.*

Frank Kathy. Hey Kath.

Kathy *sits up from where she was pretending to be a dead Linda.*

Kathy Yeah Frank.

Frank That's not my name anymore.
My name is Charles Francis Chan, Jr.
Son of Charlie Chan and the inheritor of a great shame.

Kathy Okay.

Frank So here's what I got for you, babe. I know what I gotta do now. My father and his father before him, they tried to find dignity on terms laid out by the world as it was, but that shit doesn't work.

Didn't work for them. For me. For us. And it won't work for our baby, either.

Kathy So then what does?

Frank Right? That's the trick, isn't it, babe? That's the trick. World don't change from hopes and dreams. It don't change from wishin' or talkin', it changes through action. Through revolution.

Because the world don't want to change! The world *works* for those who own it!

We've been kicked around. We've been ignored and humiliated in every chapter of our history in America, and we can't change that unless we *own* the suffering. Live inside it, accept it and understand *that's where we come from*. The children of Chan are children of shame.

So when the world kicks us in the face, we gotta kick the world right back.

And when the world ignores us we gotta get right up in its face and say:

Look at me.

I am Asian American.

We will be reborn, and if this world can't handle that then this world has gotta go.

See, we hafta be ready to destory. They gotta be afraid of us. That's the only answer, babe. They have to fear for their lives. The only way to stop racist shit from happening is to stop racist people, and the only way to stop racist people is if they're afraid. Of physical harm. Of violent death. By my hand.

Whaddya think about that, babe? How's that for a plan?

Kathy   It's a groovy plan, man.

Frank   I know it is, mama. So let's have this fuckin baby already. And we'll make him a warrior. We'll steal one of those VW buses and we'll paint it golden yellow, we'll put in there a crib and some war toys and an arsenal of weapons and pyrotechnic explosives reminiscent of ancient Chinese industry. We'll steal food and siphon gas and evade the law, we'll drive that van all over as we kill white racists and pave the road to a brand new world with the bones and hacked white flesh of every white racist person and institution we encounter, from California to the New York Island, like a Golden Yellow Black Panther Partridge Family.

Kathy   You're really on your way, aren't you, Charlie?

Frank   Yeah babe I think I am.

Kathy *stares down at her hands.*

Kathy   Well, so am I.

Frank   What's that mean.

Kathy   It means I hope you get what you want outta the war you're describing, Charlie, but I can't join your militant bus tour. At least not right now. Cause maybe you're right, maybe it's the best way to change things in this wide white world, but what if it's not?

All I know is I gotta listen to what's in my gut, and right now what's in my gut . . . is a little girl.

And there's stuff she needs. There's stuff she needs from the world but there's more she needs from me. She needs obstetrics and medical tests and stuff and scans or whatever, I don't even know what she needs but I know she needs it. And she can't get it in the theater of war.

Frank   Yeah but. I mean. What if. Um.

She gives a goodbye kiss.

Kathy   Send me a postcard from the battefield, baby.
Maybe we'll meet again in peacetime.

She starts to walk away.

Frank Wait though, where are you gonna go?

Kathy I'm going home, Charlie.

Frank Home? ...Where is that?

Kathy Canton, baby. I'm going to Canton, Ohio.

She exits.

Frank *is alone.*

Frank What's gonna happen to me, Monkey?

The **Monkey** *appears.*

Monkey You really wanna know?

Frank Yeah. Tell me the future, Monkey. Can you do that?

Monkey Course I can. I'm a monkey.

The future looks like this:

Nothing you do will ever matter.

You will forever search for ways to articulate your emptiness, and displacement. You will continue to try and reconcile the way you see yourself versus the way the world sees you.

You will continue to divide the world into the real and the fake. The authentic and the invented. And you will spend your life searching for the real. But at the end, Frank, you will understand that none of this was ever real. That none of this was ever fake either, for the things we invent might just be the realest thing we have.

But either way, it doesn't really matter.

The only thing that really matters, is the child.

What will that child invent in twenty, thirty, forty years?
What will this child know about where it comes from?
What will this child know about where it's going?

What will the world know about this child?

How will it see it?

How will it understand its history, its identity, its almond eyes and black hair, and what will that mean?

In 1980.

The year 2000.

2020.

Or beyond.

What kind of world will the world be then?

And what is that child gonna do about it?

End of play.

Postscript

A Postscript in 3 Hats

Peter Kim

I first came across Lloyd Suh's *Charles Francis Chan Jr.'s Exotic Oriental Murder Mystery* (lovingly referred to as *CHAN*) when I was working at NAATCO (National Asian American Theatre Company) as the Associate Producer back in 2014. In addition to producing the company's world premiere production in 2015 in NYC, I also originated the roles of ALFRED, CHUCK and the pivotal roles of COP and BARTENDER. Don't let the few lines these characters have fool you ... there's comedy gold in them hills! Then in 2017, my journey with this play continued when I directed a student thesis production at Princeton University.

Hat #1 aka Producer Hat

In 2008, NAATCO's Co-Founder and Actor-Manager Mia Katigbak, James Saito, and I were cast in Lloyd's play *American Hwangap* where we instantly became Lloyd fans. James suggested to Lloyd that he should adapt Agatha Christie's *Murder on the Orient Express* into a play and NAATCO should produce it. Mia was taken by the idea and *CHAN* became NAATCO's first ever commission. The play started out as an adaptation of that Agatha Christie novel but the royalties were gonna be astronomical so Lloyd had the clever idea to use *The Mysterious Affair at Styles* instead since it was in the public domain (love a pivot!). Serendipitously, it was that novel that first introduced the world-famous private detective, Hercule Poirot. This character was considered a foreigner (he's Belgian) to those around him at Styles Court in Essex, England ... sound similar to one of the characters in *CHAN*?

The script went through many iterations before it became the play you just read but you can still see these influences throughout it. Though I haven't spoken to Lloyd about this, I think a major influence on the play's transformation was his experience becoming a father (he had three kids over the course of writing *CHAN*). I see in the play themes of fatherhood and the anticipation/anxiety/apprehension of the questions a Korean American child might pose to their parents about how and whether or not they belong in this place called America.

This production received a *New York Times* Critic's Pick in large part due to the fearless and ridiculously skilled actors who were led by the relentlessly imaginative director Ed Sylvanus Iskandar. Our audiences appreciated (minus that one person who walked out during the "Orientals are more like robots" monologue) that the play sheds light on a part of American history that most don't know about and does so in a terrifyingly hilarious and non-preachy way. It allowed them to laugh at themselves but also question themselves, their expectations, and their assumptions about Asians in America.

Hat #2 aka Actor Hat

I kind of hate when actors talk about their "process" so I'll try to keep this short and not annoying. Having had the excellent fortune of working on many of Lloyd's plays in various stages of development, I feel somewhat equipped to opine on the matter, in particular about *CHAN*. First off, Lloyd tends to write in long sentences that often have tangential thoughts. There's a clear rhythm he sets out so it behooves you to honor it. I'm not saying to rush or go fast just for speed's sake, but Lloyd's pauses are intentional and often written in the script. It'll literally say, "Pause." This is, of course, something to build towards after figuring out who your character is and what they're fighting like gangbusters for. That said, keep it moving, sister!

Similar to Shakespeare, you gotta act on the line, make your argument and move with the twists and turns in the logic. Also, take BIG swings at physical and vocal transformation for these characters. They can take it and, in fact, demand it. On a more practical note, it'll help the audience keep track of all the characters of which there are many. Remember, everyone in this play plays multiple characters, even MONKEY who appears as JESUS at one point!

Hat #3 aka Director Hat

The Princeton student thesis production was the first time I ever directed a full-length play. Suzanne Agins, then a professor there and a dear colleague, had seen me in the NAATCO production and knew of my relationship with the play and Lloyd's work in general. She recommended me for the job and I'm forever grateful to her. Without her, I wouldn't have formed the bonds I continue to have with these students and the realization that I wanted to be a director. I must also give thanks to the fortuitous Kathy Zhao, who proposed the production as her senior thesis.

There was a unique bond between these students and the play. Though the play is set in 1967, the student actors felt a kinship to the college-aged characters who are trying to figure out their lives. Just as FRANK is grappling with his Asian American identity as a college student at a prestigious university, Kathy was undergoing similar struggles and ended up co-founding East West Theater, the first Asian American student theater group in Princeton University's history. Definitely, Life imitating Art and a fitting nod to the play's META-ness.

One significant difference between the professional and student productions was the age of the casts. The actors in the NAATCO production were in their 30s and 40s and the actors in the student production were in their late teens and early 20s. *CHAN* is solidly constructed that it works with the raw, chaotic charm of a student production or the razor sharp precision of a professional one. In addition to all the humor and bits (who doesn't love bits?!), the play provides rich acting opportunities for professional AAPI actors (plus one White actor) as well as a built-in access point for student theatre artists of Asian descent who might not see themselves represented in their theatre department's season programming.

Reflecting back on the two productions, we were in a kind of political golden age in 2015 and February 2017. President Obama was in office and the next President's term had only just begun. There was an optimism in the air, especially around race. Having lived through the pandemic and the anti-Asian violence instigated by the rhetoric about China from the administration under the 45th president, the play's suggestion of violence as a solution to racism speaks differently to me now:

> The only way to stop racist shit from happening is to stop racist people, and the only way to stop racist people is if they're afraid. Of physical harm. Of violent death. By my hand. . . . we'll drive that van all over as we kill white racists and pave the road to a brand new world with the bones and hacked white flesh of every white racist person and institution we encounter, from California to the New York Island, like a Golden Yellow Black Panther Partridge Family. (289)

Frank's reasoning had always seemed far-fetched to me, like he was grasping at straws. Yet now, I can empathize with where his desire comes from. I'm not proud of this but I am grateful to Lloyd for having articulated this sentiment.

Like all great plays, you find something new every time you read or work on it. I wonder and dream about what a production in 2025, the year 2030, 2050 or beyond would look like? What questions it would strive to ask and answer? Perhaps the final lines of the play sum it up best when Monkey asks, "What kind of world will the world be then? And what is that child gonna do about it?" (291)

Postscript for This Postscript

Having worked on the play as a producer, actor, and director, I want to leave you with some thoughts on what I hope may be helpful to your production. Do your homework. In addition to reading up on Agatha Christie and film noir, the characters, Frank Chan and Kathy Ching, are inspired by real life artists and activists, Frank Chin and Kathy Chang (aka Kathy Change) who were married in 1971. Chin attended University of California, Berkeley, in the 1960s and has been credited as a pioneer of the Asian American theatre. Reading about their lives, histories, and activism will benefit your understanding of the play tremendously. Remember, the play demands a wild imagination, tenacious play, and a full bleeding heart. A little optimism and kink mixed in wouldn't hurt either.

The Heart Sellers

Preface

Give Me Your Heart

Lucy Mae San Pablo Burns

Luna   . . . Coming to America. And at the end of the line it's like . . . in order to get in. To pass the gates, you know. They had to sell their hearts. . . . I imagine them saying okay sir papers look okay, now give me your heart, and then each by each these people they dig into their chest and they take out their heart and pass it over . . . . we're the heart sellers. It's us. Its our hearts, and we sell em away.

Lloyd Suh, The Heart Sellers

Lloyd Suh's *The Heart Sellers* imagines a friendship between two new immigrants, both wives to immigrant doctors who entered the United States through the Immigration and Nationality Act (INA) of 1965, also known as the Hart-Celler Act. While their husbands work, Jane, Korean, and Luna, Filipina, spend the American holiday Thanksgiving, together. Underscoring class status as constitutive of friendships and other intimate relations, Jane and Luna are folded into the category of "highly skilled, educated workers," even if they are dependents of the primary migrants. These are the contours of their immediate social circle. Set eight years after the passing of the Hart-Cellar Act, in 1973, this play focuses on the emergent relationship between two strangers as they sound out their anxieties and excitements about their new lives in a country foreign yet familiar.

Two strangers get together one night, and they rehearse unscripted roles. With each other, they become more than just wives to their doctor-husband. Both admit that they do not have many, or any, friends in America; they came with their husbands and must now figure out how to make a life in this new country. Each is an attachment to the primary migrant, the doctor-husband, who is also liminal to the state in a citizen-centric system. Of those immigrant workers and their attachments, theorist Lauren Berlant writes: "We know that just by existing, historically subordinated populations are deemed inconvenient to the privileged who made them so; the subordinated who are cast as a problem experience themselves as both necessary for and inconvenient to the production of power."[1] In a settler-colonial system that "sanctions some privileged individuals as microsovereigns," with the rest deemed "inconvenient"[2] (albeit unequally), can relations such as friendship even be possible? After all, intimacies are forged at this nexus of material and historical conditions.

The Hart-Celler Act, among others, has been noted to signal a shift from exclusionary American laws against immigrants and people of color to inclusionary and integrationist laws. The Hart-Cellar Act is celebrated as a reparative act that corrects the wrongs of restrictive and discriminatory immigration laws, such as the Page Act of 1875, the 1882 Chinese Exclusion Act, the Gentlemen's Agreement of 1907, the Asiatic Barred Zone/ The Immigration Act of 1917, the Immigration Act of 1924 (the Johnson-Reed Act), the

National Origin Act of 1929, the Tydings-McDuffie Act of 1934 (also known as the Philippine Independence Act), among others. Senator Philip Hart and Congressman Emanuel Celler, sponsors of the Immigration and Nationality Act, understood this law to be "liberalizing immigration rules" as it abolished the quota system based on national origins, prioritized family reunification, and shifted admission standards toward skills-based migration. Representative Celler, the co-author of this bill, understood INA as creating "equal opportunity for all peoples to reach this promised land." This class-based policy is often cited as significantly shaping contemporary Asian American communities.

Suh depicts migrant sociality anew in this drama about a friendship between two newly arrived immigrants who come to the United States through the Hart-Cellar Act. This play departs from previous representations (in historical accounts and creative works) of early migrant sociality that predominantly show homogeneous and homosocial migrant relations. Consequently, portrayals of migrant sociality have emphasized migrant ties as they are shaped in public spaces, including workplaces (sugar cane and pineapple plantations, agricultural fields, restaurants) and nightlife entertainment sites (taxi dancehalls, gambling halls, pool halls). Plantations, railroads, dance halls, and gambling halls have been generative sites to theorize homosocial and interethnic Asian migrant sociality of the first half of the twentieth century. Robust scholarship has been produced to understand the complexities of interethnic solidarity and alliance and multiethnic and interracial animosity, segregation, and competition. Notable dramatic works that explore migrant sociality include Genny Lim's *Bitter Cane*, Edward Sakamoto's Kamiya family trilogy, *The Taste of Kona Coffee, Manoa Valley,* and *The Life of the Land*, Lonnie Carter and Ralph Peña's adaptation of *The Romance of Magno Rubio*, David Henry Hwang's *The Dance and the Railroad* and *FOB*, and Sining Bayan's *Ti Mangyuna* and *Warbrides*.[3] Velina Hasu-Houston's *Tea* is an acclaimed play that imagines immigrant women's relationships. Set in midwest America in the 1950s, *Tea* dramatizes Japanese war brides whose lives are complexly intertwined, drawn together from their isolation in midwest America. The play emphasizes the individuality of the women, resisting the racist homogenization of those categorized as racially ethnically Asian and gendered as women in the United States.

Suh's *The Heart Sellers* shifts away from focusing on early twentieth-century migration to portray a defining moment in the formation of contemporary Asian American community. In this play, Jane's and Luna's encounter presents a hopeful beginning that maintains a skeptical distance from a successful life of assimilation through capital accumulation and seamless inclusion into American society. Throughout the Thanksgiving dinner, a national holiday repurposed as a coming together of strangers with native inhabitants acknowledging their copresence, Jane and Luna share their (bad) impressions of the social circles open to them as wives to newly recruited immigrant doctors. They commiserate about the constraints of heteronormativity bounding and binding those circles. They speak in past conditional tenses of lives they have already left and plan for alternate futures that lay a path committed to shared exploration and self-discovery. A conversation littered with affect and thoughts voiced and withheld, this interaction signals a different pathway to migrant self-imaginings and being with others, what novelist Elaine Castillo writes as "with-ing."[4]

In Luna's homophonic wordplay, turning Hart-Cellar into heart sellers, lies the profound and complex sense of migrants' loss and displacement. This homophonic paronomasia brilliantly articulates the cost of uprooting one's involuntary or voluntary life to begin another elsewhere. "Heart sellers" becomes a category that more accurately identifies their status as migrants recruited to "contribute most to this country—to its growth, to its strength, to its spirit."[5] This sound-play on words allows Luna and Jane to articulate how states and patriarchal systems articulate them.[6] It also conveys their profound grasp and insight into their experience as newly-arrived migrants.

Hart-Celler Act, the Formation of Contemporary Asian America, and Dictatorships:

President Lyndon Johnson, in his speech during the Hart-Celler Act signing ceremony, said: "This is not a revolutionary bill. It does not affect the lives of millions. It will not reshape the structure of our daily lives or add, importantly, to either our wealth or our power . . . . Yet it is still one of the most important acts of this Congress and of this administration. For it does repair a very deep and painful flaw in the fabric of American justice. It corrects a cruel and enduring wrong in the conduct of the American Nation."[7] The "enduring wrong" refers to the Immigration Act of 1924 that favored migration from western and northern European countries. Also known as the 1924 Johnson-Reed Act, this law arguably preserved the favored racial homogeneity.[8] "In 1965, whites of European descent comprised 84 percent of the U.S. population, while Hispanics accounted for 4 percent and Asians for less than 1 percent. Fifty years on, 62 percent of the U.S. population is white, 18 percent is Hispanic, and 6 percent is Asian."[9]

What have historians, politicians, and immigration scholars attributed to this immigration reform policy described to have "changed the face of America"? Hart-Celler sponsors/authors understood their policy as "liberalizing immigration rules," intent on abolishing the national origins quota system and prioritizing family reunification. At its signing, this law was presented as a reparative and corrective act to an egregious flaw in American justice: "It corrects a cruel and enduring wrong in the conduct of the American nation." This legislation revises fundamental questions of who should be allowed to enter the country: "We must . . . lift, by legislation, the bars of discrimination against those who seek entry into our country, particularly those who have much-needed skills and those joining their families. . . . A nation that was built by the immigrants of all lands can ask those who now seek admission: 'What can you do for our country?' But we should not be asking: 'In what country were you born?'"[10] (Johnson 1965)

For the first ten years of Hart-Celler, the U.S. saw increased immigrants from Italy and Southern Europe. It was in the 1980s that the shift of arrivants began, with immigrants coming from Latin America, Asia, and Africa. Between 1980 and 1990, most of the millions who immigrated to the United States came from Latin America or Asia. Historian Erika Lee writes that Asia Americans "benefited" most from this legislation. It not only increased the population, but it also shaped who would comprise Asian America.

Between 1965 and 1985, 665,000 Filipinos entered the U.S. The Philippines became among, if not the top-sending, the most significant number of professional immigrants to the U.S. (contrasting to manual laborers of the early 20th century). Nurses, doctors, and other medical personnel "to help alleviate the country's medical personnel shortage, especially in inner cities and rural areas. Twenty-five thousand nurses during this period."[11] The Hart-Celler Act also became a primary legal pathway to reunite families. For journalist Jon Melegrito, this law "enabled millions of Filipinos to make the United States their new home."[12] He also frames the law as "abolishing discriminatory national origin quotas and ushered in a time of tolerance and acceptance."[13]

Sociologists Hyun Sook Kim and Pyong Gap Min recognize the 1965 law as having the most significant effect on what would become the Korean American community. While the first significant wave began with the arrival of 102 Korean immigrants in Hawai'i, to work on pineapple and sugar plantations, on January 13, 1903, "the Korean American community before 1965 was insignificant in terms of population size." (Kim and Min 1992, 121).[14] Researching the characteristics and patterns of post-1965 immigration, Kim and Min point out that "female immigrants outnumbered male immigrants in all the years, although the sex imbalance in favor of female immigrants has been substantially moderated during recent years. This trend makes a good contrast with the earlier Korean immigrants at the turn of the century, who consisted mainly of young men" (128).

Was Hart-Celler truly liberatory? Essayist Kevin Hu expresses concern on "[t]he way we recollect and make meaning of the 1965 Immigration Act," with such a heavy focus "on the liberation of Asians from decades of exclusion that it renders invisible the furtive transferral of illegality to Mexican Americans. Whereas Mexican migrants were relatively free to move before 1965, the caps implemented by this law—limitations that were grossly incommensurate to the flow of immigration at that time—changed that."[15] For the first time in U.S. immigration history, countries from the Western Hemisphere were capped. While the law was championed as a civil rights victory for Asian Americans, Hu would argue instead that "it is the genesis of the concept of the illegal immigrant." In *Impossible Subjects: Illegal Aliens and the Making of Modern America*, historian Mae Ngai argues that the 1924 immigration law created the "illegal alien" as someone whose inclusion within the nation was "simultaneously a social reality and a legal impossibility." (2004)[16]

Critical Ethnic Studies scholar Dylan Rodriguez also challenges the celebratory and liberatory perception of Hart-Celler read against Daniel Moynihan's "The Negro Family: The Case for National Action," an influential report released in 1965. In the Hart-Celler Act and the Moynihan Report, the formation and structure of "family" played a central role. Hart-Celler sought to reunite families across seas and national borders, reinforcing heterosexual and heteronormative filial configurations. The Moynihan report presented by the U.S. Department of Labor argued that the decline of the Black nuclear family would significantly impede African Americans' progress toward economic and social equality. Arguably, "family" is an enduring category from the founding narratives of the American nation to its various U.S. immigration policies, and as a way to restore the health of the U.S. nation following war times.[17]

Philippine and South Korean dictatorial rule and labor export policies would send thousands of Filipinx and Koreans out of their countries to work elsewhere.[18] Authoritarian leaders turned full-blown dictators, President Ferdinand E. Marcos, Jr and President Park Chung Hee implemented overseas labor as part of their national development initiatives. The Korea Overseas Development Corporation (KODC), with the slogan "Planting Korea's Seeds Across the World," was established on June 10, 1965. Marcos signed Presidential Decree No. 442, the Philippine Labor Code, on May 1, 1974. These labor-exporting policies were designed to rescue the economy (and an alternative to the agricultural sector deemed "unsustainable"). Each regime identified communism as the culprit that threatened their society's demise, justifying their turn to martial rule. To this point, Ethnic and Cultural Studies scholar Crystal Baik comments on the limitation of citing the 1965 law as a single enabling factor for Korean migration to the U.S. during this period: "While the 1965 Immigration and Nationality Act 'opened' the doors of American immigration to millions of people, South Korean military dictatorial rule and the imminent threat of rekindled warfare also influenced Korean emigration. As a result, official U.S. immigration categories do not necessarily capture the complex conditions informing Koreans' decisions to migrate to the United States."[19]

Homophonic Wordplay, Strangers, and Copresence

Luna's homophonic wordplay, turning Hart-Cellar into an "imaginary sad story" of immigrants as heart sellers, translates the wrenching sacrifices and loss among immigrants as they build their lives in a new country. "You're right this is a very bad story" (329), Jane responds in a manner that may seem pithy. Interrupting with directness, perhaps delivered in a deadpan register, Jane redirects what could have become a melodramatic pity party and an evening of wallowing.[20] Suh audiates new immigrant English in Jane's and Luna's speech, how accented and English spoken by non-native English speakers from Korea and the Philippines may look in literary form. Hugging the edge of infantilization, incomprehensibility, and unintelligible exchange in this attempt to express immigrant Englishes, Suh challenges us to appreciate the literary merits of these imagined expressions and articulations. As the characters work through and try to understand each other, we (the reader and the audience) struggle with them as they "test out whether being open to knowing and being known, or just occupying the space with other people, will be worth the trouble" (Berlant 2022, 8).

Awkwardness, nervous talk, oversharing, pauses, and incomplete thoughts eventually deepen into a night of profound bonding. Luna and Jane express themselves differently. Luna talks. A lot. It may appear as if her command of English is stronger than Jane's, although her verbosity is a sign of anxiety about being with someone she does not know. At the beginning of the night, Jane would respond in one word, even just a sound. Or not respond at all. They echo each other, drop a subject, leave a topic, pause while in thought, and attempt to repeat themselves to communicate. After all, as Berlant writes, "When it comes to living in proximity, there is no such thing as passivity. Adjustment is a constant action: the grinding of the wheels of awkwardness and the bargaining with life's infrastructures" (9). Amid incomplete conversations and passing comments, of which their intended recipient may not fully understand the meaning, Jane and Luna give in and build through resonances and resounding.

Resonances and a sense of self in relation to another, "with-ing," form and make up the dynamics of their receptivity. Jane and Luna are playful with one another and test boundaries while slowly releasing what they have held in tension and suppressed to proceed with their new life. They have never cooked a turkey, celebrated Thanksgiving, much less hosted a dinner in honor of this holiday. They giggle about never having seen a penis aside from their husband's; thus, they plan an outing to a "porno movie" to remedy this. Details of their previous lives are not simply and easily divulged. They come out in pieces, chunks, fragments. They hesitate to share them. They assume the other can imagine the rest of the story, relying on unstated similarities of experiencing imperial histories and dictatorships of their countries of origin. They restrain their sadness, even as they express what and who they miss from their previous lives.

The play closes on a promise:

We make plan together. For what we do next tomorrow.
Silence.
Lingers.
End of play. (345)

Suh ends the play in abeyance, in the not-yet moment, leaving us with anticipatory hope. This budding friendship allows Jane and Luna to envision a different tomorrow. Although *not yet* is also something that has yet to happen. Will this friendship continue? Will they begin to assimilate, honor, and host "traditional" Thanksgiving holiday dinners? What, individually and together, may Jane and Luna become? Perhaps the potential of their homophonic play, one through which they could articulate how the states and patriarchal systems articulate them, will be sustained as an active choice to refuse to buy into what America has to sell.

Notes

1 Lauren Berlant, *On the Inconvenience of Other People* (Durham, NC: Duke University Press, 2022), 4.
2 Lauren Berlant, *On the Inconvenience of Other People* (Durham, NC: Duke University Press, 2022), 4.
3 Collection editor Christine Mok adds that plays about Japanese American relocation and incarceration camps during World War II, as forms of forced migration, might add another layer to theorizing intimacy in a deeply stratified and unequal society.
4 Elaine B. Castillo. *America is Not the Heart*. New York: Penguin Books, 2018, 109.
5 Lyndon B Johnson, "Remarks on Signing The Immigration Act of 1965." October 3, 1965. *Learning For Justice*. Accessed on November 14, 2023. https://www.learningforjustice.org/classroom-resources/texts/remarks-on-signing-the-immigration-act-of-1965.
6 Allan Isaac, *American Tropics: Articulating Filipino America* (Minneapolis: University of Minnesota Press, 2006).
7 Johnson, "Remarks on Signing The Immigration Act of 1965." October 3, 1965. *Learning For Justice*. Accessed on November 14, 2023.
8 Jia Lynn Yang's *One Mighty and Irresistible Tide: The Epic Struggle Over American Immigration, 1924–1965*, surmises that with the Immigration Act of 1924: "Congress instituted a system of ethnic quotas so stringent that it choked off large-scale immigration for decades, sharply curtailing arrivals from southern and eastern Europe and outright banning those from nearly all of Asia." Accessed February 4, 2024. Jia Lynn Yang, *One Mighty and Irresistible Tide: The Epic Struggle Over American Immigration, 1924–1965* (NY: W.W. Norton, 2020).

9   Muzaffar Chishti, Faye Hipsman, and Isabel Ball. "Fifty Years On, the 1965 Immigration and Nationality Act Continues to Reshape the United States." MPI: Migration Policy Institute. October 15, 2015. https://www.migrationpolicy.org/article/fifty-years-1965-immigration-and-nationality-act-continues-reshape-united-states
10 Lyndon B Johnson, "Remarks on Signing The Immigration Act of 1965." October 3, 1965. *Learning For Justice.* Accessed on November 14, 2023.
11 Aaron Talley and Dr. Sarah-SoonLing Blackburn, "The Immigration and Nationality Act of 1965 | Asian Americans." PBS Learning Media. 2022. https://ca.pbslearningmedia.org/resource/the-immigration-and-nationality-act-1965-video/asian-americans/. Accessed November 7, 2023.
12 Jon Melegrito, "Fil-Ams reflect on impact of 1965 U.S. immigration reform law." Inquirer.net. October 31, 2015. https://globalnation.inquirer.net/130175/fil-ams-reflect-on-impact-of-1965-u-s-immigration-reform-law#ixzz8IEimIuIV. Accessed November 7, 2023.
13 Jon Melegrito, "Fil-Ams reflect on impact of 1965 U.S. immigration reform law." Inquirer.net. October 31, 2015. https://globalnation.inquirer.net/130175/fil-ams-reflect-on-impact-of-1965-u-s-immigration-reform-law#ixzz8IEimIuIV. Accessed November 7, 2023.
14 Hyun Sook Kim and Pyong Gap Min, "The Post-1965 Korean Immigrants: Their Characteristics and Settlement Patterns." *Korea Journal of Population and Development.* Volume 21, Number 2, December 1992. 121–143.
15 Kevin Hu, "Seeing the Transfer of Exclusion in the 1965 Immigration Act: Asian Americans for Collective Liberation," *The Margins*, October 2020. https://aaww.org/seeing-the-transfer-of-exclusion-in-the-1965-immigration-act/ Accessed on November 7, 2023.
16 Mae Ngai, *Impossible Subjects: Illegal Aliens and the Making of Modern America* (Princeton, NJ: Princeton University Press, 2014).
17 Anna Creadick, *Perfectly Average, the Pursuit of Normality in Postwar America* (Amherst: University of Massachusetts Press, 2010).
18 These labor policies that continue to send Koreans and Filipinx laboring bodies worldwide call for a transnational analysis of Asian migrations elsewheres (ie Koreans in Germany, Argentina; Filipinx in Saudi Arabia, occupied Palestine), and thus a wider geography of immigration.
19 Crystal Mun-Hye Baik, "Korean Immigration to the United States After World War II." *Oxford Research Encyclopedia.* January 25, 2019. https://oxfordre.com/americanhistory/display/10.1093/acrefore/9780199329175.001.0001/acrefore-9780199329175-e-535.
20 For more on refusing to wallow, see Allan P. Isaac, "In a Precarious Time and Place: The Refusal to Wallow and Other Migratory Temporal Investments in *Care Divas, the Musical*." *Journal of Asian American Studies 19*(1), 5–24. https://doi.org/10.1353/jaas.2016.0007. Isaac develops their theory of refusal to wallow through the musical *Care Divas*, that centers on Filipinx migrant labor in occupied Palestine.

References

Baik, Crystal Mun-Hye. "Korean Immigration to the United States After World War II." *Oxford Research Encyclopedia.* January 25, 2019.
Berlant, Lauren. *On the Inconvenience of Other People*. Durham, NC: Duke University Press, 2022.
Castillo, Elaine B. *America is Not the Heart*. New York: Penguin Books, 2018.
Chishti, Muzaffar, Faye Hipsman, and Isabel Ball. "Fifty Years On, the 1965 Immigration and Nationality Act Continues to Reshape the United States." MPI: Migration Policy Institute.

October 15, 2015. https://www.migrationpolicy.org/article/fifty-years-1965-immigration-and-nationality-act-continues-reshape-united-states

Creadick, Anna. *Perfectly Average, the Pursuit of Normality in Postwar America.* Amherst: University of Massachusetts Press, 2010.

Hu, Kevin. "Seeing the Transfer of Exclusion in the 1965 Immigration Act: Asian Americans for Collective Liberation." *The Margins*, October 2020. https://aaww.org/seeing-the-transfer-of-exclusion-in-the-1965-immigration-act/

Isaac, Allan P. *American Tropics: Articulating Filipino America.* Minneapolis: University of Minnesota Press, 2006.

Isaac, Allan P. "In a Precarious Time and Place: The Refusal to Wallow and Other Migratory Temporal Investments in *Care Divas, the Musical*." *Journal of Asian American Studies* 19, no. 1: 5–24.

Johnson, Lyndon B. "Remarks on Signing The Immigration Act of 1965." October 3, 1965. *Learning For Justice.* Accessed on November 14, 2023. https://www.learningforjustice.org/classroom-resources/texts/remarks-on-signing-the-immigration-act-of-1965.

Kim, Hyun Sook and Pyong Gap Min, "The Post-1965 Korean Immigrants: Their Characteristics and Settlement Patterns." *Korea Journal of Population and Development.* Volume 21, Number 2, December 1992. 121–143.

Melegrito, Jon. "Fil-Ams reflect on impact of 1965 U.S. immigration reform law." Inquirer.net. October 31, 2015. https://globalnation.inquirer.net/130175/fil-ams-reflect-on-impact-of-1965-u-s-immigration-reform-law#ixzz8IEimIuIV. Accessed November 7, 2023.

Ngai, Mae. *Impossible Subjects: Illegal Aliens and the Making of Modern America.* Princeton, NJ: Princeton University Press, 2014.

Talley Aaron and Dr. Sarah-SoonLing Blackburn, "The Immigration and Nationality Act of 1965 | Asian Americans." PBS Learning Media. 2022. https://ca.pbslearningmedia.org/resource/the-immigration-and-nationality-act-1965-video/asian-americans/. Accessed November 7, 2023.

Yang, Jia Lynn. *One Mighty and Irresistible Tide: The Epic Struggle Over American Immigration, 1924–1965.* NY: W.W. Norton, 2020.

The Heart Sellers received its World Premiere production at Milwaukee Repertory Theater (Mark Clements, Artistic Director; Chad Bauman, Executive Director) from February 7 to March 19, 2023. The cast was as follows:

Luna	Nicole Javier
Jane	Narea Kang
Director	Jennifer Chang
Set Designer	Tanya Orellana
Costume Designer	Anthony Tran
Lighting Designer	Noele Stollmack
Sound Designer	Sun Hee Kil
Dramaturg	Christine Mok
Voice and Dialect Coach	Joy Lanceta Coronel
Assistant Director	Emily Newmark
Production Stage Manager	Jade Bruno

The Heart Sellers had its East Coast premiere at The Huntington Theatre Company (Loretta Greco, Artistic Director), from November 21 to December 23, 2023. The cast was as follows:

Luna	Jenna Agbayani
Jane	Juyeon Song
Director	May Adrales
Set and Costume Designer	Junghyun Georgia Lee
Lighting Designer	Kat C. Zhou
Music and Sound Designer	Fabian Obispo
Dramaturg	Christine Mok
Voice and Dialect Coach	Joy Lanceta Coronel
Assistant Director	Jenny S. Lee
Production Stage Manager	Roxanna Khan

The Heart Sellers was commissioned and developed by Milwaukee Repertory Theater as part of the John (Jack) D. Lewis New Play Development Program.

Characters

Luna. Luningning Ignacia Mangahas de la Rosario Bustos, 23, Filipina, female
Jane. Hong Jae Ha, 23, Korean, female

Setting

Luna's apartment, in a mid-sized US city.
Early evening, Thanksgiving day.
November 22, 1973.

Notes

On casting: These roles are to be performed by Asian or AAPI actors only. Further to this, because language of origin is a critical component of the play, it is essential to cast actors with specific understanding and experience with the respective dialects of the characters.

The sun is starting to set. Streaks of fading light through curtains.

An underfurnished apartment. Kitchen, living room, bedroom all occupy the same space; a bathroom just off. There is not much in the way of decoration.

The front door opens as **Luna** *enters with a single shopping bag. She wears an enormous winter coat.*

Luna   . . . but for real no kidding, I think maybe you're probably the first person we've ever had come to our apartment since we moved in, that is if you don't count people like our landlady or plumber, yes we had to have the plumber come up once but don't worry it's fixed, anyway don't count that, so for real no kidding you're the first one since we moved in, which I guess it's only been since the semester started but that's still a long time to go without visitors, huh? Back home boy it wasn't even weird to come home and somehow there's some people there you've never seen before, no kidding!, funny how different everything is, here you are just one person and it feels somehow super monumental! that you're coming into my apartment!

Jane *stands in the entryway. She wears an enormous winter coat, identical to* **Luna***'s.*

You coming in, yeah?

Jane   Mm.

She doesn't enter, but looks around the apartment.

Luna   Yeah okay, so come on in!

Luna *goes to put the shopping bag on the counter.*

Sorry sorry it's so messy!

Jane   No no not messy.

Jane *enters, tentatively. She leaves her coat on, while* **Luna** *throws hers off and just chucks it on the floor; hat and gloves too, as she moves to warm her hands on a radiator.*

Luna   Ha! You're right, I guess we'd have to have things to mess up to make a mess, and we don't have anything! So you're right its not so messy but dusty I guess? American dust is funny, it bothers me more than dust back home. Does that make sense? Have you noticed anything different about the dust?

Jane   Hm?

Luna   The dust here. Is different than the dust in Korea?

Jane   Is it?

Luna   Yeah?

Jane It is?

Luna Oh, I don't know, I'm asking you is it!?

Silence.

Jane What?

Luna Never mind! Ha! It's not important! Just small talk. Very small talk, ha? Small and insignificant. I'm nervous. This is wacky doodle. I don't have a lot of friends. It was impulsive. You must think I'm impulsive, ha? Too much so. I don't just ask strangers in the supermarket to come up to my apartment. I don't! Ever! You must think I'm goofy or something. My husband, he's definitely gonna think I'm goofy. Oh well. He's not here! You are! So I'm not the only one impulsive person. You said yes! You came up. To a stranger's apartment. So you're goofy too! Or neither one of us is goofy? Maybe it's normal, this kind of thing? Am I talking too much? I'm talking too much. Tell me if I talk too much, ha? Anyway I saw you and I was like aaah!, there's another one! Ha! In da empty supermarket on Thanksgiving! Looking at turkeys! Alone. And noticing turkeys are big. Too big to eat alone. I'm definitely talking too much. I'm glad you're here. Not to put too much pressure on this or anything. No pressure. Very casual, yes? No big deal, huh? Super cool.

Jane Mm.

Luna Can I take your coat?

Jane Coat?

Luna Yes, I can take it for you?

Jane Take it?

Luna Yes, I can – hang it up for you?

Jane Oh! Yes, yes. Um, okay.

Jane *takes off her coat,* **Luna** *helps.*

She hangs it nicely.

Luna So funny you and me we have the same same coat!

Jane Ha ha, yes, same.

Luna Itsa good coat, right?

Jane Mm. Warm.

Luna K Mart?

Jane What?

Luna I got mine at K Mart here, did you get yours same?

Jane Yes, K Mart.

Luna I love K Mart! So much things! Sometimes I go even when I don't have nothing I need to buy, I like to just look at all the things there on display like I'm at a museum, you know? Just to study all the like whatsit, the artifacts of this strange place, their jewelry and their children's toys and their decorations and things.

Silence.

Jane   Yes, K Mart.

Luna   I'm talking too much! Relax! Stay awhile!

She gestures towards the sofa.

Please have a scat! Lemme just

The only clutter in the apartment is on the sofa; she clears it.

Jane *sits.*

Luna *says the rest as she runs around the apartment to close the front door, pick up her hat and gloves, hang her own coat, move the clutter, and start to the kitchen.*

Luna   I'm so glad you're here for this, I don't even like American holidays, they're strange; like how they do Halloween, why do they do that? With these children dressed like monsters banging on your door; *why*?, but this one seems important somehow? I like the sound of it, Thanksgiving! Thanks! Giving! This seems worth it to celebrate, right?, but my husband has to work because they assume oh he's not from here he doesn't care about holidays! and since he's just a first year resident, he's gotta do whatever they say, I don't have to tell you this, you know all about it, ha? so here I am alone in the apartment all by myself, some holiday!

Jane   Mm.

Luna   So! Anyway what kinda things do you like to do, huh? Around town?

Jane   Um.

Luna   I think we've been here kinda the same time right? Semester start September, since September?

Jane   Mm, September yes.

Luna   I want to explore the city but they say don't go out alone at night so I haven't been lotsa places yet, also I dunno how to drive maybe I'll learn driving yeah?, can you imagine it me driving? I think I saw a bowling alley but I've never been bowling do you think it's fun? Have you been bowling before?

Jane   No.

Luna   Yeah me either. Are you hungry? You must be hungry! This is so embarrassing but we don't have any good snacks to offer, I was supposed to buy things at the grocery, I had a list, my husband he's gonna be surprised that instead of the list I got this turkey!

From the shopping bag, she reveals a giant turkey.

Do you like Ritz crackers? We have this, Easy Cheese, do you know this? Kinda strange. My husband it's his favorite. We have Cheetos, you like Cheetos?

Jane Oh, um. No thank you?

Luna *prepares and sets out a sad little spread.*

Luna I'm so sorry I'm so unprepared! I'm just gonna leave this out, try the Ritz they're pretty good, I know it's not much, we have a few other things here but probably we'll need them for the turkey, right? WAIT! Do you know how to cook turkey? I'm so foolish a girl, I don't know how to cook this thing do you?

Jane Yes.

Luna Wait really you do? No you don't.

Jane Yes, I do yes.

Luna You know how to cook Thanksgiving Turkey?

Jane Mm. Because Julia Child.

Silence.

Luna Wait really?

Jane Julia Child, yes. I watch, all the time I watch.

Luna You watch Julia Child all the time?

Jane Not just Julia Child, everything television, I watch. All day. Price is Right. Young and the Restless, Sanford and Son, Walter Cronkite, Archie Bunker, Sesame Street. Husband work. No friends. So. I am just same like you.

Luna Oh my goodness I have never been so happy!

Jane Can I look your cabinet?

Luna Huh?

Jane Julia Child use not too much ingredient but we see what here yes, or no?

Luna Of course! Yes! What do we need?

Jane Butter

Luna Yes! butter in the prigider

Jane Oil salt pepper

Luna Of course here

Jane Onion, celery, garlic?

Luna Ha! do not try and joke me I am Filipino!

Jane Eggs

Luna Uh-oh no eggs

Jane   Eggs so what, not important

Luna   Oh good.

Jane   Hmmm, white bread?

Luna   White bread why?

Jane   White bread forget it.

Luna   Side dish?

Jane   Mm, side dish.

Luna   Smash potato?

Jane   You have potato?

Luna   I have yams?

Jane   You have yams?!

Luna   You like yams?

Jane   I like yams!

Luna   I HAVE YAMS!!

Jane   Oh good so good!

Luna   Thanks! Giving!

Jane   Okay now. Preheat oven.

Luna   How many.

Jane   Um 400?

Luna   400 sure.

Jane *starts preparing stuff but stops as she gets to the turkey.*

Jane   Wait!

Luna   What.

Jane   Turkey frozen.

She knocks on the turkey, which is indeed audibly frozen.

Silence.

Luna   Is that bad?

Jane   Mmmm not good.

Luna   Is it needs to thaw?

Silence. **Jane** *considers. Perhaps she looks at her watch.*

Jane   No! So what?, gonna be fine!

Luna   Really?

Jane   Not perfect but is okay. Just cook more longer!

Luna   Really?

Jane   My mother, she say food? Always there is some way.

Luna   She's a good cook?

Jane   Mm. Best.

Luna   She makes turkey?

Jane   No, turkey no. But she live, you know, very poor, when I am born this is war time, have to eat whatever, so she teach me: okay, you have food, no matter perfect, just make some way, always there is way.

Luna   Wow.

Jane   I know everybody say this, their mother best cook but this is no, maybe their mother second place okay but my mother number one.

Luna   I would never say my mother is the best cook.

Jane   Ha!

Luna   But I lived with a big family, so many titas and lolas – aunties and grand-aunties, I mean—so we still had good food all the time, oh it's been so long!

Jane   Mm.

Silence.

Luna   I miss them.

Jane   Mm.

Silence.

Luna   Especially since it's a holiday. Even though it's not our holiday, you know, it seems silly, I could call and say Happy Thanksgiving but they'd say what is that?, why you waste money long distance silly girl, this is ordinary Thursday, ha? so it's funny to miss them when I know they don't miss me the same.

Silence.

Jane   Yes, they miss. Same. Of course they miss same.

Silence.

Luna   What does your. Do your parents, they

Jane   Mm no, my parents they . . . they die.

Luna   I'm so sorry.

Jane   My brother, I have one brother, so yes. He have nice wife, kids, such funny kids, so yes I miss too.

Luna I know it's . . . in Korea these days. It's a hard time, right?

Jane Mm.

Luna Also in the Philippines too. Hard times everywhere.

Jane You know Korea?

Luna Oh no I've never been there, no, but I follow along. I know they did something similar, military coup, right?

Jane Military coup, yes.

Luna So scary. News is always so scary I guess, but still I like to read about it. I just like to know. I go to the library here, the university library and believe it or not they have newspapers from everywhere, I betcha they have em from Korea too, I read the ones from Manila sometimes. And my family whenever I call, even though I can't call a lot it's expensive, I don't have to tell you that, they tell me things too.

Jane Mm.

Luna About Marcos you know.

Jane Marcos, mm.

Silence.

Luna But we don't have to talk about that!

Jane In Korea, yes is bad time. But when I am little was bad time too, so. Cannot say which one is worser time. And you know, here? America. America is . . .

Luna Bad time too.

Jane Yes.

Silence.

Luna Hey hey do you like to ah . . . you know, drinky drinky?

Jane Drink?

Luna I have wine.

Jane's face lights up. But:

Jane Ah! No, I should. No.

Luna Are you sure? It's not fancy fancy wine but.

Silence.

Jane Hee hee ya, little bit okay.

*They giggle as **Luna** prepares wine in novelty coffee mugs.*

Luna We don't have proper proper wine glasses but these are cute, right?

Jane Mm.

Luna Cheers?

Jane Cheers!

Luna To Thanksgiving?

Jane To Thanksgiving.

They drink.

Jane Wow.

Luna Do you don't drink much?

Jane No no, my husband, no.

Luna He's not a drinker?

Jane No he is yes drinker. Yes. But.

Luna Oh.

Jane Is not something . . .

Luna Ugh I know what you mean. My husband he drinks too, but yes it's one of those things, huh? That a good wife's not supposed to do.

Jane Mm.

They drink.

Luna You said he has late night?

Jane Mm yes, he say gonna come home around 3 o'clock morning.

Luna Ah.

Jane Your husband?

Luna All night, he has to stay until 6.

Jane Wow.

Luna Maybe they'll see each other?

Jane Maybe!

Luna Maybe they'll become best friends!

Jane Ha! Yes.
But probably no.

Luna Oh.

Jane Just because, my husband, you know, he is . . . he is kind of shy.

Luna So is mine!

Jane Really?

Luna I mean at least over here he is, back in Philippines he wasn't but you know, over here it's different.

Jane Mm.

Luna So I can't imagine he'd ever start a conversation with someone, you know? A casual conversation. On his own.

Jane Yes, true, my husband same way.

Luna I mean I can't blame him, after all it's hard to make friends.

Silence.

Jane Yes.

They drink.

Luna Say do you have any pets?

Jane Pets?

Luna Back in the Philippines I had a dog called Paco, he was like my best friend in the whole world. I've been thinking about getting a dog, have you thought about it?

Jane Oh no, me no I don't like.

Luna You don't like dogs?

Jane I don't like pick up the poop.

Luna Ha! Yeah I can see that, funny I don't mind it? What about cats, do you like cats?

Jane Cats okay.

Luna Yeah maybe I'll get a cat. I like dogs better but I look at this apartment and I think boy Paco wouldn't like it here, compared to home? This maybe isn't the best kind of life for a dog, living in an apartment, always on a leash. I don't think Paco ever wore a leash even once in his whole life. And he's been a part of our family since I was a little girl. He's super old now, he must like 16 or 17 at least. When I left, he was the last person I said goodbye to. Or I guess he's not a person but you know what I mean. And I realized boy this dog is so old, probably he's gonna . . . you know, probably he's gonna die soon.

Jane Oh.

Luna And probably I won't be there when he does.

Silence.

Why am I saying this?! Hoy I'm such a drag! I'm sorry sorry!, I'll shut up now, let's have more wine. More wine?

Jane No no no, oh no, I am not using to drink so. No, my face it – you see, turning red already.

Luna Stop it your face looks great.

Jane Ha no, I have to get good rest, when husband come home cannot be ah, you know, stinky. Make breakfast, long time in hospital, need to be yes, responsibility.

Silence.

Luna Okay.

Jane But you can drink! Drink more! Drink many! I like.

Silence.

Luna Is Jane your real name?

Jane What?

Luna Jane. That's not your real name right, what's your real name I wanna know.

Jane Mm, yes my name is Jae Ha. Hong Jae Ha.

Luna Hong Jae Ha.

Jane Change to Jane. For easier, for American, Jane Hong.

Luna Why Jane?

Jane Because Jane Fonda.

Luna Shut up.

Jane Ha! No, serious. Jane Fonda I like Jane Fonda.

Luna Everybody likes Jane Fonda.

Jane Jane sound almost like Jae Ha so Jane Fonda Jane Hong.

Luna That's amazing.

Jane Your name always Luna?

Luna Always? Kinda, ha, I am Luningning so when I'm a kid everybody calls me Nening or Ning Ning, my friends call me Luna, my husband calls me Lulu sometimes (and I only like it sometimes), but officially yes I am Luningning. Luningning Ignacia Mangahas de la Rosario Bustos.

Jane Oh my God.

Luna I know. Luningning Ignacia Mangahas de la Rosario Bustos, Luningning Ignacia because two names, confirmation name Ignacia, my mother's last name Mangahas and my dad's name de la Rosario and my husband he is Bustos. Aurelio Bustos.

Jane Aureli?

Luna Aurelio, don't worry you don't have to try and pronounce it, people just call him Leo.

Jane This also hard for to say.

Luna Leo and Luna! Lulu and Leo! Cute, ha? What's your husband's name?

Jane Young Chul.

Luna Oh! Okay.

Jane Mm.

Silence.

Luna   Hoy, do you want to lookit my photo album?

Jane   Photo?

Luna   Don't worry it's not big, film it's expensive I don't have to tell you that.

Jane   Mm.

Luna *gets a photo album, pours herself another glass of wine.*

Luna   Here's from our wedding see.

Jane   Mm, handsome.

Luna   He shaved the moustache.

Jane   Okay.

Luna   This is when we went to Disneyland.

Jane   Disneyland!

Luna   Yes we went to Disneyland! Our honeymoon. Sorta kinda. We got married in the Philippines just before we came to America, so he said pick a place, anyplace, we will go early, of course I said Disneyland!

Jane   Wow.

Luna   I know! But of course I mean we didn't go inside, tickets are expensive I don't have to tell you that, but anyway we got to be there! Right there, you know? Just outside of everything, and we could see almost all of it. The train and the hotel, the big mountain and the water slide, for real, we could almost see everything.

Silence.

Jane   Mm.

Luna   Anyway this one is my father, he still has the moustache. My mother. My brother. Look there's Paco! See him?

Jane   Ah Paco!, good Paco.

Luna   This one's my other brother. My sisters with my cousins blah blah blah this is making me sad and missing my family too much let's talk about something else.

She puts the book away.

Jane   You have nice family.

Luna   Too many moustaches.

They laugh.

How did you and your husband meet?

Jane   Oh no exciting story. My brother knows, they meet when together in Army? My brother he say hey, this boy probably he is going to be doctor, go for school to America. You should meet.

Luna And so you met.

Jane And so we marry.

Silence.

Luna Oh! You must have been . . .

Silence.

I mean, you must have . . . To come to America. That your brother would . . . to say, he's going to go to America, this is. This makes him . . .

Jane Hm?

Luna A good person to marry.

Jane Yes.

Silence.

Luna He must have had a lot of choices then.

Jane Mm.

Luna But he picked you.

Jane Hm. Yes.

Silence.

Your husband, same?

Luna *nods her head.*

Luna So we're the lucky ones.

Jane Mm.

Silence.

Luna Do you ever . . . no, never mind.

Jane What?

Luna Nothing, no. I just.
Except yes, actually yes, I was gonna ask:
Do you ever wonder.
What did I do, did I really did that? Like I look at my husband and I know I married him because he . . . because I wanted to. But. Like if you met someone who didn't have . . . let's say a job or a future you'd say no thank you sir but if that same person somehow then they got a job and a future you'd maybe give him a chance?, and when you give him a chance then bam one day you look at him and say yeah okay chance worked out, I can see it okay let's get married and stuff, well even if you didn't get married to the guy *because* of the job and the future you still kinda back of your mind know those things . . . they mattered?

Silence.

And so you can't tell yourself anymore they don't matter?

Silence.

Jane   What?

Silence.

Luna   Ha! Nothing, I just. You're right I'm silly, it's just a silly . . .
But anyway hey.
Is it . . . is it what you expected?

Jane *laughs.*

Then **Luna** *laughs.*

Jane *laughs louder.*

They laugh and laugh and laugh.

They can't stop laughing.

This time, **Jane** *pours herself another glass of wine.*

They drink.

Eventually they stop laughing.

What *did* you expect?

Silence.

Jane   American GI in Korea, you know . . . so much American GI in Korea, and they have chocolate? Little chocolate, they carry. Little candy piece. Whenever see children, give candy, when I am small girl this – Wow. I never see this. So special taste, I think is like magic. You know?

Luna   Yeah.

Jane   I am no stupid, I know come to America, this will not be same like magic, I know this will be hard time, husband work hard so important, stay home, English bad, I know this. But.

Luna   You know . . .
We could leave.

Silence.

We could. We could leave.

Silence.

Jane   How you—I don't understand.

Silence.

Luna   Never mind, I was just. Never mind.

Silence.

How long will it take for the turkey to be ready?

Silence.

Jane   Maybe I don't know because frozen, but probably more than two hour.

Luna   Mm.

Silence.

Jane   Where?

Luna   What?

Jane   Where? Where you would go.

Luna   Noplace! Ha, I'm not going noplace don't be so serious all the sudden you, ha!

Silence.

Why?, is there um.

Jane   Hm?

Luna   Is there someplace you'd go?

Jane   Me?! No! No no, oh no.

Silence.

Luna   Yeah. But don't you just sometimes think about hey, big country big world so much to see, like we come to America and Disneyland for just one day, and then we sit at home watch tv see so many places where all the other people are. Leo he says I have a too big big imagination, well this time is he yes!, correct!, just a big big silly imagination, ha? Just a daydream, like maybe I go learn to drive and go somewhere I never been. Go dancing. Go fishing. Go to the beach.

Silence.

Jane   Too cold for beach.

Luna   Ha! Yes beach end of November maybe not so fun.

Jane   But dancing, this idea I like.

Luna   You do?

Jane   What I like, I like Soul Train.

Luna   You like Soul Train?

Jane   Of course so good Soul Train yes!

Luna   Oh I love it!

Jane   So am I!

They dance.

Luna Maybe it's on now!

Jane No Soul Train only Saturday 2pm.

Luna Radio!

Jane Yes!

Luna *goes to a clock radio from the bedside.*

Luna Stupid thing gets no good signal antenna busted but I'm gonna open it anyway and fingers crossed!

She tries to find something good, at some point she finds a decent dance song but it's way too in and out with static to be useful.

Come on come on you dummy old radio!

She gives up on that station and searches more, catches the tail end of a decent pop song but it's one of those slow-dance love songs.

Hm? Maybe huh?

The song ends though. And a DJ comes on, saying:

> You're listening to 98.7 lite fm on this national day of Thanksgiving, as we mark the 10th anniversary of the assassination of former President John F. Kennedy. In other news today, a White House spokesperson confirmed that President Nixon will not release his tax records for the years 1970 and 1971-amidst ongoing speculation about the source of payments related to the Waterg—

Luna *shuts off the radio.*

Luna Say hey you know how to drive?

Jane What?

Luna Driver's license, do you have it?

Jane No.

Luna Oh.

Silence.

Jane How much is taxi?

Luna Taxi?

Jane You buy turkey, maybe I buy taxi?

Luna Oh golly really?

Jane You know how much?

Luna I dunno, I never paid for a taxi before but how much can it be?

Jane Yellow pagee!

Luna   Yes!

Jane   Yellow pagee look and we find dance club we call taxi find out how much?

Luna   Yes!

Luna *gets the Yellow Pages.*

Jane *hums a song, starts dancing again.*

How do I find this? Dance club?

Jane   Nightclub.

Luna   Yes maybe under nightclub!

She finds something, but **Jane** *suddenly stops dancing.*

Jane   Wait.

Luna   I found it. Nightclub! It says they got a dance floor!

Jane   Thanksgiving.

Luna   What huh?

Jane   Not gonna open. Thanksgiving so gonna be close.

Silence.

Luna   I'm gonna call anyway and find out.

She calls.

Jane *checks on the turkey.*

Silence.

Luna *hangs up the phone.*

I guess noplace fun is gonna be open, yeah?

Silence.

Jane   Here is fun.

Jane *smiles.*

So does **Luna**.

Luna   How's turkey looking?

Jane   Mm, no, no close.

Luna   Okay.

Jane   But yam is almost close!

Luna   Yams!

Jane   Gonna be good!

Silence.

Luna   I'm just gonna use da CR, kay? Be right back.

Jane   Hm?

Luna   Da comfort room. Ha! Bathroom.

Jane   Ah!

Luna   Just a quick one!

Luna *starts towards the restroom.*

Don't miss me too much, 'kay?

She goes into the restroom, closes the door.

Jane *stands there within the quiet.*

She takes a long breath.

Looks around. Studies the apartment in a way she didn't before.

Looks at the bed, unmade, tussled sheets and haphazard pillows.

Perhaps she peeks inside a cabinet or two.

Looks out the window at the fading light.

We hear the toilet flush and the sink start up, as **Jane** *goes back to the spot she had been standing before.*

Luna   I'm back!

Jane   Mm.

Luna   Dja miss me?

Jane *smiles.*

Joke.

Silence.

Why how come you look so serious whatcha thinkin about?

Silence.

Jane   Oh. Nothing, just stupid think. You no want to know.

Luna   I do want to know!

Jane   No.

Luna   I do though!

Jane   Okay okay, I dunno why for somehow I was think about Richard Nixon.

Luna   NO WAY SO WAS I.

Jane No you are, stop it!

Luna For serious I was!

Jane No!, inside bathroom you think about Richard Nixon?!

Luna Always!

Jane What ha why? What you think when you think Richard Nixon!?

Luna I think he makes me wanna make a poo poo yeah?

Jane What?

Luna He makes me wanna pee pee all over everyplace and stuff ya know?

Jane Ha!

They laugh and laugh.

Oh so terrible why, I don't wanna think Richard Nixon!

Luna Oh so true!

They drink.

Jane But, uh. You say you like to know about news, yes?

Luna I do! I try anyhow, to pay attention yes, I have a sister back home don't tell anyone kay because she's a . . .

she whispers
A communist.

Jane Mm.

Luna Yeah, she's my older sister so when I was a kid and stuff she'd always talk about it, mosta my friends in school none of em were too interested interested but my sister well here's the thing, first of all she made it all seem kinda cool? Ya know? The way everything an older sister does seems super cool? But then I really started paying attention because the things she said, about what was gonna happen in Philippines, well they started coming true. No foolin. They all started happening!, and I don't just mean little things and things, but like big things, big important scary things like martial law and suspension of constitution and all that, so. Back home mosta my friends and family where I come from they'd be like ay nako so what?, government it's always corrupt no surprise!, but I guess it felt surprising to me. Also I worry about my sister yeah?, cause if your sister's a communist in the Philippines you kinda gotta worried she might get ya know

Luna *makes a finger-across-the-neck gesture of getting killed*

Jane Mm.

Silence.

Luna Oh gosh I didn't offend you just now did I, maybe you hate communisits, stupid girl why do I say such a thing!

Jane   Ha! No it's okay!

Luna   I gotta remember nobody likes talking bout communism!

Jane   Luna!

Luna   What?

Jane   My sister, she communist too!

Luna   NO SHE'S NOT.

Jane   Yes!

They laugh and laugh.

Luna   Wait though you didn't say you had a sister!

Jane   I know.

Luna   You said you had a brother you didn't say you had a sister?

Jane   Yes first time I don't say her!

Luna   But I guess every family's got one!

Jane   Ha!

Luna   A communist I mean, not a sister!

Jane   Yes but my sister I didn't say her first time because she died.

Silence.

Luna   Oh no.

Jane   Yeah.

Luna   Oh I'm such a dummy I gotta put my foot in mouth I'm so sorry!

Jane   Is okay is okay, long time ago.

Luna   Oh no wait was she

Luna *makes a finger-across-the-neck gesture of getting killed*

Jane   No she were got hit by a bus.

Silence.

Somehow this makes **Jane** *laugh.*

Or maybe no. Maybe yes? But maybe no.
Hit by bus this is anyway, this is what they tell to us is happen.

Silence.

But of course yes bus. There are many bus in Korea. So is possible, very possible.

Luna   Jane I'm so sorry.

Jane No no be sorry.

Silence.

They drink.

What your sister think about you come to America?

Luna She was happy? I think so anyway. She says she's happy for me, anyway I guess if you're communist you're probably not gonna like America much?, but then again I guess an older sister's gotta like it their little Luna's someplace far away from Marcos.

Silence.

You know she told me this something, I guess they passed a law here in USA, this law what made it so we can come here, you know what is it?

Jane Law?

Luna Yeah my sister says they call it the Hart Celler Act because somebody whos name is Hart and somebody whos name is Celler they wrote this thing and it got made into law and stuff, just a few years ago and I guess before it happened hardly nobody could come from Philippines or from Korea or noplace where there's people like, you know, like us?, before it everybody whos coming to USA they come pretty much just from Europe and white people places, but after Hart Celler all of a sudden we can come here. Our husbands anyway, they can come here to study. Work and study.

Jane Hart Celler?

Luna I know. When she told me I pictured this . . . it's silly I know but I pictured this little old lady with a little stand on the side of the road sellling hearts. All kindsa hearts, little paper hearts and plastic toy hearts, red with lacies and doilies.

Jane American lady?

Luna That's the funny thing!, she wasn't American but a little old lola, and it wasn't even in America but right down the street from our old house!, like it was there one day when it wasn't before, and because these guys Hart and Celler I could just go down there and take my pick.

Jane Wait for real?

Luna Ha!, no not for real, just imagination.

Silence.

But I had this . . . another image? I was at the airport, when we came here?, not this airport, but the one to Disneyland where we got to first, we landed and they put us in this big big room, I'm sure you know it, all the people from flights coming in from other countries, they're all there together and I look around and see these folks from everyplace and I think about Hart Celler, but this time it's not some little old lady but a big line of people all waiting to get checked in, and I was looking at all the USA police, though I guess they're not police but immigration workers, they're looking over everyone's papers and actually never mind this is kinda too sad a story I don't wanna be this kind of sad right now.

Silence.

Jane   Huh?

Luna   Never mind my sillly story! Let's talkabout something else, huh?

Jane   Luna you crazy whats matter with you, no way you having to finish!

Luna   Nah.

Jane   Oh my god Luna, finish sad story!

Luna   It's not even really sad just imaginary sad!

Jane   I don't care, you start story you finish story okay?!

Luna   Okay! Okay. So. Um. I just watched all these people. Coming to America. Going to the front, standing and waiting while these immigration officers look at their papers, and I imagine them saying okay sir papers look okay, now give me your heart. And then each by each these people they dig into their chest and they take out their heart and pass it over. That this Hart Cellar it's not somebody who's gonna give you a heart, but we're the heart sellers. It's us, it's our hearts, and we sell em away.

Silence.

Jane   You're right this is very bad story.

Luna   I told you!

Jane   Oh my God Luna!

Luna   I tried to stop! Your fault!

Jane   Okay my fault, my fault yes!

They laugh and laugh.

Silence. They drink.

Jane   You know, sometime I am think. If I was . . . If I was a man. I would be good at this. I would. Hm. I don't how is best way to say.

Luna   I think I know what you mean.

Jane   How to make best of. Choices. Man have so much more choices. So much times, I see man is make worser one. And so I think. If I am a man. Man, but with still my brain. With my feeling. I make better one.

Luna   Yeah.

Jane   But then maybe if I am a man, I make bad choice because if I become man, then I become all of sudden so bad at make choice? I don't know.

Luna   Ha!

Jane But my husband, you know, sometime he make such wrong choice I think how . . . how this man? How this man think?

Luna Like what kind of choices?

Silence.

Jane No nothing, is not important.

Silence.

But point of story is. Richard Nixon! Oh my God how so stupid he is!

Luna I know right?!

Jane When man is have power. Yes? Why? . . . Why they . . .?

Luna They don't know what to do with power!

Jane No!

Luna Why why then do they want so much anyway!?

Jane If I am Richard Nixon I mean God I am think I have best job, wife so much more pretty than me, how I even get such pretty wife, I have so ugly face and things?, power of nice country and money money money why how come I wanna throw all to trash can?

Luna Penis!

Jane Heh?

Luna It's the penis the penis! When they have this little tiny itty bitty titi, they think they gotta grow something big someplace else, yeah?, so all this missles and rockets penis; atomic bomb testes; cause their penis it's not good enough even when they got a pretty wife they think they have to prove something to the world or something, I mean lookit you and lookit me we're kinda foxy ya?

Jane Yes foxy!

Luna But even my husband, yeah, sometimes he does this macho thing and I think why how come, huh?

Silence.

I mean I'm not saying my husband has a little bitty penis.

Silence.

I'm not saying he *doesn't* either, I mean how would I even know I've never seen any other one, oh my golly gosh stop it Luna please tell me to shut up!

Jane Ha, no!

Luna Why am I talking about this no one wants to talk about penis!

June But I am same way! I don't know too! I mean sometimes it seem too big like monster like aaaah! get away from me! but also I never see another one so

Luna Right?!

They laugh and laugh.

Luna *has an idea!*

Luna Hey hey let's go to a porno movie!

Jane Heh?

Luna We should go to a porno movie and look at the peeners!

Jane Er.

Luna Then we can compare to our husbands!

Silence.

Jane This idea . . . Luna, this is so terrible idea!

Luna Oh my gosh it is!

Jane I mean!

Luna Can you imagine?

Jane No!

Luna What if someone from the department

Jane Our husband supervisor!

Luna Or a patient!

They laugh and laugh.

Jane This is problem!

Luna Super duper problem!

Jane You know this, whenever someone see us

Luna I know!

Jane They know who are we!

Luna Right away!

Jane No one else here looking like this, so

Luna Sus maria josep!

Jane No porno!

Luna No porno.

Jane No porno.

Silence.

Did you know?

Luna Know what?

Jane Who am I.

Luna You mean . . .

Jane When you see me supermarket today. Look at turkey?

Silence.

Luna I did.

Silence.

Jane I know you too.

Luna You did?

Jane Mm.

Luna You noticed me? Before?

Jane Yes.

Luna At K Mart?

Jane K Mart, yes.

Luna You saw me?

Jane Of course.

Luna I thought you did!

Jane Mm.

Luna And before that. At the

Jane Picnic.

Luna The resident picnic.

Jane Mm.

Luna I wanted to talk to you then.

Jane Mm, same. I am too.

Silence.

I dunno why but my husband . . . he say. He think better we don't make only friend of you, people maybe they think.

Luna Yeah.

Jane Already everyone think we are . . . um, strange, so. He say we should try to make American people friend more better.

Silence.

Luna Oh.

Jane   Stupid suck cock bullshit!

Luna   Oh my gosh!

Jane   Only one thing worser thing than person who is have too much power, you know what is?

Luna   What.

Jane   Person who is not have any.

Silence.

They drink.

Luna   When you were a girl. What did you want to become?

Silence.

Jane   I go to school for to be painter.

Luna   You're a painter?

Jane   Not really no, just student. Art school.

Luna   Art school wow.

Jane   Mm. But. Most of time I paint just simple thing, whole time I think is just beginning, so. Paint tree. Paint river. Think someday later I paint forest. Practice paint hand, paint leg, think maybe one day I paint sometime whole body, but this, I never do this. Just read about it. See book, so much book, so much famous good painting, I think maybe someday I go Paris, go Louvre, see real thing, but this no real dream. Real dream maybe someday I paint. Paint something like this, I do it. Marc Chagall. Van Gogh. Monet. Me?

Silence.

Luna   I love to sing.

Silence.

Luna *starts to laugh.*

So does **Jane**.

Jane   Sing for me.

Luna   Okay goody I'm gonna, but yes I know how tacky this girl is!, she says I love to sing and I know you're just being polite to say sing for me, but I do really really wanna sing so here it goes!

Silence.

Luna *sings.*

It doesn't have to be a sad song. Maybe it is, but even if it's not, it sounds sad when she sings it.

When the song ends, she begins to cry.

Softly.

Jane *takes her hand. Comforts her.*

A moment.

Luna Jane.

Jane Mm.

Luna I feel so . . . so . . . hungry.

They laugh.

Jane Yams gotta be ready now.

Luna Gimme gimme.

They get up and go to the oven.

Jane Okay let's see.

She takes the yams out of the oven.

Hm.

Luna No?

Jane No perfect but you know, we eat anyway!

She shuts the oven and starts preparing the yams.

Luna More wine!

She finishes off the bottle and opens another.

Jane Taste.

Jane *holds out a piece of yam.*

Hot hot . . .

Jane *blows on it.*

Luna *does too.*

They take tiny tentative bites.

It tastes amazing.

Luna Ah.

Jane Mm.

Luna Ooh!

Jane Yaaaa.

They eat.

Luna In the Philippines yams are different.

Jane Mm, in Korea too, little bit different.

Luna They taste kinda the same? But somehow the smell is different?

Jane Mm.

Luna I miss so many smells. Not just food, but you know. Like . . . plants. Beaches.

Jane Yes, I am same way, Korea smell different.

Luna Trees, different trees smell different.

Jane Pepper.

Luna Mm yes, different red pepper.

Jane Yes red.

Luna Rain.

Jane Hm, rain.

Luna Yeah, the way the rain smells, it's different here isn't it?

Jane Mm yes!, because. Because rain, yes. It take all whole of city, take smell of air, take smell of ground, mix all together, yes I know this you are right, rain smell yes is big difference.

Silence.

Luna Do you have to pee?

Jane Huh?

Luna I have to pee again but I don't wanna pee twice before you pee once so if you hafta pee you should go first.

Silence.

Jane Yes I have to pee!

They laugh and laugh.

Luna Okay go go go hurry up hey!, so I can go after!

Jane Okay okay!

Jane *goes into the restroom, shuts the door.*

Luna *takes a moment alone.*

Perhaps she hums to herself. Perhaps she dances.

Perhaps she laughs, perhaps she cries.

She blows on a yam.

Takes a bite.

When **Jane** *returns:*

Luna   Hey finally! My turn!

Luna *rushes into the restroom as* **Jane** *laughs.*

The door closes.

Jane *has a moment alone.*

She looks concerned.

Checks the clock. Smells her clothes.

Rubs her temples, her eyes. Deep breath sigh.

She sits on the sofa.

Begins to relax a bit.

Curls up with a pillow.

When **Luna** *returns, she sits next to her.*

They sit in silence just long enough to note that this is a comfortable silence. Perhaps the first one they've had.

Luna   Have you ever played tennis?

Jane   No.

Luna   Yeah me either.

Silence.

Jane   Only sports I know, I know soccer.

Luna   You play soccer?

Jane   I play? Ha!, no no, but okay maybe little bit yes but not serious. My father, yes, when I am elementary school time he was teacher? High school teacher, yes, so for this school he teach, they have soccer team, and he um . . . coach, you know what is coach, am I say right?

Luna   Oh my goodness yes, that's so cool!

Jane   Yes coach for boy soccer team. But most of time they lose. Not good team. This school, my father, he teach school good for academic, but no for soccer.

Luna   But still, that's so exciting!

Jane   Yes.

Luna   And so he taught you soccer?, you have to teach me!

Jane   Oh no, he no teach to me. Because . . . mm. When I am grow up, even when there is chance for me do something like this, my father he wanting always do just safe choice. Soccer game maybe too rough, this is not right thing for girl? So just I watch. And pretend play.

Luna Oh.

Jane My mother my father, after they are die, I understand more? They think best way to protect, yes? When they are same age like me, they live such hard time, so only want for me do safe way, protect me.

Luna But look at you now.

Jane Mm, yes.

Luna What do you think they'd say if . . . if they could see you now, in America?

Silence.

Jane I don't know. Sometimes America, you know, seems like big adventure. But sometimes seems like . . .

Luna The opposite?

Jane Yes sometimes seems like safe way. Because just I am do same like everybody say is best way. Whole my life, prepare for become best wife, good support, follow husband even to most far place can imagine, yes?

Luna Yeah.

Jane Seems like just same. Like one more soccer game I watch somebody else play.

Silence.

Luna Yeah.

Silence.

Jane Okay, anyway!, so. If. If we leave. Where we go?

Luna Paris France. The Louvre.

Jane Yes!

Luna YES!

Jane This is not safe choice!

They laugh together.

When the laughter subsides:

Luna I don't feel safe.

Jane I know.

Luna Back home I felt like people, we had the same . . . we came from the same place huh?, so I felt. What is it? Confidence, yeah. That if something happened. If something bad. Then I could count on someone to care. But here. I don't have to tell you. I'm sure the things that happen to me, these things that happen every day, the way people . . . the way they talk the things they say the way they look at . . . I'm sure they happen to you too, yeah?

Jane Mm.

Luna So it's the opposite. The opposite of confidence.

Jane Mm.

Luna I would like to take you to the Louvre. But this is not my really real answer. My really real answer is that if we left for really real we would go to a place I saw once in the countryside.

Silence.

When we first came here, from the airport, at one point, we pulled off the highway to some kinda side road?, and I saw this place. I didn't see it all at once. First a little barn it was?, and I said oh lookit such a cute little barn, fresh paint, it was yellow and I never saw a yellow barn before. And then we passed a little garden, so full of flowers like you couldn't imagine, purple pink yellow and the deepest red any person's ever seen. Then a basketball thing you know whatsit called, hoop, on the side of a house and children. Laughing children and now I'm sitting straight up in my seat, yeah, and looking out the window of the car like I'm on a Disneyland ride, but it's real life. I see a little market off the side of the road, buckets and baskets of corn carrots even pumpkins and then we turn the corner and there are all these people, all gathered around. I look around to try and find what is it these people are here for?, and then I see it's a band. A band playing music and I can hear it so faint only through the car window, it's a music I never heard before, and the people they're dancing and there are kids on the shoulders of their parents and they're clapping and swaying with the music, and the car it passes so slow. So slow I can hear just enough of the song to remember a few seconds of it today, like:

She hums a little. Just a little.

And as we pulled away, we passed a big open field, and there were still more people. There were children just running. And dogs, without any leashes, running side by side with the kids, but we passed it too quickly. Too too quickly, but I saw enough to know these children with their dogs weren't running to anywhere in particular. They were running in a circle, they were running just to run. Because they're already right where they're supposed to be.

Silence.

This place. I know it can't be like this always, I know it was some special day, some special situation in the town and I know if I go there probably it's not the same kind of fun for a goofy Filipino girl who's super ignorant of their particular music, but I think about it just the same. I think about what it would feel like to be in the middle of it. To be a part of it somehow.

Silence.

Jane You tell this your husband?

Silence.

Luna Yeah.

Jane He should take. Go.

Luna He doesn't . . . he. He doesn't trust the countryside.

Jane Mm.

Luna He's heard bad things about

Jane Mm-hm.

Luna About how they. For people like us, what they.
Anyway, it's probably good advice.

Silence.

Jane You and husband, you talk about what you gonna do after residency?

Luna Sometimes. Yeah, not as often as we should.

Jane What you think gonna happen?

Silence.

Luna Well, we talk about maybe we'll go home.

Jane Back to Philippine?

Luna But we won't.

Jane No?

Luna No. Even if things are better over there when he's finished, we still won't go back. Because he'll become a doctor, and he can already see the way doctors live here; he knows how doctors live back home and how can somebody resist the difference?

Jane Mm.

Luna And so I've seen what happens, he'll go where they tell him to go, they'll tell him which such and such place will take him, and we'll move there; he'll work long hours and every holiday. And maybe if everything goes how they say it's gonna go, we'll have money. All of a sudden we'll be people who have money? Which maybe it will but how can we trust this, right?, how can we trust that everything's gonna go the way they say it will when everything is different than we thought it would be, when it rains and I say this, no this isn't rain, it doesn't smell like rain so then how can I trust what they say is true? And anyway, I'll make babies, and those babies will be babies who grow up with parents who have money, and they will be more American than I am, and I'll struggle to make them understand where they come from. I won't understand how to love them the same way my mother loved me, because they won't understand me the way I understand my mother. My mother won't understand me either, because I'll change too, I've already changed I can feel it, I changed the minute I stepped off the plane, because I sold it, my heart, I sold it didn't I?, I sold it to the man at the place in the room in the airport, and I can't ever get it back, and without my heart my old heart my real heart my heart my heart I will stop understanding my mother, my communist sister, my home, my past, more and more every day until there's no one left who understands me. No one left. Not even myself.

Silence.

Jane Holy shit Luna NO!, you gotta shutting up so sad whine whine stupid wow!

Luna I'm sorry!

Jane You gotta need eat something or something now okay!

Luna I'm sorry!

Jane No be sorry just shut up, my God you are so bad terrible!

Luna Sorry.

Jane No!

Luna Okay!

Jane Eat more yam!

Luna Okay!

Jane *gets yams and basically shoves them at* **Luna**.

Jane Drink! More drink!

Luna *drinks.*

Luna Okay!

Jane More faster!

Luna But

Jane Stop no talking just eat drink stop so sad wah wah poor Luna bullshit be happy!

Luna Okay!

Jane Thanksgiving! Thanks! Giving!

Luna *can't help laugh with her mouth full, gets yams all over.*

Good! Now more drinky fast!

Luna *drinks.*

Yes now smile be happy okay fuck!

Total wine spit take all over **Jane**'s *face.*

Point blank bullseye in the middle of her face.

Jane *is covered in a mixture of spit wine and yams.*

Silence.

And then they laugh and laugh.

Jane   Wow.

Luna   I am so sorry sorry!

Jane   No!, is my fault!

Luna   No it's mine!

Jane   I am too funny!

Luna   I'm too sad!

Jane   Yes true!

Luna   You're true too, too funny you!

Jane & Luna   Your fault!

They laugh and laugh.

Luna *gets* **Jane** *a towel, tries to clean her off.*

Luna   Oh gosh

Jane   Is okay!

Luna   I ruined your clothes!

Jane   I hate this clothe anyway!

Luna   Lemme just

Luna *awkwardly tries to wipe,* **Jane** *swats her away.*

Jane   Ah-ah! No I can do, I can do

Jane *takes the towel.*

Luna *runs to the closet, digs around.*

Luna   I can wash your clothes and give you some of mine for now

Jane   No no no no problem

Luna   No it's good! I can wash your clothes in the tub and I can give you some of – yes, here you can change into da home clothes!

Jane   Heh?

Luna   Da home clothes! Ha! PJs! We callem da home clothes.

Jane   Home clothes?

Luna   Home clothes!

Silence.

Make yerself at home! In da home clothes!

Silence.

Jane Yeah okay, I like, yes, home clothes okay!

Luna *gives her a pair of home clothes, which* **Jane** *takes into the restroom.*

While she's in there, **Luna** *changes into home clothes too.*

Luna Hoy, just leave your dirties in the tub, yah? I'll wash it.

Once **Luna** *is changed she goes to the oven.*

Checks the turkey.

It's still frozen, audibly so as **Luna** *pokes at it.*

Luna *laughs and laughs.*

She moves to the wine mess, gets a towel and starts to clean up, but changes her mind and leaves it.

Tosses the towel onto the floor.

She flops down on the sofa and turns on the television (or radio).

Richard Nixon *is on.*

It catches him mid-sentence, as he says:

Nixon (*V.O.*) . . . where the money came from. Let me just say this, and I want to say this to the television audience: I made my mistakes, but in all my years of public life, I have never profited, never profited from public service. I have earned every cent. And in all my years of public life, I have never obstructed justice. And I think, too, that I could say that in my years of public life, that I welcome this kind of examination, because people have got to know whether or not their President is a crook. Well, I am not a—

Near the end of this, we hear the sound of water running from the tub.

At this, **Luna** *abruptly turns off the television and runs to the restroom door.*

Luna Hey no way leave it! I'll wash it later huh!?

Jane (*off*) No problem!

Luna No housework tonight! Hey serious! I'm even gonna leave the wine and this and everything out here, not tonight okay!? Just for tonight. No cleaning. For tonight.

The water stops.

Silence.

Jane *opens the restroom door.*

Jane Yes. Deal. I like it, good deal.

Jane *is dressed in da home clothes.*

Luna Lookit you look good in da home clothes!

Jane Yes good more comfort.

Luna   We look twinsies, yeah?

They pose in their home clothes.

Jane *notices the wine mess.*

Jane   Oh wow big messy.

Luna   Not tonight!

Jane   Okay.

Silence.

They smile and sit on the sofa.

And then now what.

Silence.

Luna   Hm. Put on da home clothes means we probably not going anyplace.

Silence.

Jane   Tomorrow. Tomorrow we can go.

Silence.

Luna   Tomorrow.

Silence.

Jane   Where we can go tomorrow?

Silence.

Luna   I dunno.

Silence.

Jane   First we go porno movie.

Luna   Shut up.

Jane   You shut up. First we go porno movie. Then nightclub.

Luna   Okay.

Jane   We dance. We dance big because feel funny little bit from porno movie.

Luna   Ha!

Jane   Dance until so tired, so eat lunch someplace nice.

Luna   Lunch ha, you mean dinner?

Jane   No, lunch!

Luna   Tomorrow we can't go anywhere daytime with husbands coming home in the morning

Jane Quiet

Luna And besides if we're going to a nightclub it's night

Jane I say quiet this is imagination okay let me do as imagination!

Luna Okay.

Jane So. For lunch we go take taxi to town of purple flower and corn bucket, and yes because day after Thanksgiving everybody so full and happy big belly tired they so good mood, and when they see two foxy us lady they say hey we can play music together. And you sing song, sing such beautiful song with funny countryside American people, and we sit in field eat pie, pumpkin pie, all together, look out at field of basketball hoop and new yellow barn and I think, okay Jane maybe I can paint this. Yes. This barn this field this moment. So I paint every whole thing. Barn yes, field yes. I paint music people. Also, also I paint music. So can see music in painting.

And you, I paint you. You whole thing of you, not just you face but you smile. And you sadness. And all of everything you are dreaming. I paint this.
This picture of my friend.

Luna *leans into* **Jane**, *puts her head on her shoulder.*

Luna Keep going.

Jane And is good! Is so good, this day, this picture, so good that everything inside that make you want . . . that make us want . . . to leave? All of this it is . . . it just, it go away. It go away. And you look at me and I look at you and we say okay, let's go home.

Silence.

But and then! When are we come back, we not ready yet to come all of way home, not yet, day so good not ready to over. So we go . . . we go K Mart. Look at all of things there. Laugh, we laugh, so much at all so many strange things are coming from this people, this people who are live in this place. And maybe we buy some. Buy some dress, match dress, we look same together, and we dress like this, like this people. We dress like this people but we know it is pretend. Like costume.

And in this costume together we go . . . we go library. Library, at library you show me how to find all news from all whole world, news from real our home. You show me news of you home, and we read about place we know already, sound so familiar but already it feel so long time ago, and we read about . . . yes, we read about how so many power of man, these man who keep hurt our home. How they hurt our long ago home, and we know also here too, in America, are person just like this, hurt new our home, so we know, we see, see how whole world all around us everything everywhere, how it is all fall apart. Yes? Little bit, little bit, how all world is break. Burn. Crumble. Tumble. Crash. Fall apart.

Silence.

And then we come home.

Silence.

Luna And then what?

Silence.

Jane And then. Before we are say goodbye. We make plan together. For what we do next tomorrow.

Silence.

Linger.

End of play.

Postscript

A Promise and A Wish

May Adrales

My mom, Jocelyn Deramos Divinagracia Adrales, was able to watch the Huntington Theatre's 2023 production of *The Heart Sellers*. She knew very little about the play except that one character, the loquacious Luna, was very loosely based on her. Upon watching the production, the only thing she said to me was, "She's definitely from Manila." I laughed lightly—my mother, who prizes her graceful reserve, so typical of the Visayan people—"Well, I said she was very *loosely* based!"

While Luna may not have been like my mother in personality, there were many things that they shared. They both came to the United States under the auspices of the Hart-Celler Act. They both came at age 22. Their husbands were both residents at a hospital. My mom, like Luna, came from "a big family, so many titas and lolas—aunties and grand-aunties" (314) – from a home that was always filled with conversation, friends, music, and food. They both had quite the transition coming to a one-bedroom apartment in a new foreign city with very few people who looked like them.

While I was Director of New Play Development at Milwaukee Rep, I initiated a commission with Lloyd after a successful production of *The Chinese Lady*. We began to have conversations about supporting his next play. In those conversations, we spoke of our parents' immigration to the US, in particular our mothers' experiences. The play was inspired by those conversations, and Lloyd provided me with some questions to ask my mom, such as *what were your first impressions of America? How was it different from your expectations? Did you think you would stay? Did you want to?* I was so grateful for this time, to talk with my mom about her experience coming to the US. It made me feel closer to her, knowing and listening firsthand about the expectations, fears, and small joys that she had in her first few years in America.

My mother came with many expectations of the promises this new land would bring. She spoke about the perceived wealth of Americans, the manicured lawns and large houses, so different from the compound she occupied with her seven brothers and sisters and extended family. What a shock it must have been to arrive at hospital housing in downtown Newark, New Jersey, just before the Newark riots, as civil unrest spread throughout the US. She worked 12-hour shifts as a nurse, often at night. She once unwittingly cared for a mafia boss, only realizing why this man was always surrounded by men in suits when he gave her $200 ($1800 today). But more often, her days were spent nursing the nation's poor. She and my father lamented that they had never seen greater poverty and violence than their time in Newark. What struck my mother the hardest was how alone her patients were. Patients with traumatic fatal injury without the comfort of family. Alone and thousands of miles away from her own, she feared this utter loneliness herself.

In our talks, she shared with me a photo of their arrival from Manila, at their port of entry in Vancouver, Washington, in June 1965. The picture was taken in front of what appears to be a parking lot. My dad is in a lovely black suit, the only one he owned, with my mother looking elegant in a matching sweater and skirt set. My mother looked at the photo. I watched her as she looked at the image. Wistfully? With sadness? With longing? With hope? She stared in silence. After a while, she said simply, "So young and full of . . . anxiety."

It has been the work of the play to unpack that silence. I wondered, as Luna does in the play, if my mother, upon looking at the photograph, recognized the young woman in the picture, or if she seemed almost a stranger. I am grateful that two intrepid actors, Jenna Agbayani and Juyeon Song, were willing to excavate what might be behind her silence. Through the play, I was able to transport myself to the time and circumstance that my mother lived through. I found myself seeing aspects of a woman I had never known. For instance, I had always thought my mother to be a shy and diffident woman. But I remember when I went with her to the Philippines as a young adult, I saw how boisterous and outgoing and charismatic she was, speaking her native tongue, so easy and popular among her friends. There was a side of my mother that I will never know because we know a different language, a different home, a different sense of family.

As theater artists, we are asked to step into the experience of others and see the world from their perspective. With this play, I was asked to do that every day: to imagine seeing the US through my mother's eyes. A cathartic experience, this was my chance to get to know my mother—the spirited young woman I had glimpsed in her homeland. Early rehearsals centered on rendering the truth of that lived experience. I asked the actors to write journal entries from their character's point of view. I offered Jenna and Juyeon prompts, similar to the questions I had asked my mother: *Describe your final goodbye from home. What was the first quarrel you had with your husband? What was your last dinner at home?* I invited the actors to conjure images with their words in sense memory explorations. I had them walk through their rituals at home, to more deeply personalize how this Thanksgiving Day was different from any other. In rehearsal, we shared memories of our families. We related to one another by sharing our own experiences of "otherness." As the weeks went on, the distance between character and actor became less and less. And somehow, I believe, all of us in the rehearsal room got much closer not only to these two extraordinary characters, but to our mothers, and in doing so, most surprisingly, to ourselves.

The magic of the theater is that the final product is vastly different from the starting point. The writer draws experience from real life, but then in the act of writing creates from a different point of view. The director interprets the text to best uplift the words on the page. The actors make the characters their own, blurring the line between their own self and the character. Thus, it was true that the character of Luna was very different from my mother, and the character of Jane was unlike Lloyd's mother. Perhaps the only real-life truth is my and Lloyd's sincere *wish* that our mothers had found a friend as Luna and Jane do. That somehow their first year in America was filled with less . . . anxiety. That each of our mothers had a friend who understood their hardship intimately. For even just one night, to be free from the loneliness that would come to define their initial years in America, so that each woman could feel the promise of tomorrow.

The Long Answer: A Conversation with Lloyd Suh

The following conversation between playwright Lloyd Suh and editor Christine Mok took place over the phone on June 11, 2024. The transcript has been edited for clarity and concision.

Christine Mok: Your inaugural collection brings together five history plays, four of which are an extended exploration of Asian American history, and one set during the geopolitical precondition for many Korean Americans. Can you share how these works came together?

Lloyd Suh: I should give you the long answer, right? There's a long answer, which is that it started with *Charles Francis Chan Jr.'s Exotic Oriental Murder Mystery*.

I was at a holiday party at The Lark [formerly the Lark Play Development Center (1994–2021) where Lloyd was director of artistic programs from 2011–2020]. Mia Katigbak and James Saito were there, and James was talking about how obsessed he was with true crime murder mystery TV shows. I repeated a fun fact I'd heard about how the second most produced playwright in history, by a longshot, is Agatha Christie. Mia got very excited because her company, the National Asian American Theatre Company (NAATCO), is founded on staging classics with all-Asian American casts. The idea of doing an Agatha Christie adaptation became really enticing to her. She was commissioning Asian American playwrights to reimagine and reinterpret classics, so she said, "Hey, you should do an Agatha Christie," and that intrigued me.

I looked at the Agatha Christies in the public domain; Mia was excited by the idea of Hercule Poirot, because he is a foreigner. He's underestimated—his brilliance comes from, in large part, being underestimated. I looked into those, but I went back to her and said: "I don't think I can do this, because if I do Poirot, the underestimated, overweight funny guy, who everybody thinks is comic, solving murders as an Asian American guy, it's immediately Charlie Chan." To which she said, "Yes, exactly. That is why you have to do it."

CM: The facial hair.

LS: Yes! Exactly, right? There are so many similarities that my first impulse was that it's impossible—I cannot. Yet, what led me away was exactly what Mia was excited about. What if I force myself to go there? Generationally, I don't have a direct relationship with Charlie Chan. I didn't grow up watching those movies and it wasn't part of the cultural conversation. My understanding of Charlie Chan is historical, through the literature of the 1970s, which I consumed as a college student. This became the frame for *Chan*, the birth of the Asian American movement in the 1970s, so, it became a history play.

Researching *Chan*, I got into new Asian American scholarship, which wasn't around when I was growing up, that kept introducing me to stories, facts, and moments in time that I felt I had to sit with. Spend time really thinking about. The first of those was Afong Moy. Reading about Afong Moy haunted me in a way that I had to process. And the way I process things is to get into a room with peers and wrestle with it together. I started writing around Afong Moy, beginning with just some exploratory writing. And that's how *Chan* led to *Chinese Lady*. Then came *Bina's Six Apples*, which was a separate process. I don't know if that's true. Was it a separate process?

CM: There's something about how you framed it: you didn't have a direct generational relationship to Chan, so you pinged back to the 1970s through Frank Chin and Kathy Change, to touch Charlie Chan. I wonder for *Bina's Six Apples* if there is a similar generational reach.

LS: I had done a play for young audiences for Children's Theatre Company and Ma-Yi, called *The Wong Kids in the Secret of the Space Chupacabra Go!* It was my first play for young audiences, and it was such a fun and rewarding process. I had just had kids. Writing for the demographic of my kids, my niece and nephew, that felt like it paralleled my life.

The origin story of *Bina's Six Apples* is that it is a piece of family lore. My father grew up on an apple orchard in Daegu, South Korea. When the Korean War broke out, he has this memory of being about five. He was the youngest of ten and when his family left the orchard to go to Busan, they all carried stuff. They gave my dad a little backpack filled with a handful of apples. In his memory—and in his retelling—it was a happy memory because it made him feel useful. It made him feel valuable.

On opening night for *The Wong Kids,* Elissa Adams, who was then Director of New Play Development at Children's Theatre Company, came up to me and said, "That story about the apples. That's a play for young audiences." I didn't see it at the time. As a piece of family lore, maybe I was holding onto it too tightly. I had blocks about it, but I gave it a shot. It was one of the easiest plays to write.

CM: In delving into family lore, I see how that connects with the familial excavations that you undertook for *The Heart Sellers*. But what came next, after *Bina's Six Apples*?

LS: Next came the pandemic—the pandemic is important to this chronology. Through all my reading, I had been circling the exclusion era. In research for *Chan* and *Chinese Lady*, the exclusion era looms so large as a pivot, and I wanted to interrogate that pivot for myself. Just prior to the pandemic, I got a commission from Atlantic Theatre Company, and they said, "Yeah, you can write about anything you want." I took the leap. I said, "Okay, I'm gonna write about the exclusion era." I didn't know how, I didn't know what it would look like, but I said I was gonna do it.

I started with some exploratory writing prior to lockdown. But once lockdown hit, adding an extra layer of isolation, of waiting, of being displaced, I realized I can use that energy. The bulk of *The Far Country* was written during lockdown and then developed over Zoom. *The Heart Sellers* also came during lockdown. I wrote them one after the other.

There was a production of *The Chinese Lady* at Milwaukee Rep [in 2018] that May Adrales directed. On opening night, Mark Clements, the artistic director of Milwaukee Rep, approached me and said, "Hey, you, do you want to write a play for us?" And I said, "Yeah, totally." May was there, and she and I started talking about what that might be. We remembered a conversation about our mothers, because they came to the United States at about the same time, the late 60s/early 70s, in the wake of the Hart-Celler Act.

I hadn't been thinking about the Hart-Celler Act as the engine for that play. Through talking about our mothers, and the similarities in how they navigated being newly in the US, I thought I'd start there. It wasn't until we put them into historical context that I realized it was a bookend to *The Far Country*. The plays are rooted in two pieces of legislation that changed the demographics of the US. The exclusion acts and the Hart-Celler Act created the conditions for which people like my mother, May's mother, the poets of Angel Island, and generations of Asians in America arrived here to live and struggle and thrive.

CM: You name the pandemic as a historical event. It is also one that has had a large impact on Asians in America. I'm curious what your thoughts are on the simultaneity of the resurgence in anti-Asian violence and *The Chinese Lady*, which, according to theater critic Diep Tran, writing in *American Theater*, was the most produced play of the 2021-2022 season. What do you make of this convergence? How the history of the present converged with your plays and how you navigated that?

LS: I felt it experientially. Delving into that history and then seeing it play out. It was all connected, right? When I read the news, because of the research and the interrogating I had been doing, I could see the roots of it. See where it all came from. Connect those dots in a way that was a little bit frightening, a little bit inevitable. It was definitely a critical part of the way I navigated that time. The thing about those productions of *The Chinese Lady* and being in the pandemic—it changed my relationship to my writing.

I'd never had the experience of having a play produced in multiple cities, in the same moment. To watch variations. To watch the differences from one production to the next, especially how they related to that moment in time. How they became really present tense and how they became very local to a particular community. And very personal to those performers.

It made me crave a theater that's portable—plays that can exist in different times. If you write a play during a time when there are no theaters, when theater is not happening anywhere, then you can't say that you know the audience you're writing for. You have to imagine a future-tense audience. You have to imagine what theater will look like when theaters exist again.

That changed everything about how I wrote. I wanted to leave space for a production to bring the news of that day into the room with them. For actors to be able to bring themselves, but also their time, their city, their local community, into the theater with them.

CM: I want to return to *The Heart Sellers* as a bookend and connect it to how you make generational ties to the material. You once said to me how it's in *The Heart Sellers* that you see the glimmer of yourself, the potential of you, in writing a life for your mother from before you were born.

LS: That was big, and I didn't realize it at the time. There are certain things I try not to overthink. I have a tendency to overthink a lot—in terms of situation, character, setting, all that stuff. But I try not to overthink the emotional part of it, the part that's personal. I try to let that be subconscious. I want to know that it's there, but I don't want to name it.

It wasn't until after the first draft [of *The Heart Sellers*] where I realized, wow, I'm in this, I'm there. I can locate myself. And if I can locate me, then I can locate my children. And that made me feel like I was ready to move on from history. It satisfied some subconscious impulse.

∽

CM: You spoke of exploratory writing. Give us a view into how you construct these worlds on the page. What is that like? What are you like when you're drafting plays? Do you have rituals?

LS: I think for a long time before I sit down and start writing. I first studied playwriting at Indiana University, with Dennis Reardon, who was an amazing teacher. One of the things I remember him saying in class was that a great approach is to know absolutely everything about the play you're going to write. You know all of it: why you're writing it, what it's about, what it means, what happens, know who it's about, what changes, where it is. *Then* you start writing. And absolutely under no circumstances are you allowed to follow what you had planned.

When I went to graduate school, I realized that this idea is the parallel of an actor's process. For an actor, that's what rehearsal is, what memorizing lines is, what learning an accent and learning a physicality is. You do all of this preparatory work. And you do enough that it becomes a part of you. So when you go on stage, you can let all of it go and respond to whatever's happening in real time.

Since it mirrors an actor's process, I try to write in synergy to that. I try to have everything that I need defined and internalized so that I can trust that it's there and then just write impulsively. So that I'm not thinking too much while I'm writing because I've already done that part.

Maybe a good example is *The Chinese Lady*. I didn't know that I wanted to write about Afong Moy. I only knew that I wanted to wrestle with why this little paragraph I read about her was haunting me. I was set to fly out to the Magic Theatre in San Francisco to do a benefit. And Loretta Greco, who was artistic director at the time said, "Hey, if you're gonna fly all the way out here, I can give you time in a room with some actors, you can do whatever you want, try something new." So, I impulsively wrote a version of the first scene. Looking back, it is remarkably similar to the first scene now. Not much is different from what I did that day.

This actually isn't a good example, because I hadn't thought about the structure of the play or what I was writing or any of that practical stuff yet. But it is a good example because I had sat with Afong Moy for a long time before I wrote that first page. And I had thought quite a lot, in particular, about the theatricality.

CM: …that this is a performance: I'm not saying what you think I'm saying, this is not my body, this is not my voice.

The Long Answer: A Conversation with Lloyd Suh   353

LS: Yeah. That was all there. When I started writing that play, I had no idea where it was gonna end up. I had no idea we were going to get that direct about her being in the present tense. And yet, in that first scene that I wrote, I had that line, "This is not my body. This is not my voice." So you could say I did know, on some level. But I have to believe process-wise that that's the result of time beforehand, to feel like I had enough to start with *before* I began to write.

CM: In that preparatory work, your homework, is this where exploratory writing comes in?

LS: The exploratory writing comes after, when I'm ready to throw things up on the page. More than half of the time what I start with, I throw away. I remember with *Chan,* I wrote scene one. And I got actors in a room and we read it and then I threw it away. I wrote another scene one, got actors in the room, we read it, and I threw that away. Writing the scene, hearing it, throwing it away. It's those attempts, the trying *again* that leads you to where a play starts. Now I have forward energy. I can go on to the next scene. That's what exploratory writing is. It's looking for the thing that propels you to the next scene.

CM: I am interested in what draws you to projects and what propels you. For *Chan* and *Bina,* with Mia and Elissa, there is your initial no to their yes, which leads to "Okay, I'm gonna do it." You also name the impulse to get into a room with peers and figure things out. Tell us about the process when you get to be with others collaboratively, not just in play development, but in production. How do you see that step? Or all those steps from page-to-stage?

LS: That's a big one. Because that's what theater is, right? When it's popping, it's drawing on many, many people who are making it personal. I can make it personal for myself. But it has to be personal for everybody in the room.

The exploration of trying to find it in the room is an exploration of seeing what resonates with actors. In the case of Afong Moy, it had to be actors, because she was a performer. So much of what I was grappling with was in recognition of conversations I'd had with peers about what it's like to be on display. What it's like to walk into a room knowing that you carry something with you.

If you walk onto a stage or an audition room, in particular, there is an expectation of what I am, what I carry with me. How much of that actually changes who you are? Even if it's not who you are. It can't help but become part of your identity. I knew with *Chinese Lady* that actors are key. Finding those resonances and letting people respond with their own impulses. I have to create the conditions where an actor can make it personal so that an audience can, too.

CM: Of the plays in this collection, is there a character that you've written that sticks out to you for whatever reason?

LS: As soon as you asked, two immediately popped into mind, which are Jane from *The Heart Sellers* and Bina [from *Bina's Six Apples*] because they're family.

CM: I know why Jane is family – because Jane is based on your mother – but with Bina, I'm curious, why transform the story of your father from a young boy to a young girl?

LS: When I wrote that play, my daughter was eight or nine years old. It's dumb that this wasn't obvious to me, because I always imagined my dad and my daughter watching the play together. That was an image that I carried with me throughout the process. What would appeal to them both? It seems ridiculous that I wasn't able to see that I was putting my daughter into my dad's story. I was imagining her into that scenario. Once I saw it, of course, that's what I'm doing.

CM: You have a knack for offering audiences a window into the lives of Asian women, their aspirations and disappointments, whether it's Afong Moy in *The Chinese Lady*, or Luna and Jane in *The Heart Sellers*. How do you do that?

LS: This is part of a conversation that's happening in the American theatre: how do you write outside your particular social location? As a teacher, I come across this question a lot. If you go into a project saying, "I'm going to write a play about immigrant women," and you are not an immigrant woman, then you are dead in the water. You're in a lot of trouble. It's not going to work. So you have to make it really, really personal. I never thought of this as "I'm writing a play about immigrant women." I thought of it as, "I am writing a play about my mother." Suddenly, you become the only person who can tell that story. You have to create the conditions where you are the only person who can write it. You have to make it yours.

***

CM: With all these history plays, you have pulled together, as directors, designers and cast, the widest net of Asian American talent. There are certainly collaborators you work with repeatedly, but because your work is produced across the country, so many people have had the opportunity to make work.

LS: When you put it that way, there's nothing better. It's so meaningful to me. I don't even know how to talk about that. When I think about the people I've been able to meet and work with, in the different cities I've been able to go to. There's an expansiveness that's always kind of a goal. The sense of reaching people. Especially in terms of quality because you want to reach people deeply. I don't know how to talk about this. Like, it's just, it's the best.

I always think of actors as my first audience. Like, that's who I write for. I can theoretically write for an audience, but there's an interpretive layer. I can't write for an audience if I'm not writing for actors. So I really do think first about actors, and the whole team, directors, designers. When I imagine how a play will manifest, I think about the people who are working on it first.

It's extraordinary to think about. You write a play and then somebody memorizes it. Somebody spends real emotional labor in actualizing and understanding and getting deep, deep into the skin of these characters. It's a level of engagement that I feel no other writing—no other art form—requires. The fact that actors do this, it blows my mind. I feel like the relationship between my writing and actors is the most profound.

That they're going to do that is so extraordinary. That's always the starting place for me.

CM: I've also noticed that you like to workshop your plays with playwrights first. I'm also reminded that for about five years, you were co-director of the Ma-Yi Writers Lab, which was a convivial and formidable scribble of playwrights. In thinking about the expansiveness of theater, we're really talking about community. What is it that you find generative about such a community?

LS: There's probably another really long answer here. Writing for me always started with writers. In classroom settings, in workshops, I spent most of my time in writers groups, before I ever went into production or any kind of rehearsal environment. It's sitting in a room with a handful of other writers, sharing work, and talking about it. That's a lot more of what playwrights do than being in rehearsal.

I was very lucky, coming out of graduate school, to be in writers groups: Youngblood at Ensemble Studio Theatre, the Ma-Yi Writers Lab, The Lark's Playwrights Workshop. I was able to develop groups of peers where we understood each other. I knew their work really intimately; they knew my work really intimately. When we respond to each other, there is context. If somebody makes a comment, I know where they're coming from. If I make a comment, they know where I'm coming from. With early writing, when you have that relationship, they can see what you're trying to do without you having to articulate it. I've always thrived on that.

The beginning, for me, is delicate because I'm exploring. And when you're exploring, you're trying to pull something together. It can be sensitive, so in the early going, I like to have people in the room who have context. Once I've explored enough to feel a shape, that is when I'm ready for actors.

CM: I've asked questions about pre-production, play development, process, etc. I am curious what it's like for you once a production is open and running.

LS: At that point, it's out of my hands. I feel like it's theirs. It's theirs before that, too. Part of the impulse to want actors, directors, designers, crews to make it personal is that if they don't, if you don't leave enough room to let it be theirs, then you're limiting every aspect of production and impact. I very much want them to own it. The rehearsal process for me is trying to allow that.

CM: You said that in locating yourself in *Heart Sellers,* you're ready to move on from history. Where do you go from here? What comes next?

LS: Yeah, now I'm writing about the future.

Acknowledgements

The author and editor would like to thank the team at Bloomsbury including Dom O'Hanlon, Sam Nicholls, and Mark Jones for their patience and editorial guidance. We are grateful to the agents who advocated for the commission and production of the plays collected in this volume, as well as the volume itself: Beth Blickers and Noah Ezell.

Thank you to Elissa Adams, May and Jocelyn Adrales, Brittany K. Allen, Nissy Aya, Irene Borger and the Herb Alpert Award in the Arts, Judy Bowman, Peter Brosius, Jennifer Chang, Jiyoun Chang, Kathy Change, Frank Chin, Dustin Chinn, Mark Clements, Catherine Coray, Joy Lanceta Coronel, Jane Cox and the Program in Theater and Music Theater at Princeton University, Curt Dempster, Ensemble Studio Theatre and Youngblood, Suzy Fay, Jody Feldman, Francesca Fernandez McKenzie, Hallie Foote and the Horton Foote Prize, Kyle Frisina, Graeme Gillis, Loretta Greco, Andrea Hiebler, AK Howard, Daniel K. Isaac, Mia Katigbak and NAATCO, Peter Kim, Arthur Kopit, Anna Kull, The Lark, Junghyun Georgia Lee, Kimber Lee, Ken Leung, Genny Lim, Teresa Avia Lim, Romulus Linney, Yilong Liu, Ma-Yi Theater Company, Annie MacRae, Emily Morse and New Dramatists, Christopher Moses, Gregg Mozgala, Qui Nguyen, Fabian Obispo, Diana Oh "Zaza D", Jorge Z. Ortoll, A. Rey Pamatmat, Ralph B. Peña, Neil Pepe, Annika Perez-Krikorian, Suzette Porte, Dennis J. Reardon, Sung Rno and the Ma-Yi Writers Lab, James Saito, Maureen Sebastian, Ralph Sevush, Jim Steinberg and the Harold & Mimi Steinberg Charitable Trust, Haleh Roshan Stillwell, Shannon Tyo, Ching Valdes-Aran, Deanie Vallone, Paula Vogel, Miriam Weisfeld, Krista Williams, Eugene Young, Fan Zhang, and Kathy Zhao.

Finally, we are indebted to our families who are our present, past, and future: Young and Oliva Suh, Ron, Andrea, Vivian and Beckett Suh, and Matilda, Elliot, Lewis and Jeanie Lee Suh; Jung Lai Mok, and Eldon Grant Porter.